NEW INTRODUCTORY
LECTURES ON
PSYCHOANALYSIS

By SIGMUND FREUD

AN AUTOBIOGRAPHICAL STUDY

BEYOND THE PLEASURE PRINCIPLE

CIVILIZATION AND ITS DISCONTENTS

THE COMPLETE INTRODUCTORY LECTURES ON PSYCHOANALYSIS

THE EGO AND THE ID

FIVE LECTURES ON PSYCHOANALYSIS

THE FUTURE OF AN ILLUSION

GROUP PSYCHOLOGY AND THE ANALYSIS OF THE EGO

INHIBITIONS, SYMPTOMS AND ANXIETIES

INTRODUCTORY LECTURES ON PSYCHOANALYSIS

JOKES AND THEIR RELATION TO THE UNCONSCIOUS

LEONARDO DA VINCI AND A MEMORY OF HIS CHILDHOOD

NEW INTRODUCTORY LECTURES ON PSYCHOANALYSIS

ON DREAMS

ON THE HISTORY OF THE PSYCHOANALYTIC MOVEMENT

AN OUTLINE OF PSYCHOANALYSIS

THE PSYCHOPATHOLOGY OF EVERYDAY LIFE

THE QUESTION OF LAY ANALYSIS

TOTEM AND TABOO

THE STANDARD EDITION
OF THE COMPLETE PSYCHOLOGICAL WORKS OF
SIGMUND FREUD
24 VOLUMES

New Introductory Lectures on Psychoanalysis

SIGMUND FREUD

Newly Translated and Edited by
JAMES STRACHEY

NEW YORK

W · W · NORTON & COMPANY · INC ·

ISBN 0 393 01064 3 Cloth Edition
ISBN 0 393 00743 X Paper Edition

PRINTED IN THE UNITED STATES OF AMERICA
3 4 5 6 7 8 9 0

CONTENTS

Editor's Note   3

Preface   5

LECTURES

XXIX   Revision of the Theory of Dreams   7

XXX   Dreams and Occultism   28

XXXI   The Dissection of the Psychical Personality   51

XXXII   Anxiety and Instinctual Life   72

XXXIII   Femininity   99

XXXIV   Explanations, Applications and Orientations 120

XXXV   The Question of a *Weltanschauung*   139

Bibliography and Author Index   161

List of Abbreviations   168

General Index   169

NEW INTRODUCTORY
LECTURES ON
PSYCHOANALYSIS

EDITOR'S NOTE

THIS WORK—*Neue Folge der Vorlesungen zur Einführung in die Psychoanalyse,* ("New Series of the Lectures to Serve as an Introduction to Psychoanalysis")—was first published at the beginning of 1933, some fifteen years after the original series of lectures to which it was to be a supplement. The first English translation, by W. J. H. Sprott, appeared in the same year.

In the early part of 1932 the financial affairs of the psychoanalytic publishing business in Vienna had been in a parlous state, and the idea occurred to Freud of coming to its help with a new series of the *Introductory Lectures.* The first and last lectures were ready by the end of May, and the whole book was finished by the end of August. It was actually issued on December 6, a month before the official date of publication.

These lectures differ from the original set in various ways and not merely in that they were never meant to be delivered. As Freud pointed out in his own preface (and as he insisted by his numeration of the lectures), they do not stand on their own legs but are essentially supplementary. What is especially noticeable about them, however, is the way in which they differ in character among themselves. The first lecture, on dreams, is scarcely more than a recapitulation of the dream section of the original series. On the other hand, the third, fourth, and fifth lectures (on the structure of the mind, on anxiety and the theory of the instincts, and on the psychology of women) introduce entirely new material and theories and, in the case of the third and fourth lectures, plunge into theoretical and metapsychological discussions of a difficulty which had been studiously avoided fifteen years earlier. The remaining lectures (the second and the last two) are of a very different order. They deal with a number of miscellaneous topics only indirectly related to psychoanalysis and, moreover, deal with them in what might almost be described as a popular manner. This is not to suggest that they are trivial or uninteresting—far from it. But they call for a very different kind and degree of attention than do their fellows. Nevertheless, whatever the reader's choice may be—whether he wishes to know what Freud thought about telepathy, education, religion, or Communism, or whether he wishes to learn Freud's final views on the super-ego, on anxiety, on the death instinct, or on the pre-Oedipus phase in girls—he

3

will certainly find plenty to occupy him in these lectures.

The text of the present translation is the same as that in Volume XXII of the Standard Edition of *The Complete Psychological Works of Sigmund Freud* (London, 1964; the Hogarth Press and the Institute of Psycho-Analysis). The footnotes and references have, however, been adjusted for this edition.

The editor wishes to express his gratitude to Miss Anna Freud for her critical advice throughout the preparation of the work. A large share in the editorial details involved has been undertaken by Miss Angela Richards.

JAMES STRACHEY

PREFACE

My *Introductory Lectures on Psycho-Analysis* were delivered during the two Winter Terms of 1915–16 and 1916–17 in a lecture room of the Vienna Psychiatric Clinic before an audience gathered from all the Faculties of the University. The first half of the lectures were improvised, and written out immediately afterwards; drafts of the second half were made during the intervening summer vacation at Salzburg, and delivered word for word in the following winter. At that time I still possessed the gift of a phonographic memory.

These new lectures, unlike the former ones, have never been delivered. My age had in the meantime absolved me from the obligation of giving expression to my membership of the University (which was in any case a peripheral one) by delivering lectures; and a surgical operation had made speaking in public impossible for me. If, therefore, I once more take my place in the lecture room during the remarks that follow, it is only by an artifice of the imagination; it may help me not to forget to bear the reader in mind as I enter more deeply into my subject.

The new lectures are by no means intended to take the place of the earlier ones. They do not in any sense form an independent entity with an expectation of finding a circle of readers of its own; they are continuations and supplements, which, in relation to the former series, fall into three groups. A first group contains fresh treatments of subjects which were already dealt with fifteen years ago but which, as a result of a deepening of our knowledge and an alteration in our views, call for a different exposition to-day—that is to say, critical revisions. The two other groups contain what are true extensions, for they deal with things which either did not exist in psycho-analysis at the time of the first lectures or which were too little in evidence to justify a special chapter-heading. It is inevitable, but not to be regretted, if some of the new lectures unite the characteristics of more than one of these groups.

I have also given expression to the dependence of these new lectures on the *Introductory Lectures* by giving them a numbering continuous with theirs. The first lecture in this volume is accordingly called No. XXIX. Like their predecessors, they offer the professional analyst little that is new; they are addressed to the multitude of educated people to whom we may perhaps attribute a benevolent, even though cautious, interest in the characteristics and discoveries of the young science. This time once again it has been my chief aim to make no sacrifice to an appearance of being simple, complete or rounded-off, not to disguise problems and not to deny the existence of gaps and uncertainties. In no other field of scientific work would it be necessary to boast of such modest intentions. They are universally regarded as self-evident; the public expects nothing else. No reader of an account of astronomy will feel disappointed and contemptuous of the science if he is shown the frontiers at which our knowledge of the universe melts into haziness. Only in psychology is it otherwise. There mankind's constitutional unfitness for scientific research comes fully into the open. What people seem to demand of psychology is not progress in knowledge, but satisfactions of some other sort; every unsolved problem, every admitted uncertainty is made into a reproach against it.

Whoever cares for the science of mental life must accept these injustices along with it.

FREUD

VIENNA, *Summer* 1932

REVISION OF THE THEORY OF DREAMS

LADIES AND GENTLEMEN,—If, after an interval of more than fifteen years, I have brought you together again to discuss with you what novelties, and what improvements it may be, the intervening time has introduced into psycho-analysis, it is right and fitting from more than one point of view that we should turn our attention first to the position of the theory of dreams. It occupies a special place in the history of psycho-analysis and marks a turning-point; it was with it that analysis took the step from being a psychotherapeutic procedure to being a depth-psychology. Since then, too, the theory of dreams has remained what is most characteristic and peculiar about the young science, something to which there is no counterpart in the rest of our knowledge, a stretch of new country, which has been re-claimed from popular beliefs and mysticism. The strangeness of the assertions it was obliged to put forward has made it play the part of a shibboleth, the use of which decided who could become a follower of psycho-analysis and to whom it remained for ever incomprehensible. I myself found it a sheet-anchor during those difficult times when the unrecognized facts of the neuroses used to confuse my inexperienced judgement. Whenever I began to have doubts of the correctness of my wavering conclusions, the successful transformation of a senseless and muddled dream into a logical and intelligible mental process in the dreamer would renew my confidence of being on the right track.

It is therefore of special interest to us, in the particular instance of the theory of dreams, on the one hand to follow the vicissitudes through which psycho-analysis has passed during this interval, and on the other hand to learn what advances it has made in being understood and appreciated by the contemporary world. I may tell you at once that you will be disappointed in both these directions.

Let us look through the volumes of the *Internationale Zeitschrift für (ärztliche) Psychoanalyse* [*International Journal of (Medical) Psycho-Analysis*], in which, since 1913, the authoritative writings in our field of work have been brought together. In the earlier volumes you will find a recurrent sectional heading 'On Dream-Interpretation', containing numerous contributions on

---

[1] [Cf. Freud's Preface, pp. 5–6 above.]

various points in the theory of dreams. But the further you go
the rarer do these contributions become, and finally the sectional heading disappears completely. The analysts behave as
though they had no more to say about dreams, as though there
was nothing more to be added to the theory of dreams. But if
you ask how much of dream-interpretation has been accepted
by outsiders—by the many psychiatrists and psychotherapists
who warm their pot of soup at our fire (incidentally without
being very grateful for our hospitality), by what are described
as educated people, who are in the habit of assimilating the
more striking findings of science, by the literary men and by the
public at large—the reply gives little cause for satisfaction. A
few formulas have become generally familiar, among them
some that we have never put forward—such as the thesis that
all dreams are of a sexual nature—but really important things
like the fundamental distinction between the manifest content
of dreams and the latent dream-thoughts, the realization that
the wish-fulfilling function of dreams is not contradicted by
anxiety-dreams, the impossibility of interpreting a dream unless
one has the dreamer's associations to it at one's disposal, and,
above all, the discovery that what is essential in dreams is the
process of the dream-work—all this still seems about as foreign
to general awareness as it was thirty years ago. I am in a
position to say this, since in the course of that period I have
received innumerable letters whose writers present their dreams
for interpretation or ask for information about the nature of
dreams and who declare that they have read my *Interpretation
of Dreams*, though in every sentence they betray their lack of
understanding of our theory of dreams. But all this shall not
deter us from once more giving a connected account of what
we know about dreams. You will recall that last time we devoted a whole number of lectures to showing how we came to
understand this hitherto unexplained mental phenomenon.[1]

Let us suppose, then, that someone—a patient in analysis,
for instance—tells us one of his dreams. We shall assume that
in this way he is making us one of the communications to which
he has pledged himself by the fact of having started an analytic
treatment. It is, to be sure, a communication made by inappropriate means, for dreams are not in themselves social utterances,
not a means of giving information. Nor, indeed, do we understand what the dreamer was trying to say to us, and he himself

---

[1] [Cf. the whole of Part II of *Introductory Lectures on Psycho-Analysis*
(1916–17).]

is equally in the dark. And now we have to make a quick decision. On the one hand, the dream may be, as non-analytic doctors assure us, a sign that the dreamer has slept badly, that not every part of his brain has come to rest equally, that some areas of it, under the influence of unknown stimuli, endeavoured to go on working but were only able to do so in a very incomplete fashion. If that is the case, we shall be right to concern ourselves no further with the product of a nocturnal disturbance which has no psychical value: for what could we expect to derive from investigating it that would be of use for our purposes? Or on the other hand—but it is plain that we have from the first decided otherwise. We have—quite arbitrarily, it must be admitted—made the assumption, adopted as a postulate, that even this unintelligible dream must be a fully valid psychical act, with sense and worth, which we can use in analysis like any other communication. Only the outcome of our experiment can show whether we are right. If we succeed in turning the dream into an utterance of value of that kind, we shall evidently have a prospect of learning something new and of receiving communications of a sort which would otherwise be inaccessible to us.

Now, however, the difficulties of our task and the enigmas of our subject rise before our eyes. How do we propose to transform the dream into a normal communication and how do we explain the fact that some of the patient's utterances have assumed a form that is unintelligible both to him and to us?

As you see, Ladies and Gentlemen, this time I am taking the path not of a genetic but of a dogmatic exposition. Our first step is to establish our new attitude to the problem of dreams by introducing two new concepts and names. What has been called the dream we shall describe as the text of the dream or the *manifest* dream, and what we are looking for, what we suspect, so to say, of lying behind the dream, we shall describe as the *latent* dream-thoughts. Having done this, we can express our two tasks as follows. We have to transform the manifest dream into the latent one, and to explain how, in the dreamer's mind, the latter has become the former. The first portion is a *practical* task, for which dream-interpretation is responsible; it calls for a technique. The second portion is a *theoretical* task, whose business it is to explain the hypothetical dream-work; and it can only be a theory. Both of them, the technique of dream-interpretation and the theory of the dream-work, have to be newly created.

With which of the two, then, shall we start? With the technique of dream-interpretation, I think; it will present a more concrete appearance and make a more vivid impression on you.

Well then, the patient has told us a dream, which we are to interpret. We have listened passively, without putting our powers of reflection into action.[1] What do we do next? We decide to concern ourselves as little as possible with what we have heard, with the *manifest* dream. Of course this manifest dream exhibits all sorts of characteristics which are not entirely a matter of indifference to us. It may be coherent, smoothly constructed like a literary composition, or it may be confused to the point of unintelligibility, almost like a delirium; it may contain absurd elements or jokes and apparently witty conclusions; it may seem to the dreamer clear and sharp or obscure and hazy; its pictures may exhibit the complete sensory strength of perceptions or may be shadowy like an indistinct mist; the most diverse characteristics may be present in the same dream, distributed over various portions of it; the dream, finally, may show an indifferent emotional tone or be accompanied by feelings of the strongest joy or distress. You must not suppose that we think nothing of this endless diversity in manifest dreams. We shall come back to it later and we shall find a great deal in it that we can make use of in our interpretations. But for the moment we will disregard it and follow the main road that leads to the interpretation of dreams. That is to say, we ask the dreamer, too, to free himself from the impression of the manifest dream, to divert his attention from the dream as a whole on to the separate portions of its content and to report to us in succession everything that occurs to him in relation to each of these portions—what associations present themselves to him if he focuses on each of them separately.

That is a curious technique, is it not?—not the usual way of dealing with a communication or utterance. And no doubt you guess that behind this procedure there are assumptions which have not yet been expressly stated. But let us proceed. In what order are we to get the patient to take up the portions of his dream? There are various possibilities open to us. We can simply follow the chronological order in which they appeared in the account of the dream. That is what may be called the strictest, classical method. Or we can direct the dreamer to begin by looking out for the 'day's residues' in the dream; for experience has taught us that almost every dream includes the remains of a memory or an allusion to some event (or often to several events) of the day before the dream, and, if we follow these connections, we often arrive with one blow at the tran-

[1] [Some illuminating remarks on reflection will be found, in a similar connection, in Chapter II of *The Interpretation of Dreams* (1900a).]

sition from the apparently far remote dream-world to the real life of the patient. Or, again, we may tell him to start with those elements of the dream's content which strike him by their special clarity and sensory strength; for we know that he will find it particularly easy to get associations to these. It makes no difference by which of these methods we approach the associations we are in search of.[1]

And next, we obtain these associations. What they bring us is of the most various kinds: memories from the day before, the 'dream-day', and from times long past, reflections, discussions, with arguments for and against, confessions and enquiries. Some of them the patient pours out; when he comes to others he is held up for a time. Most of them show a clear connection to some element of the dream; no wonder, since those elements were their starting-point. But it also sometimes happens that the patient introduces them with these words: 'This seems to me to have nothing at all to do with the dream, but I tell it you because it occurs to me.'

If one listens to these copious associations, one soon notices that they have more in common with the content of the dream than their starting-points alone. They throw a surprising light on all the different parts of the dream, fill in gaps between them, and make their strange juxtapositions intelligible. In the end one is bound to become clear about the relation between them and the dream's content. The dream is seen to be an abbreviated selection from the associations, a selection made, it is true, according to rules that we have not yet understood: the elements of the dream are like representatives chosen by election from a mass of people. There can be no doubt that by our technique we have got hold of something for which the dream is a substitute and in which lies the dream's psychical value, but which no longer exhibits its puzzling peculiarities, its strangeness and its confusion.

Let there be no misunderstanding, however. The associations to the dream are not yet the latent dream-thoughts. The latter are contained in the associations like an alkali in the mother-liquor, but yet not quite completely contained in them. On the one hand, the associations give us far more than we need for formulating the latent dream-thoughts—namely all the explanations, transitions, and connections which the patient's intellect is bound to produce in the course of his approach to the dream-thoughts. On the other hand, an association often comes

---

[1] [A slightly different list of these alternative methods is given in 'Remarks on the Theory and Practice of Dream-Interpretation' (1923c).]

to a stop precisely before the genuine dream-thought: it has only come near to it and has only had contact with it through allusions. At that point we intervene on our own; we fill in the hints, draw undeniable conclusions, and give explicit utterance to what the patient has only touched on in his associations. This sounds as though we allowed our ingenuity and caprice to play with the material put at our disposal by the dreamer and as though we misused it in order to interpret *into* his utterances what cannot be interpreted *from* them. Nor is it easy to show the legitimacy of our procedure in an abstract description of it. But you have only to carry out a dream-analysis yourselves or study a good account of one in our literature and you will be convinced of the cogent manner in which interpretative work like this proceeds.

If in general and primarily we are dependent, in interpreting dreams, on the dreamer's associations, yet in relation to certain elements of the dream's content we adopt a quite independent attitude, chiefly because we have to, because as a rule associations fail to materialize in their case. We noticed at an early stage that it is always in connection with the same elements that this happens; they are not very numerous, and repeated experience has taught us that they are to be regarded and interpreted as *symbols* of something else. As contrasted with the other dream-elements, a fixed meaning may be attributed to them, which, however, need not be unambiguous and whose range is determined by special rules with which we are unfamiliar. Since *we* know how to translate these symbols and the dreamer does not, in spite of having used them himself, it may happen that the sense of a dream may at once become clear to us as soon as we have heard the text of the dream, even before we have made any efforts at interpreting it, while it still remains an enigma to the dreamer himself. But I have said so much to you in my earlier lectures about symbolism, our knowledge of it and the problems it poses us, that I need not repeat it to-day.[1]

That, then, is our method of interpreting dreams. The first and justifiable question is: 'Can we interpret *all* dreams by its help?'[2] And the answer is: 'No, not all; but so many that we feel confident in the serviceability and correctness of the procedure.' 'But why not all?' The answer to this has something important to teach us, which at once introduces us into the psychical determinants of the formation of dreams: 'Because the work of interpreting dreams is carried out against a resistance,

---

[1] [See *Introductory Lectures* (1916–17), Lecture X.]

[2] [Freud had recently written a special note on 'The Limits to the Possibility of Interpretation' (1925*i*).]

which varies between trivial dimensions and invincibility (at
least so far as the strength of our present methods reaches).' It
is impossible during our work to overlook the manifestations of
this resistance. At some points the associations are given without hesitation and the first or second idea that occurs to the
patient brings an explanation. At other points there is a stop-
page and the patient hesitates before bringing out an association, and, if so, we often have to listen to a long chain of ideas
before receiving anything that helps us to understand the
dream. We are certainly right in thinking that the longer and
more roundabout the chain of associations the stronger the
resistance. We can detect the same influence at work in the
forgetting of dreams. It happens often enough that a patient,
despite all his efforts, cannot remember one of his dreams. But
after we have been able in the course of a piece of analytic work
to get rid of a difficulty which had been disturbing his relation
to the analysis, the forgotten dream suddenly re-emerges. Two
other observations are also in place here. It very frequently
comes about that, to begin with, a portion of a dream is
omitted and added afterwards as an addendum. This is to be
regarded as an attempt to forget that portion. Experience shows
that it is that particular piece which is the most important; there
was a greater resistance, we suppose, in the path of communicating it than the other parts of the dream.[1] Furthermore, we
often find that a dreamer endeavours to prevent himself from
forgetting his dreams by fixing them in writing immediately
after waking up. We can tell him that that is no use. For the
resistance from which he has extorted the preservation of the
text of the dream will then be displaced on to its associations
and will make the manifest dream inaccessible to interpretation.[2] In view of these facts we need not feel surprised if a
further increase in the resistance suppresses the associations
altogether and thus brings the interpretation of the dream to
nothing.

From all this we infer that the resistance which we come
across in the work of interpreting dreams must also have had a
share in their origin. We can actually distinguish between
dreams that arose under a slight and under a high pressure of
resistance.[3] But this pressure varies as well from place to place
within one and the same dream; it is responsible for the gaps,

[1] [Cf. *The Interpretation of Dreams* (1900a), Chapter VII (A).]
[2] [Cf. 'The Handling of Dream-Interpretation in Psycho-Analysis'
(1911e).]
[3] [Cf. Section II of 'Remarks on the Theory and Practice of Dream-
Interpretation' (1923c).]

obscurities and confusions which may interrupt the continuity of even the finest of dreams.

But what is creating the resistance and against what is it aimed? Well, the resistance is the surest sign to us of a conflict. There must be a force here which is seeking to express something and another which is striving to prevent its expression. What comes about in consequence as a manifest dream may combine all the decisions into which this struggle between two trends has been condensed. At one point one of these forces may have succeeded in putting through what it wanted to say, while at another point it is the opposing agency which has managed to blot out the intended communication completely or to replace it by something that reveals not a trace of it. The commonest and most characteristic cases of dream-construction are those in which the conflict has ended in a compromise, so that the communicating agency has, it is true, been able to say what it wanted but not in the way it wanted—only in a softened down, distorted and unrecognized form. If, then, dreams do not give a faithful picture of the dream-thoughts and if the work of interpretation is required in order to bridge the gap between them, that is the outcome of the opposing, inhibiting and restricting agency which we have inferred from our perception of the resistance while we interpret dreams. So long as we studied dreams as isolated phenomena independent of the psychical structures akin to them, we named this agency the *censor*[1] *of dreams*.

You have long been aware that this censorship is not an institution peculiar to dream-life. You know that the conflict between the two psychical agencies, which we—inaccurately—describe as the 'unconscious repressed' and the 'conscious', dominates our whole mental life and that the resistance against the interpretation of dreams, the sign of the dream-censorship, is nothing other than the resistance due to repression by which the two agencies are separated. You know too that the conflict between these two agencies may under certain conditions produce other psychical structures which, like dreams, are the outcome of compromises; and you will not expect me to repeat to you here everything that was contained in my introduction to the theory of the neuroses in order to demonstrate to you what we know of the determinants of the formation of such compromises. You have realized that the dream is a pathological product, the first member of the class which includes hysterical

---

[1] [This is one of the very rare occasions on which Freud uses the personified form '*Zensor*' instead of the impersonal '*Zensur*' (censorship).]

symptoms, obsessions and delusions,[1] but that it is distinguished
from the others by its transitoriness and by its occurrence under
conditions which are part of normal life. For let us bear firmly
in mind that, as was already pointed out by Aristotle, dream-
life is the way in which our mind works during the state of
sleep.[2] The state of sleep involves a turning-away from the real
external world, and there we have the necessary condition for
the development of a psychosis. The most careful study of the
severe psychoses will not reveal to us a single feature that is
more characteristic of those pathological conditions. In psychoses, however, the turning-away from reality is brought about
in two kinds of way: either by the unconscious repressed becoming excessively strong so that it overwhelms the conscious,
which is attached to reality,[3] or because reality has become so
intolerably distressing that the threatened ego throws itself into
the arms of the unconscious instinctual forces in a desperate
revolt. The harmless dream-psychosis is the result of a withdrawal from the external world which is consciously willed and
only temporary, and it disappears when relations to the external world are resumed. During the isolation of the sleeping
individual an alteration in the distribution of his psychical
energy also sets in; a part of the expenditure on repression,
which is normally required in order to hold the unconscious
down, can be saved, for if the unconscious makes use of its
relative liberation for active purposes, it finds its path to
motility closed and the only path open to it is the harmless one
leading to hallucinatory satisfaction. Now, therefore, a dream
can be formed; but the fact of the dream-censorship shows that
even during sleep enough of the resistance due to repression is
retained.

Here we are presented with a means of answering the question of whether dreams have a function too, whether they are
entrusted with any useful achievement. The condition of rest
free from stimulus, which the state of sleep wishes to establish,
is threatened from three directions: in a relatively accidental
manner by external stimuli during sleep, and by interests of the
previous day which cannot be broken off, and in an unavoid-
able manner by unsated repressed instinctual impulses which

---

[1] [This part of the sentence is repeated almost word for word from the
second sentence in Freud's preface to the first edition of *The Interpretation
of Dreams* (1900a).]

[2] [*The Interpretation of Dreams*, Chapter I.]

[3] [The notion occurs already in one of Freud's very earliest psychological papers, his first one on 'The Neuro-Psychoses of Defence'
(1894a).]

are on the watch for an opportunity of finding expression. In consequence of the diminishing of repressions at night there would be a risk that the rest afforded by sleep would be interrupted whenever an instigation from outside or from inside succeeded in linking up with an unconscious instinctual source. The process of dreaming allows the product of a collaboration of this kind to find an outlet in a harmless hallucinatory experience and in that way assures a continuation of sleep. The fact that a dream occasionally awakens the sleeper, to the accompaniment of a generation of anxiety, is no contradiction of this function but rather, perhaps, a signal that the watchman regards the situation as too dangerous and no longer feels able to control it. And very often then, while we are still asleep, a consolation occurs to us which seeks to prevent our waking up: 'But after all it's only a dream!'

This was what I wanted to say to you, Ladies and Gentlemen, about dream-interpretation, whose task it is to lead the way from the manifest dream to the latent dream-thoughts. When this has been achieved, interest in a dream, so far as practical analysis is concerned, is for the most part at an end. We add the communication we have received in the form of a dream to the rest of the patient's communications and proceed with the analysis. We, however, have an interest in dwelling a little longer on the dream. We are tempted to study the process by which the latent dream-thoughts were transformed into the manifest dream. We call this the 'dream-work'. As you will recall, I described it in such detail in my earlier lectures[1] that I can restrict my present survey to the most concise summary.

The process of the dream-work, then, is something entirely new and strange, nothing resembling which was known before. It has given us our first glimpse of the processes which take place in the unconscious system and has shown us that they are quite other than what we know from our conscious thinking and are bound to appear to the latter preposterous and incorrect. The importance of this finding was then increased by the discovery that in the construction of neurotic symptoms the same mechanisms (we do not venture to say 'processes of thought') are operative as those which have transformed the latent dream-thoughts into the manifest dream.

In what follows I shall not be able to avoid a schematic method of exposition. Let us assume that in a particular case we have before us all the latent thoughts, charged with a greater

[1] [*Introductory Lectures*, XI.]

or less amount of affect, by which the manifest dream has been replaced after its interpretation has been completed. We shall then be struck by one difference among these latent thoughts, and that difference will take us a long way. Almost all these dream-thoughts are recognized by the dreamer or acknowledged by him; he admits that he has thought this, now or at some other time, or that he might have thought it. There is only one single thought that he refuses to accept; it is strange to him or even perhaps repellent; he may possibly reject it with passionate feeling. It now becomes evident to us that the other thoughts are portions of a conscious, or, more accurately, a preconscious train of thinking. They might have been thought in waking life too, and indeed they were probably formed during the previous day. This one repudiated thought, however, or, properly speaking, this one impulse, is a child of night; it belongs to the dreamer's unconscious and on that account it is repudiated and rejected by him. It had to wait for the nightly relaxation of repression in order to arrive at any kind of expression. And in any case this expression is a weakened, distorted and disguised one; without our work of dream-interpretation we should not have found it. This unconscious impulse has to thank its link with the other, unobjectionable, dream-thoughts for the opportunity of slipping past the barrier of the censorship in an inconspicuous disguise. On the other hand, the preconscious dream-thoughts have to thank this same link for the power to occupy mental life during sleep as well. For there is no doubt about it: this unconscious impulse is the true creator of the dream; it is what produces the psychical energy for the dream's construction. Like any other instinctual impulse, it cannot strive for anything other than its own satisfaction; and our experience in interpreting dreams shows us too that that is the sense of all dreaming. In every dream an instinctual wish has to be represented as fulfilled. The shutting-off of mental life from reality at night and the regression to primitive mechanisms which this makes possible enable this wished-for instinctual satisfaction to be experienced in a hallucinatory manner as occurring in the present. As a result of this same regression, ideas are transformed in the dream into visual pictures: the latent dream-thoughts, that is to say, are dramatized and illustrated.

This piece of the dream-work gives us information about some of the most striking and peculiar features of dreams. I will repeat the course of events in dream-formation. As an introduction: the wish to sleep and intentional turning away from the external world. Next, two consequences of this for the mental apparatus: first, the possibility for older and more primitive methods of working to emerge in it—regression; secondly, the lowering of the resistance due to repression which weighs down upon the unconscious. As a result of this last factor the possibility arises for the formation of a dream and this is taken advantage of by the precipitating causes, the internal and external stimuli which have become active. The dream which originates in this way is already a compromise-structure. It has a double function; on the one hand it is ego-syntonic,[1] since, by getting rid of the stimuli which are interfering with sleep, it serves the wish to sleep; on the other hand it allows a repressed instinctual impulse to obtain the satisfaction that is possible in these circumstances, in the form of the hallucinated fulfilment of a wish. The whole process of forming a dream which is permitted by the sleeping ego is, however, subject to the condition of the censorship, which is exercised by the residue of the repression still in operation. I cannot present the process more simply: it is not more simple. But I can proceed now with my description of the dream-work.

Let us go back once more to the latent dream-thoughts. Their most powerful element is the repressed instinctual impulse which has created in them an expression for itself on the basis of the presence of chance stimuli and by transference on to the day's residues—though an expression that is toned down and disguised. Like every instinctual impulse, it too presses for satisfaction by action; but its path to motility is blocked by the physiological regulations implied in the state of sleep; it is compelled to take the backwards course in the direction of perception and to be content with a hallucinated satisfaction. The latent dream-thoughts are thus transformed into a collection of sensory images and visual scenes. It is as they travel on this course that what seems to us so novel and so strange occurs to them. All the linguistic instruments by which we express the subtler relations of thought—the conjunctions and prepositions, the changes in declension and conjugation—are dropped, because there are no means of representing them; just as in a primitive language without any grammar, only the raw material of thought is expressed and abstract terms are taken back to the concrete ones that are at their basis. What is left over after this may well appear disconnected. The copious employment of symbols, which have become alien to conscious thinking, for representing certain objects and processes is in harmony alike with the archaic regression in the mental apparatus and with the demands of the censorship.

[1] [In conformity with the ego.]

But other changes made in the elements of the dream-thoughts go far beyond this. Such of those elements as allow any point of contact to be found between them are *condensed* into new unities. In the process of transforming the thoughts into pictures, preference is unmistakably given to such as permit of this putting-together, this condensation; it is as though a force were at work which was subjecting the material to compression and concentration. As a result of condensation, one element in the manifest dream may correspond to numerous elements in the latent dream-thoughts; but, conversely too, one element in the dream-thoughts may be represented by several images in the dream.

Still more remarkable is the other process—*displacement* or shifting of accent—which in conscious thinking we come across only as faulty reasoning or as means for a joke. The different ideas in the dream-thoughts are, indeed, not all of equal value; they are cathected with quotas of affect of varying magnitude and are correspondingly judged to be important and deserving of interest to a greater or less degree. In the dream-work these ideas are separated from the affects attaching to them. The affects are dealt with independently; they may be displaced on to something else, they may be retained, they may undergo alterations, or they may not appear in the dream at all. The importance of the ideas that have been stripped of their affect returns in the dream as sensory strength in the dream-pictures; but we observe that this accent has passed over from important elements to indifferent ones. Thus something that played only a minor part in the dream-thoughts seems to be pushed into the foreground in the dream as the main thing, while, on the contrary, what was the essence of the dream-thoughts finds only passing and indistinct representation in the dream. No other part of the dream-work is so much responsible for making the dream strange and incomprehensible to the dreamer. Displacement is the principal means used in the *dream-distortion* to which the dream-thoughts must submit under the influence of the censorship.

After these influences have been brought to bear upon the dream-thoughts the dream is almost complete. A further, somewhat variable, factor also comes into play—known as 'secondary revision'—after the dream has been presented before consciousness as an object of perception. At that point we treat it as we are in general accustomed to treat the contents of our perception: we fill in gaps and introduce connections, and in doing so are often guilty of gross misunderstandings. But this activity, which might be described as a rationalizing one and which at best provides the dream with a smooth façade that cannot fit its true content, may also be omitted or only be expressed to a very modest degree—in which case the dream will display all its rents and cracks openly. It must not be forgotten, on the other hand, that the dream-work does not always operate with equal energy either; it often restricts itself to certain portions of the dream-thoughts only and others of them are allowed to appear in the dream unaltered. In such cases an impression is given of the dream having carried out the most delicate and complex intellectual operations, of its having speculated, made jokes, arrived at decisions and solved problems, whereas all this is a product of our normal mental activity, may have been performed equally well during the day before the dream as during the night, has nothing to do with the dream-work and brings nothing to light that is characteristic of dreams. Nor is it superfluous to insist once more on the contrast within the dream-thoughts themselves between the unconscious instinctual impulse and the day's residues. While the latter exhibit all the multiplicity of our mental acts, the former, which becomes the motive force proper of the forming of the dream, finds its outlet invariably in the fulfilment of a wish.

I could have told you all this fifteen years ago, and indeed I believe I did in fact tell it you then. And now let me bring together such changes and new discoveries as may have been made during the interval. I have said already that I am afraid you will find that it amounts to very little, and you will fail to understand why I obliged you to listen to the same thing twice over, and obliged myself to say it. But fifteen years have passed meanwhile and I hope that this will be my easiest way of re-establishing contact with you. Moreover, these are such fundamental things, of such decisive importance for understanding psycho-analysis, that one may be glad to hear them a second time, and it is in itself worth knowing that they have remained so much the same for fifteen years.

In the literature of this period you will of course find a large quantity of confirmatory material and of presentation of details, of which I intend only to give you samples. I shall also, incidentally, be able to tell you a few things that were in fact already known earlier. What is in question is principally the symbolism in dreams and the other methods of representation in them. Now listen to this. Only quite a short while ago the medical faculty in an American University refused to allow psycho-analysis the status of a science, on the ground that it did not admit of any experimental proof. They might have raised

the same objection to astronomy; indeed, experimentation with
the heavenly bodies is particularly difficult. There one has to
fall back on observation. Nevertheless, some Viennese investi-
gators have actually made a beginning with experimental con-
firmation of our dream symbolism. As long ago as in 1912 a
Dr. Schrötter found that if instructions to dream of sexual
matters are given to deeply hypnotized subjects, then in the
dream that is thus provoked the sexual material emerges with
its place taken by the symbols that are familiar to us. For instance, a woman was told to dream of sexual intercourse with a
female friend. In her dream this friend appeared with a travelling-bag on which was pasted the label 'Ladies Only'. Still
more impressive experiments were carried out by Betlheim and
Hartmann in 1924. They worked with patients suffering from
what is known as the Korsakoff confusional psychosis. They
told these patients stories of a grossly sexual kind and observed
the distortions which appeared when the patients were instructed to reproduce what they had been told. Once more
there emerged the symbols for sexual organs and sexual intercourse that are familiar to us—among them the symbol of the
staircase which, as the writers justly remark, could never have
been reached by a conscious wish to distort.[1]

In a very interesting series of experiments, Herbert Silberer
[1909 and 1912] has shown that one can catch the dream-work
red-handed, as it were, in the act of turning abstract thoughts
into visual pictures. If he tried to force himself to do intellectual
work while he was in a state of fatigue and drowsiness, the
thought would often vanish and be replaced by a vision, which
was obviously a substitute for it.

Here is a simple example. 'I thought', says Silberer, 'of
having to revise an uneven passage in an essay.' The vision: 'I
saw myself planing a piece of wood.' It often happened during
these experiments that the content of the vision was not the
thought that was being dealt with but his own subjective state
while he was making the effort—the state instead of the object.
This is described by Silberer as a 'functional phenomenon'. An
example will show you at once what is meant. The author was
endeavouring to compare the opinions of two philosophers on a
particular question. But in his sleepy condition one of these
opinions kept on escaping him and finally he had a vision that
he was asking for information from a disobliging secretary who
was bent over his writing-table and who began by disregarding

---

[1] [Longer descriptions of these experiments will be found in Chapter
VI (E) of *The Interpretation of Dreams* (1900a).]

him and then gave him a disagreeable and uncomplying look.
The conditions under which the experiments were made probably themselves explain why the vision that was induced represented so often an event of self-observation.[1]

We have not yet finished with symbols. There are some which
we believed we recognized but which nevertheless worried
us because we could not explain how *this* particular symbol
had come to have *that* particular meaning. In such cases confirmations from elsewhere—from philology, folklore, mythology
or ritual—were bound to be especially welcome. An instance of
this sort is the symbol of an overcoat or cloak [German '*Mantel*'].
We have said that in a woman's dreams this stands for a man.[2]
I hope it will impress you when you hear that Theodor Reik
(1920) gives us this information: 'During the extremely ancient
bridal ceremonial of the Bedouins, the bridegroom covers the
bride with a special cloak known as "Aba" and speaks the
following ritual words: "Henceforth none save I shall cover
thee!"' (Quoted from Robert Eisler [1910, **2**, 599 f.]). We
have also found several fresh symbols, at least two of which
I will tell you of. According to Abraham (1922) a spider in
dreams is a symbol of the mother, but of the *phallic* mother, of
whom we are afraid; so that the fear of spiders expresses dread
of mother-incest and horror of the female genitals. You know,
perhaps, that the mythological creation, Medusa's head, can be
traced back to the same *motif* of fright at castration.[3] The other
symbol I want to talk to you about is that of the *bridge*, which
has been explained by Ferenczi (1921 and 1922). First it means
the male organ, which unites the two parents in sexual intercourse; but afterwards it develops further meanings which
are derived from this first one. In so far as it is thanks to the
male organ that we are able to come into the world at all, out
of the amniotic fluid, a bridge becomes the crossing from the
other world (the unborn state, the womb) to this world (life);
and, since men also picture death as a return to the womb (to the
water), a bridge also acquires the meaning of something that
leads to death, and finally, at a further remove from its original
sense, it stands for transitions or changes in condition generally.

[1] [Freud gave a very much fuller account of Silberer's experiments,
with a great many quotations, in some passages added in 1914 to *The
Interpretation of Dreams* (1900a), Chapter VI (D) and (I).]

[2] [The symbol is referred to in the *Introductory Lectures*, Lecture X,
but the fact that this applies to *women's* dreams is only mentioned
among some 'Observations and Examples' published earlier (Freud,
1913h).]

[3] [Cf. a posthumously published note by Freud on the subject (1940c
[1922]).]

It tallies with this, accordingly, if a woman who has not over-come her wish to be a man has frequent dreams of bridges that are too short to reach the further shore.

In the manifest content of dreams we very often find pictures and situations recalling familiar themes in fairy tales, legends and myths. The interpretation of such dreams thus throws a light on the original interests which created these themes, though we must at the same time not forget, of course, the change in meaning by which this material has been affected in the course of time. Our work of interpretation uncovers, so to say, the raw material, which must often enough be described as sexual in the widest sense, but has found the most varied application in later adaptations. Derivations of this kind are apt to bring down on us the wrath of all non-analytically schooled workers, as though we were seeking to deny or undervalue everything that was later erected on the original basis. Never-theless, such discoveries are instructive and interesting. The same is true of tracing back the origin of particular themes in plastic art, as, for instance, when M. J. Eisler (1919), following indications in his patients' dreams, gave an analytic interpre-tation of the youth playing with a little boy represented in the Hermes of Praxiteles. And lastly I cannot resist pointing out how often light is thrown by the interpretation of dreams on mythological themes in particular. Thus, for instance, the legend of the Labyrinth can be recognized as a representation of anal birth: the twisting paths are the bowels and Ariadne's thread is the umbilical cord.

The methods of representation employed by the dream-work —fascinating material, scarcely capable of exhaustion—have been made more and more familiar to us by closer study. I will give you a few examples of them. Thus, for instance, dreams represent the relation of frequency by a multiplication of simi-lar things. Here is a young girl's remarkable dream. She dreamt she came into a great hall and found some one in it sitting on a chair; this was repeated six or eight times or more, but each time it was her father. This is easy to understand when we dis-cover, from accessory details in the interpretation, that this room stood for the womb. The dream then becomes equivalent to the phantasy, familiarly found in girls, of having met their father already during their intra-uterine life when he visited the womb while their mother was pregnant. You should not be confused by the fact that something is reversed in the dream— that her father's 'coming-in' is displaced on to herself; incident-ally, this has a special meaning of its own as well. The multi-plication of the figure of the father can only express the fact that the event in question occurred repeatedly. After all, it must be allowed that the dream is not taking very much on itself in expressing frequency by multiplicity.[1] It has only needed to go back to the original significance of the former word; to-day it means to us a repetition in time, but it is derived from an accumulation in space. In general, indeed, where it is possible, the dream-work changes temporal relations into spatial ones and represents them as such. In a dream, for instance, one may see a scene between two people who look very small and a long way off, as though one were seeing them through the wrong end of a pair of opera-glasses. Here, both the smallness and the remoteness in space have the same significance: what is meant is remoteness in *time* and we are to understand that the scene is from the remote past.

Again, you may remember that in my earlier lectures I already told you (and illustrated the fact by examples) that we had learnt to make use for our interpretations even of the purely *formal* features of the manifest dream—that is, to transform them into material coming from the latent dream-thoughts.[2] As you already know, all dreams that are dreamt in a single night belong in a single context. But it is not a matter of indifference whether these dreams appear to the dreamer as a continuum or whether he divides them into several parts and into how many. The number of such parts often corresponds to an equal number of separate focal points in the structural formation of the latent dream-thoughts or to contending trends in the dreamer's mental life, each of which finds a dominant, even though never an exclusive, expression in one particular part of the dream. A short introductory dream and a longer main dream following it often stand in the relation of protasis and apodosis [conditional and consequential clauses], of which a very clear instance will be found in the old lectures.[3] A dream which is described by the dreamer as 'somehow interpolated' will actually correspond to a dependent clause in the dream-thoughts. Franz Alexander (1925) has shown in a study on pairs of dreams that it not infrequently happens that two dreams in one night share the carrying-out of the dream's task by producing a wish-fulfilment in two stages if they are taken together, though each dream separately would not effect that result. Suppose, for instance, that the dream-wish had as its con-

---

[1] ['*Häufigkeit*' and '*Häufung*' in German. Both words are derived from '*Haufen*'—a 'heap'.]

[2] [Cf. *Introductory Lectures*, XI.]

[3] [*Introductory Lectures*, XII.]

tent some illicit action in regard to a particular person. Then in the first dream the person will appear undisguised, but the action will be only timidly hinted at. The second dream will behave differently. The action will be named without disguise, but the person will either be made unrecognizable or replaced by someone indifferent. This, you will admit, gives one an impression of actual cunning. Another and similar relation between the two members of a pair of dreams is found where one represents a punishment and the other the sinful wish-fulfilment. It amounts to this: 'if one accepts the punishment for it, one can go on to allow oneself the forbidden thing.'

I cannot detain you any longer over such minor discoveries or over the discussions relating to the employment of dream-interpretation in the work of analysis. I feel sure you are impatient to hear what changes have been made in our fundamental views on the nature and significance of dreams. I have already warned you that precisely on this there is little to report to you. The most disputed point in the whole theory was no doubt the assertion that all dreams are the fulfilments of wishes. The inevitable and ever recurring objection raised by the layman that there are nevertheless so many anxiety-dreams is, I think I may say, completely disposed of in my earlier lectures.[1] With the division into wishful dreams, anxiety-dreams and punishment dreams, we have kept our theory intact.

Punishment-dreams, too, are fulfilments of wishes, though not of wishes of the instinctual impulses but of those of the critical, censoring and punishing agency in the mind. If we have a pure punishment-dream before us, an easy mental operation will enable us to restore the wishful dream to which the punishment-dream was the correct rejoinder and which, owing to this repudiation, was replaced as the manifest dream. As you know, Ladies and Gentlemen, the study of dreams was what first helped us to understand the neuroses, and you will find it natural that our knowledge of the neuroses was later able to influence our view of dreams. As you will hear,[2] we have been obliged to postulate the existence in the mind of a special critical and prohibiting agency which we have named the 'super-ego'. Since recognizing that the censorship of dreams is also a function of this agency, we have been led to examine the part played by the super-ego in the construction of dreams more carefully.

[1] [See *Introductory Lectures*, XIV.]
[2] [In Lecture XXXI below.]

Only two serious difficulties have arisen against the wish-ful-filment theory of dreams. A discussion of them leads far afield and has not yet, indeed, brought us to any wholly satisfying conclusion.

The first of these difficulties is presented in the fact that people who have experienced a shock, a severe psychical trauma —such as happened so often during the war and such as affords the basis for traumatic hysteria—are regularly taken back in their dreams into the traumatic situation. According to our hypotheses about the function of dreams this should not occur. What wishful impulse could be satisfied by harking back in this way to this exceedingly distressing traumatic experience? It is hard to guess.

We meet with the second of these facts almost every day in the course of our analytic work; and it does not imply such an important objection as the other does. One of the tasks of psycho-analysis, as you know, is to lift the veil of amnesia which hides the earliest years of childhood and to bring to conscious memory the manifestations of early infantile sexual life which are contained in them. Now these first sexual experiences of a child are linked to painful impressions of anxiety, prohibition, disappointment and punishment. We can understand their having been repressed; but, that being so, we cannot under-stand how it is that they have such free access to dream-life, that they provide the pattern for so many dream-phantasies and that dreams are filled with reproductions of these scenes from childhood and with allusions to them. It must be admitted that their unpleasurable character and the dream-work's wish-fulfilling purpose seem far from mutually compatible. But it may be that in this case we are magnifying the difficulty. After all, these same infantile experiences have attached to them all the imperishable, unfulfilled instinctual wishes which through-out life provide the energy for the construction of dreams, and to which we may no doubt credit the possibility, in their mighty uprush, of forcing to the surface, along with the rest, the material of distressing events. And on the other hand the manner and form in which this material is reproduced shows unmistakably the efforts of the dream-work directed to denying the unpleasure by means of distortion and to transforming dis-appointment into attainment.

With the traumatic neuroses things are different. In their case the dreams regularly end in the generation of anxiety. We should not, I think, be afraid to admit that here the function of the dream has failed. I will not invoke the saying that the ex-ception proves the rule: its wisdom seems to me most questionable. But no doubt the exception does not overturn the rule. If, for the sake of studying it, we isolate one particular psychical function, such as dreaming, from the psychical machinery as a whole, we make it possible to discover the laws that are peculiar to it; but when we insert it once more into the general context we must be prepared to discover that these findings are obscured or impaired by collision with other forces. We say that a dream is the fulfilment of a wish; but if you want to take these latter objections into account, you can say nevertheless that a dream is an *attempt* at the fulfilment of a wish. No one who can properly appreciate the dynamics of the mind will suppose that you have said anything different by this. In certain circumstances a dream is only able to put its intention into effect very incompletely, or must abandon it entirely. Unconscious fixation to a trauma seems to be foremost among these obstacles to the function of dreaming. While the sleeper is obliged to dream, because the relaxation of repression at night allows the upward pressure of the traumatic fixation to become active, there is a failure in the functioning of his dream-work, which would like to transform the memory-traces of the traumatic event into the fulfilment of a wish. In these circumstances it will happen that one cannot sleep, that one gives up sleep from dread of the failure of the function of dreaming. Traumatic neuroses are here offering us an extreme case; but we must admit that childhood experiences, too, are of a traumatic nature, and we need not be surprised if comparatively trivial interferences with the function of dreams may arise under other conditions as well.[1]

[1] [The topic of the last three paragraphs was first raised by Freud in Chapters II and III of *Beyond the Pleasure Principle* (1920g). Further allusions to it will be found in Lecture XXXII, p. 94 below.]

LECTURE XXX

DREAMS AND OCCULTISM[1]

LADIES AND GENTLEMEN,—To-day we will proceed along a narrow path, but one which may lead us to a wide prospect.

You will scarcely be surprised by the news that I am going to speak to you on the relation of dreams to occultism. Dreams have, indeed, often been regarded as the gateway into the world of mysticism, and even to-day are themselves looked on by many people as an occult phenomenon. Even we, who have made them into a subject for scientific study, do not dispute that one or more threads link them to those obscure matters. Mysticism, occultism—what is meant by these words? You must not expect me to make any attempt at embracing this ill-circumscribed region with definitions. We all know in a general and indefinite manner what the words imply to us. They refer to some sort of 'other world', lying beyond the bright world governed by relentless laws which has been constructed for us by science.

Occultism asserts that there are in fact 'more things in heaven and earth than are dreamt of in our philosophy'. Well, we need not feel bound by the narrow-mindedness of academic philosophy; we are ready to believe what is shown to us to deserve belief.

We propose to proceed with these things as we do with any other scientific material: first of all to establish whether such events can really be shown to occur, and then and only then, when their factual nature cannot be doubted, to concern ourselves with their explanation. It cannot be denied, however, that even the putting of this decision into action is made hard for us by intellectual, psychological and historical factors. The case is not the same as when we approach other investigations.

First, the intellectual difficulty. Let me give you a crude and obvious explanation of what I have in mind. Let us suppose that the question at issue is the constitution of the interior of the earth. We have, as you are aware, no certain knowledge about it. We suspect that it consists of heavy metals in an incandescent state. Then let us imagine that someone puts forward an asser-

---

[1] [Ernest Jones has given a comprehensive survey of Freud's attitude to occultism in Chapter XIV of the third volume of his biography (1957).]

tion that the interior of the earth consists of water saturated
with carbonic acid—that is to say, with a kind of soda-water.
We shall no doubt say that this is most improbable, that it
contradicts all our expectations and pays no attention to the
known facts which have led us to adopt the metal hypothesis.
Nevertheless it is not inconceivable; if someone were to show
us a way of testing the soda-water hypothesis we should follow
it without objecting. But suppose now that someone else comes
along and seriously asserts that the core of the earth consists of
jam. Our reaction to this will be quite different. We shall tell
ourselves that jam does not occur in nature, that it is a product
of human cooking, that, morover, the existence of this material
presupposes the presence of fruit-trees and their fruit, and that
we cannot see how we can locate vegetation and human cookery
in the interior of the earth. The result of these intellectual
objections will be a switching of our interest: instead of starting
upon an investigation of whether the core of the earth really
consists of jam, we shall ask ourselves what sort of person this
must be who can arrive at such a notion, or at most we shall ask
him where he got it from. The unlucky inventor of the jam
theory will be very much insulted and will complain that we
are refusing to make an objective investigation of his assertion
on the ground of a pretendedly scientific prejudice. But this
will be of no help to him. We perceive that prejudices are not
always to be reprobated, but that they are sometimes justified
and expedient because they save us useless labour. In fact they
are only conclusions based on an analogy with other well-
founded judgements.

A whole number of occultist assertions have the same sort
of effect on us as the jam hypothesis; so that we consider ourselves justified in rejecting them at sight, without further investigation. But all the same, the position is not so simple. A
comparison like the one I have chosen proves nothing, or proves
as little as comparisons in general. It remains doubtful whether
it fits the case, and it is clear that its choice was already determined by our attitude of contemptuous rejection. Prejudices are
sometimes expedient and justified; but sometimes they are
erroneous and detrimental, and one can never tell when they
are the one and when the other. The history of science itself
abounds in instances which are a warning against premature
condemnation. For a long time it was regarded as a senseless
hypothesis to suppose that the stones, which we now call meteo-
rites, could have reached the earth from outer space or that the
rocks forming mountains, in which the remains of shells are

imbedded, could have once formed the bed of the sea. Incidentally, much the same thing happened to our psycho-
analysis when it brought forward its inference of there being
an unconscious. Thus we analysts have special reason to be
careful in using intellectual considerations for rejecting new
hypotheses and must admit that they do not relieve us from
feelings of antipathy, doubt and uncertainty.

I have spoken of the second factor [that complicates our
approach to the subject] as the psychological one. By that I
mean the general tendency of mankind to credulity and a belief
in the miraculous. From the very beginning, when life takes
us under its strict discipline, a resistance stirs within us against
the relentlessness and monotony of the laws of thought and
against the demands of reality-testing.[1] Reason becomes the
enemy which withholds from us so many possibilities of pleasure.
We discover how much pleasure it gives us to withdraw from
it, temporarily at least, and to surrender to the allurements of
nonsense. Schoolboys delight in the twisting of words; when a
scientific congress is over, the specialists make fun of their own
activities; even earnest-minded men enjoy a joke.[2] More serious
hostility to 'Reason and Science, the highest strength possessed
by man',[3] awaits its opportunity; it hastens to prefer the
miracle-doctor or the practitioner of nature-cures to the 'qualified' physician; it is favourable to the assertions of occultism so
long as those alleged facts can be taken as breaches of laws and
rules; it lulls criticism to sleep, falsifies perceptions and en-
forces confirmations and agreements which cannot be justified.
If this human tendency is taken into account, there is every
reason to discount much of the information put forward in
occultist literature.

I have called the third doubt the historical one; and by it I
mean to point out that there is in fact nothing new in the world
of occultism. There emerge in it once more all the signs,
miracles, prophecies and apparitions which have been reported
to us from ancient times and in ancient books and which we
thought had long since been disposed of as the offspring of un-
bridled imagination or of tendentious fraud, as the product of
an age in which man's ignorance was very great and the scientific spirit was still in its cradle. If we accept the truth of what,

[1] [I.e. the process of testing things to see if they are real. This is discussed in 'A Metapsychological Supplement to the Theory of Dreams',
(1917d). See also Introductory Lectures, XXIII.]

[2] [This 'pleasure in nonsense' had been fully discussed by Freud in
Chapter IV of his book on jokes (1905c), (Norton, 1961) pp. 125–7.]

[3] [Goethe, Faust, Part I, Scene 4.]

according to the occultists' information, still occurs to-day, we must also believe in the authenticity of the reports which have come down to us from ancient times. And we must then reflect that the tradition and sacred books of all peoples are brimful of similar marvellous tales and that the religions base their claim to credibility on precisely such miraculous events and find proof in them of the operation of superhuman powers. That being so, it will be hard for us to avoid a suspicion that the interest in occultism is in fact a religious one and that one of the secret motives of the occultist movement is to come to the help of religion, threatened as it is by the advance of scientific thought. And with the discovery of this motive our distrust must increase and our disinclination to embark on the examination of these supposedly occult phenomena.

Sooner or later, however, this disinclination must be overcome. We are faced by a question of fact: is what the occultists tell us true or not? It must, after all, be possible to decide this by observation. At bottom we have cause for gratitude to the occultists. The miraculous stories from ancient times are beyond the reach of our testing. If in our opinion they cannot be substantiated, we must admit that they cannot, strictly speaking, be disproved. But about contemporary happenings, at which we are able to be present, it must be possible for us to reach a definite judgement. If we arrive at a conviction that such miracles do not occur to-day, we need not fear the counter-argument that they may nevertheless have taken place in ancient times: in that case other explanations will be much more plausible. Thus we have settled our doubts and are ready to take part in an investigation of occult phenomena.

But here unluckily we are met by circumstances which are exceedingly unfavourable to our honest intentions. The observations on which our judgement is supposed to depend take place under conditions which make our sensory perceptions uncertain and which blunt our power of attention; they occur in darkness or in dim red light after long periods of blank expectation. We are told that in fact our unbelieving—that is to say, critical—attitude may prevent the expected phenomena from happening. The situation thus brought about is nothing less than a caricature of the circumstances in which we are usually accustomed to carry out scientific enquiries. The observations are made upon what are called 'mediums'—individuals to whom peculiarly 'sensitive' faculties are ascribed, but who are by no means distinguished by outstanding qualities of intellect or character, and who are not, like the miracle-workers of the past, inspired by any great idea or serious pur-

pose. On the contrary, they are looked upon, even by those
who believe in their secret powers, as particularly untrustworthy; most of them have already been detected as cheats and
we may reasonably expect that the same fate awaits the remainder. Their performances give one the impression of children's
mischievous pranks or of conjuring tricks.[1] Never has anything
of importance yet emerged from *séances* with these mediums—
the revelation of a new source of power, for instance. We do
not, it is true, expect to receive hints on pigeon-breeding from
the conjurer who produces pigeons by magic from his empty
top-hat. I can easily put myself in the place of a person who
tries to fulfil the demands of an objective attitude and so takes
part in occult *séances*, but who grows tired after a while and
turns away in disgust from what is expected of him and goes
back unenlightened to his former prejudices. The reproach
may be made against such a person that this is not the right way
of behaving: that one ought not to lay down in advance what
the phenomena one is seeking to study shall be like and in what
circumstances they shall appear. One should, on the contrary,
persevere, and give weight to the precautionary and super-
visory measures by which efforts have recently been made to
provide against the untrustworthiness of mediums. Unfortunately this modern protective technique makes an end of the easy
accessibility of occult observations. The study of occultism
becomes a specialized and difficult profession—an activity one
cannot pursue alongside of one's other interests. And until
those concerned in these investigations have reached their conclusions, we are left to our doubts and our own conjectures.

Of these conjectures no doubt the most probable is that there
is a real core of yet unrecognized facts in occultism round which
cheating and phantasy have spun a veil which it is hard to
pierce. But how can we even approach this core? at what point
can we attack the problem? It is here, I think, that dreams come
to our help, by giving us a hint that from out of this chaos we
should pick the subject of *telepathy*.

What we call 'telepathy' is, as you know, the alleged fact
that an event which occurs at a particular time comes at about
the same moment to the consciousness of someone distant in
space, without the paths of communication that are familiar
to us coming into question. It is implicitly presupposed that this
event concerns a person in whom the other one (the receiver

[1] [Cf. the similar remarks in Chapter V of *The Future of an Illusion*
(1927*c*).]

of the intelligence) has a strong emotional interest. For instance, Person A may be the victim of an accident or may die, and Person B, someone nearly attached to him—his mother or daughter or fiancée—learns the fact at about the same time through a visual or auditory perception. In this latter case, then, it is as if she had been informed by telephone, though such was not the case; it is a kind of psychical counterpart to wireless telegraphy. I need not insist to you on the improbability of such events, and there is good reason for dismissing the majority of such reports. A few are left over which cannot be so easily disposed of in this way. Permit me now, for the purpose of what I have to tell you, to omit the cautious little word 'alleged' and to proceed as though I believed in the objective reality of the phenomenon of telepathy. But bear firmly in mind that that is not the case and that I have committed myself to no conviction.

Actually I have little to tell you—only a modest fact. I will also at once reduce your expectations still further by saying that at bottom dreams have little to do with telepathy. Telepathy does not throw any fresh light on the nature of dreams nor do dreams give any direct evidence of the reality of telepathy. Moreover the phenomenon of telepathy is by no means bound up with dreams; it can occur as well during the waking state. The only reason for discussing the relation between dreams and telepathy is that the state of sleep seems particularly suited for receiving telepathic messages. In such cases one has what is called a telepathic dream and, when it is analysed, one forms a conviction that the telepathic news has played the same part as any other portion of the day's residues and that it has been changed in the same way by the dream-work and made to serve its purpose.

During the analysis of one such telepathic dream, something occurred which seems to me of sufficient interest in spite of its triviality to serve as the starting-point of this lecture. When in 1922 I gave my first account of this matter I had only a single observation at my disposal. Since then I have made a number of similar ones, but I will keep to the first example, because it is easiest to describe, and I will take you straight away *in medias res*.[1]

An obviously intelligent man, who from his own account was not in the least 'inclined towards occultism', wrote to me

[1] [This was first published in very much greater detail, in 'Dreams and Telepathy' (1922a).]

about a dream he had had which seemed to him remarkable. He began by informing me that his married daughter, who lived at a distance from him, was expecting her first confinement in the middle of December. This daughter meant a great deal to him and he knew too that she was very much attached to him. During the night of November 16–17, then, he dreamt that his wife had given birth to twins. A number of details followed, which I may here pass over, and all of which were never in fact explained. The wife who in the dream had become the mother of twins was his *second* wife, his daughter's stepmother. He did not wish to have a child by his present wife who, he said, had no aptitude for bringing up children sensibly; moreover, at the time of the dream he had long ceased to have sexual relations with her. What led him to write to me was not doubt about the theory of dreams, though the manifest content of his dream would have justified it, for why did the dream, in complete contradiction to his wishes, make his wife give birth to children? Nor, according to him, was there any reason to fear that this unwished-for event might occur. What induced him to report this dream to me was the circumstance that on the morning of November 18 he received a telegram announcing that his daughter had given birth to twins. The telegram had been handed in the day before and the birth had taken place during the night of November 16–17, at about the same time at which he had had the dream of his wife's twin birth. The dreamer asked me whether I thought the coincidence between dream and event was accidental. He did not venture to call the dream a telepathic one, since the difference between its content and the event affected precisely what seemed to him essential in it—the identity of the person who gave birth to the children. But one of his comments shows that he would not have been astonished at an actual telepathic dream: he believed his daughter would have thought particularly of him during her labour.

I feel sure, Ladies and Gentlemen, that you have been able to explain this dream already and understand too why I have told it you. Here was a man who was dissatisfied with his second wife and who would prefer his wife to be like the daughter of his first marriage. This 'like' dropped out, of course, so far as the unconscious was concerned. And now the telepathic message arrived during the night to say that his daughter had given birth to twins. The dream-work took control of the news, allowed the unconscious wish to operate on it—the wish that he could put his daughter in the place of his second wife—and thus arose the puzzling manifest dream, which disguised the wish and distorted the message. We must admit that it is only the *interpretation* of the dream that has shown us that it was a telepathic one: psycho-analysis has revealed a telepathic event which we should not otherwise have discovered.

But pray do not let yourselves be misled! In spite of all this, dream-interpretation has told us nothing about the objective reality of the telepathic event. It may equally be an illusion which can be explained in another way. The man's latent dream-thoughts may have run: 'To-day is the day the confinement should take place if my daughter is really out in her reckoning by a month, as I suspect. And when I saw her last she looked just as though she was going to have twins. How my dead wife who was so fond of children would have rejoiced over twins!' (I base this last factor on some associations of the dreamer's which I have not mentioned.) In that case the instigation to the dream would have been well-grounded suspicions on the dreamer's part and not a telepathic message; but the outcome would remain the same. You see then that even the interpretation of this dream has told us nothing on the question of whether we are to allow objective reality to telepathy. That could only be decided by a thorough-going investigation of all the circumstances of the case—which was unfortunately no more possible in this instance than in any of the others in my experience. Granted that the telepathy hypothesis offers by far the simplest explanation, yet that does not help us much. The simplest explanation is not always the correct one; the truth is often no simple matter, and before deciding in favour of such a far-reaching hypothesis we should like to have taken every precaution.

We may now leave the subject of dreams and telepathy: I have nothing more to say to you on it. But kindly observe that what seemed to us to teach us something about telepathy was not the dream but the interpretation of the dream, its psycho-analytic working-over. Accordingly, in what follows we may leave dreams entirely on one side and may follow an expectation that the employment of psycho-analysis may throw a little light on other events described as occult. There is, for instance, the phenomenon of thought-transference, which is so close to telepathy and can indeed without much violence be regarded as the same thing. It claims that mental processes in one person—ideas, emotional states, conative impulses—can be transferred to another person through empty space without employing the familiar methods of communication by means of words and signs. You will realize how remarkable, and perhaps even of what great practical importance, it would be if something of the kind really happened. It may be noted, incidentally, that strangely enough precisely this phenomenon is referred to least frequently in the miraculous stories of the past.

I have formed an impression in the course of the psycho-analytic treatment of patients that the activities of professional fortune-tellers conceal an opportunity for making particularly unobjectionable observations on thought-transference. These are insignificant and even inferior people, who immerse themselves in some sort of performance[1]—lay out cards, study writing or lines upon the palm of the hand, or make astrological calculations—and at the same time, after having shown themselves familiar with portions of their visitor's past or present circumstances, go on to prophesy their future. As a rule their clients exhibit great satisfaction over these achievements and feel no resentment if later on these prophecies are not fulfilled. I have come across several such cases and have been able to study them analytically, and in a moment I will tell you the most remarkable of these instances. Their convincingness is unfortunately impaired by the numerous reticences to which I am compelled by the obligation of medical discretion. I have, however, of set purpose avoided distortions. So listen now to the story of one of my women patients, who had an experience of this kind with a fortune-teller.[2]

She had been the eldest of a numerous family and had grown up with an extremely strong attachment to her father. She had married young and had found entire satisfaction in her mar-

[1] [In Section I of his earlier, posthumously published, paper, 'Psycho-Analysis and Telepathy' (1941d [1921]), Freud had elaborated on the significance of the fortune-teller's distracting his attention by some meaningless activity as a means of releasing an unconscious mental process. He there compared the use of a similar 'distracting contrivance' in the making of some kinds of jokes; see for this Chapter V of his book on jokes (1905c), pp. 151–3. Much earlier, in his technical contribution to Studies on Hysteria (1895d), he had brought forward the same explanation for certain techniques for producing hypnosis, and in particular for his own early method of eliciting forgotten facts by pressure on the patient's forehead; and this he afterwards developed in a discussion of hypnotism in Chapter X of his Group Psychology (1921c). Compare also some remarks near the end of Chapter VI of The Psychopathology of Everyday Life (1901b) on the fact that attention directed to an automatic action interferes with its performance, p. 132.]

[2] [This case is reported at greater length, with some slight variations, in 'Psycho-Analysis and Telepathy', and much more briefly in Section C of 1925i.]

riage. Only one thing was wanting to her happiness: she had remained childless, so she could not bring her beloved husband completely into the place of her father. When, after long years of disappointment, she decided to undergo a gynaecological operation, her husband revealed to her that the blame was his: an illness before their marriage had made him incapable of procreating children. She took the disappointment badly, became neurotic and clearly suffered from fears of being tempted [into unfaithfulness to her husband]. To cheer her up, he took her with him on a business trip to Paris. They were sitting there one day in the hall of their hotel when she noticed a stir among the hotel servants. She asked what was going on and was told that Monsieur le Professeur had arrived and was giving consultations in a little room over there. She expressed a wish to have a try. Her husband rejected the idea, but while he was not watching she slipped into the consulting-room and faced the fortune-teller. She was 27 years old, but looked much younger and had taken off her wedding-ring. Monsieur le Professeur made her lay her hand on a tray filled with ashes and carefully studied the imprint; he then told her all kinds of things about hard struggles that lay before her, and ended with the comforting assurance that all the same she would still get married and would have two children by the time she was 32. When she told me this story she was 43 years old, seriously ill and without any prospect of ever having a child. Thus the prophecy had not come true; yet she spoke of it without any sort of bitterness but with an unmistakable expression of satisfaction, as though she were recalling a cheerful event. It was easy to establish that she had not the slightest notion of what the two numbers in the prophecy [2 and 32] might mean or whether they meant anything at all.

You will say that this is a stupid and incomprehensible story and ask why I have told it you. I should be entirely of your opinion if—and this is the salient point—analysis had not made it possible to arrive at an interpretation of the prophecy which is convincing precisely from the explanation it affords of the details. For the two numbers find their place in the life of my patient's *mother*. She had married late—not till she was over thirty, and in the family they had often dwelt on the fact of the success with which she had hastened to make up for lost time. Her two first children (with our patient the elder) had been born with the shortest possible interval between them, in a single calendar year; and she had in fact two children by the time she was 32. What Monsieur le Professeur had said to my patient meant therefore: 'Take comfort from the fact of being so young. You'll have the same destiny as your mother, who also had to wait a long time for children, and you'll have two children by the time you're 32.' But to have the same destiny as her mother, to put herself in her mother's place, to take her place with her father—that had been the strongest wish of her youth, the wish on account of whose non-fulfilment she was just beginning to fall ill. The prophecy promised her that the wish would still be fulfilled in spite of everything; how could she fail to feel friendly to the prophet? Do you regard it as possible, however, that Monsieur le Professeur was familiar with the facts of the intimate family history of his chance client? Out of the question! How, then, did he arrive at the knowledge which enabled him to give expression to my patient's strongest and most secret wish by including the two numbers in his prophecy? I can see only two possible explanations. Either the story as it was told me is untrue and the events occurred otherwise, or thought-transference exists as a real phenomenon. One can suppose, no doubt, that after an interval of 16 years the patient had introduced the two numbers concerned into her recollection from her unconscious. I have no basis for this suspicion, but I cannot exclude it, and I imagine that you will be readier to believe in a way out of that kind than in the reality of thought-transference. If you do decide on the latter course, do not forget that it was only analysis that created the occult fact—uncovered it when it lay distorted to the point of being unrecognizable.

If it were a question of *one* case only like that of my patient, one would shrug it aside. No one would dream of erecting upon a single observation a belief which implies taking such a decisive line. But you must believe me when I assure you that this is not the only case in my experience. I have collected a whole number of such prophecies and from all of them I gained the impression that the fortune-teller had merely brought to expression the thoughts, and more especially the secret wishes, of those were were questioning him, and that we were therefore justified in analysing these prophecies as though they were subjective products, phantasies or dreams of the people concerned. Not every case, of course, is equally convincing and in not every case is it equally possible to exclude more rational explanations; but, taking them as a whole, there remains a strong balance of probability in favour of thought-transference as a fact. The importance of the subject would justify me in producing all my cases to you; but that I cannot do, owing to the prolixity of description that would be involved and to the

inevitable breach of the obligations of discretion. I will try so
far as possible to appease my conscience in giving you a few
more examples.

One day I was visited by a highly intelligent young man, a
student preparing for his final examinations for a doctorate, but
unable to take them since, as he complained, he had lost all
interest and power of concentration and even any faculty for
orderly memory.[1] The previous history of this condition of
quasi-paralysis was soon revealed: he had fallen ill after carrying
out a great act of self-discipline. He had a sister, to whom he
was attached by an intense but always restrained devotion, just
as she was to him. 'What a pity we can't get married!' they
would often say to each other. A respectable man fell in love
with the sister; she responded to his affection, but her parents
did not assent to the union. In their difficulty the young couple
turned to her brother, nor did he refuse his help. He made it
possible for them to correspond with each other, and his influence eventually persuaded the parents to consent. In the
course of the engagement, however, an occurrence took place
whose meaning it was easy to guess. He went with his future
brother-in-law on a difficult mountain-climb without a guide;
they lost their way and were in danger of not returning safe and
sound. Shortly after his sister's marriage he fell into this condition of mental exhaustion.

The influence of psycho-analysis restored his ability to work
and he left me in order to go in for his examinations; but after
he had passed them successfully he came back to me for a short
time in the autumn of the same year. It was then that he
related a remarkable experience to me which he had had before
the summer. In his University town there lived a fortune-teller
who enjoyed great popularity. Even the Princes of the Royal
House used to consult her before important undertakings. Her
mode of operation was very simple. She asked to be given the
date of the relevant person's birth; she required to know
nothing else about him, not even his name. She then proceeded
to consult her astrological books, made long calculations and
finally uttered a prophecy relating to the person in question.
My patient decided to call upon her mystical arts in connection
with his brother-in-law. He visited her and told her the relevant
date. After carrying out her calculations she made her prophecy: 'The person in question will die in July or August of this

[1] [This case too appears in rather greater detail in 'Psycho-Analysis
and Telepathy'.]

year of crayfish- or oyster-poisoning.' My patient finished his
story with the words: 'It was quite marvellous!'

From the first I had listened with irritation. After this excla-
mation of his I went so far as to ask: 'What do you see that's so
marvellous in this prophecy? Here we are in late autumn and
your brother-in-law isn't dead or you'd have told me long
ago. So the prophecy hasn't come true.' 'No doubt that's so,' he
replied, 'but here is what's marvellous. My brother-in-law is
passionately devoted to crayfish and oysters and in the previous
summer—that's to say, *before* my visit to the fortune-teller—he
had an attack of oyster-poisoning[1] of which he nearly died.'
What was I to say to this? I could only feel annoyed that this
highly-educated man (who had moreover been through a successful analysis) should not have a clearer view of the position. I
for my part, rather than believe that it is possible to calculate
the onset of an attack of crayfish- or oyster-poisoning from astrological tables, prefer to suppose that my patient had not yet
overcome his hatred for his rival, the repression of which had
earlier led to his falling ill, and that the fortune-teller was
simply giving expression to his own expectation: 'a taste of that
kind isn't to be given up, and one day, all the same, it will be the
end of him.' I must admit that I cannot think of any other
explanation for this case, unless, perhaps, that my patient was
having a joke with me. But neither then nor at a later time did
he give me grounds for such a suspicion, and he seemed to be
meaning what he said seriously.

Here is another case.[2] A young man in a position of consequence was involved in a *liaison* with a *demi-mondaine* which
was characterized by a curious compulsion. He was obliged
from time to time to provoke her with derisive and insulting
remarks till she was driven to complete desperation. When he
had brought her to that point, he was relieved, became recon-
ciled with her and made her a present. But now he wanted to be
free of her: the compulsion seemed to him uncanny. He noticed
that this *liaison* was damaging his reputation; he wanted to have
a wife of his own and to raise a family. But since he could not
get free from this *demi-mondaine* by his own strength, he called
analysis to his help. After one of these abusive scenes, when the
analysis had already started, he got her to write something on a

---

[1] ['Crayfish-poisoning' in the 'Psycho-Analysis and Telepathy' version.]
[2] [Also reported with some further details in 'Psycho-Analysis and
Telepathy', though the present account is in some respects fuller.]

piece of paper, so as to show it to a graphologist. The report that
he received from him was that the writing was that of someone
in extreme despair, who would certainly commit suicide in the
next few days. This did not, it is true, occur and the lady remained alive; but the analysis succeeded in loosening his bonds.
He left the lady and turned to a young girl who he expected
would be able to make him a good wife. Soon afterwards a
dream appeared which could only hint at a dawning doubt as to
the girl's worthiness. He obtained a specimen of her writing
too, took it to the same authority, and was given a verdict on her
writing which confirmed his apprehensions. He therefore abandoned the idea of making her his wife.

In order to form an opinion of the graphologist's reports,
especially the first one, we must know something of our subject's secret history. In his early youth he had (in accordance
with his passionate nature) fallen in love to the pitch of frenzy
with a married woman who was still young but nevertheless
older than he was. When she rejected him, he made an attempt
at suicide which, there can be no doubt, was seriously intended.
It was only by a hair's breadth that he escaped death and he
was only restored after a long period of nursing. But this wild
action made a deep impression on the woman he loved; she
granted him her favours, he became her lover and thenceforward remained secretly attached to her and served her with
a truly chivalrous devotion. More than twenty years later, when
they had both grown older—but the woman, naturally, more
than he—the need was awakened in him to detach himself from
her, to make himself free, to lead a life of his own, to set up a
house and raise a family. And along with this feeling of satiety
there arose in him his long-suppressed craving for vengeance on
his mistress. As he had once tried to kill himself because she had
spurned him, so he wished now to have the satisfaction of her
seeking death because he left her. But his love was still too
strong for it to be possible for this wish to become conscious in
him; nor was he in a position to do her enough harm to drive
her into death. In this frame of mind he took on the *demi-
mondaine* as a sort of whipping-boy, to satisfy his thirst for
revenge *in corpore vili*; and he allowed himself to practise upon
her all the torments which he might expect would bring about
with her the result he wished to produce on his mistress. The
fact that the vengeance applied to the latter was betrayed by his
making her into a confidante and adviser in his *liaison* instead of
concealing his defection from her. The wretched woman, who
had long fallen from giving to receiving favours, probably suffered more from his confidences than the *demi-mondaine* did

from his brutalities. The compulsion of which he complained in regard to this substitutive figure, and which drove him to analysis, had of course been transferred on to her from his old mistress; it was from her that he wanted to free himself but could not. I am not an authority on handwriting and have no high opinion of the art of divining character from it; still less do I believe in the possibility of foretelling the writer's future in this way. You can see, however, whatever one may think of the value of graphology, that there is no mistaking the fact that the expert, when he promised that the writer of the specimen presented to him would commit suicide in the next few days, had once again only brought to light a powerful secret wish of the person who was questioning him. Something of the same kind happened afterwards in the case of the second report. What was there concerned, however, was not an unconscious wish; it was the questioner's dawning doubt and apprehension that found a clear expression from the graphologist's mouth. Incidentally, my patient succeeded, with the help of analysis, in finding an object for his love outside the magic circle in which he had been spellbound.

Ladies and Gentlemen,—You have now heard how dream-interpretation and psycho-analysis in general assist occultism. I have shown you from examples that by their application occult facts have been brought to light which would otherwise have remained unknown. Psycho-analysis cannot give a direct answer to the question that no doubt interests you the most—whether we are to believe in the objective reality of these findings. But the material revealed by its help makes an impression which is at all events favourable to an affirmative reply. Your interest will not come to a stop at this point, however. You will want to know what conclusions are justified by the incomparably richer material in which psycho-analysis has no part. But I cannot follow you there: it lies outside my province. The only further thing I could do would be to report observations to you which have at least so much relation to analysis that they were made during psycho-analytic treatment and were even perhaps made possible by its influence. I will tell you one such example—the one which has left the strongest impression behind on me. I shall tell it at great length and shall ask for your attention to a large number of details, though even so I shall have to suppress much that would have greatly increased the convincing force of the observation. It is an example in which the fact came clearly to light and did not need to be developed by analysis. In discussing it, however, we shall not be able to do without the help of analysis. But I will tell you in advance that this example too of apparent thought-transference in the analytic situation is not exempt from all doubts and that it does not allow us to take up an unqualified position in support of the reality of occult phenomena.[1]

Listen then:—One autumn day in the year 1919, at about 10.45 a.m., Dr. David Forsyth,[2] who had just arrived from London, sent in his card to me while I was working with a patient. (My respected colleague from London University will not, I feel sure, regard it as an indiscretion if in this way I betray the fact that he spent some months being initiated by me into the arts of psycho-analytic technique.) I only had time to greet him and to make an appointment to see him later. Dr. Forsyth had a claim to my particular interest; he was the first foreigner to come to me after I had been cut off by the war-years and to bring a promise of better times. Soon afterwards, at eleven o'clock, Herr P., one of my patients, arrived—an intelligent and agreeable man, between forty and fifty years of age, who had originally come to me on account of difficulties with women. His case did not promise any therapeutic success; I had long before proposed our stopping the treatment, but he had wished to continue it, evidently because he felt comfortable in a well-tempered father-transference to me. At that period money played no part: there was too little of it about. The sessions which I spent with him were stimulating and refreshing for me as well, and consequently, in disregard of the strict rules of medical practice, analytic work was being carried on up to a foreseen time-limit.

That day P. returned to his attempts at having erotic relations with women and once again mentioned a pretty, piquante, penniless girl, with whom he felt he might succeed, if the fact of her being a virgin did not scare him off any serious attempt. He had often talked of her before but that day he told me for the first time that, though of course she had no notion of the true

---

[1] [This case is the one which should have been the 'third case' to be included in 'Psycho-Analysis and Telepathy'. The circumstances of its omission were explained by Freud in that paper. As was indicated there, the original draft survived. It resembled the version given here so closely that it was doubtful whether it was necessary to print it separately. It should be added, however, that the manuscript has once again unaccountably disappeared.]

[2] [Dr. David Forsyth (1877–1941), Consulting Physician to Charing Cross Hospital, London, was an original member of the London Society for Psycho-Analysis, founded in 1913.]

grounds of his impediment, she used to call him 'Herr von
Vorsicht' [Mr. Foresight]. I was struck by this information; Dr.
Forsyth's visiting card lay beside me, and I showed it to him.

These are the facts of the case. I expect they will seem to you
paltry; but listen a little longer, there is more behind them.

When he was young, P. had spent some years in England and
since then had retained a permanent interest in English literature. He possessed a rich English library and used to bring me
books from it. I owe to him an acquaintance with such authors
as Bennett and Galsworthy, of whom till then I had read little.
One day he lent me a novel of Galsworthy's with the title *The
Man of Property*, whose scene is laid in the bosom of a family
invented by the author, bearing the name of 'Forsyte'. Galsworthy himself was evidently captivated by this creation of his,
for in later volumes he repeatedly came back to the members of
this family and finally collected all the tales relating to them
under the title of *The Forsyte Saga*. Only a few days before the
occurrence I am speaking of, he had brought me a fresh volume
from this series. The name 'Forsyte', and everything typical
that the author had sought to embody in it, had played a part,
too, in my conversations with P. and it had become part of the
secret language which so easily grows up between two people
who see a lot of each other. Now the name 'Forsyte' in these
novels differs little from that of my visitor 'Forsyth' and, as
pronounced by a German, the two can scarcely be distinguished; and there is an English word with a meaning—'fore-
sight'—which we should also pronounce in the same way and
which would be translated '*Voraussicht*' or '*Vorsicht*'. Thus P.
had in fact selected from his personal concerns the very name
with which I was occupied at the same time as a result of an
occurrence of which he was unaware.

That begins to look better, you will agree. But we shall, I
think, receive a stronger impression of the striking phenomenon
and even obtain an insight into its determinants, if we throw
some analytic light upon two other associations brought up by
P. during the same session.

Firstly: One day of the previous week I had waited in vain for
Herr P. at eleven o'clock, and had then gone out to visit Dr.
Anton von Freund[1] in his *pension*. I was surprised to find that
Herr P. lived on another floor of the same building in which the
pension was located. In connection with this I had later told P.
that I had in a sense paid him a visit in his house; but I know
definitely that I did not tell him the name of the person I visited

---

[1] [A prominent Hungarian psycho-analyst.]

in the *pension*. And now, shortly after mentioning 'Herr von Vorsicht' he asked me whether perhaps the Freud-Ottorego who was giving a course of lectures on English at the Volks-universität[1] was my daughter. And for the first time during our long period of intercourse he gave my name the distorted form to which I have indeed become habituated by functionaries, officials and compositors: instead of 'Freud' he said 'Freund'.

Secondly: At the end of the same session he told me a dream, from which he had woken in a fright—a regular '*Alptraum*', he said. He added that not long ago he had forgotten the English word for that, and when someone had asked him said that the English for '*Alptraum*' was 'a mare's nest'. This was nonsense, of course, he went on; 'a mare's nest' meant something incredible, a cock-and-bull story: the translation of '*Alptraum*' was 'nightmare'. The only element in common between this association and the previous one seemed to be the element 'English'. I was however reminded of a small incident which had occurred about a month earlier. P. was sitting with me in the room when another visitor, a dear friend from London, Dr. Ernest Jones, unexpectedly came in after a long separation. I signed to him to go into the next room while I finished with P. The latter, however, had at once recognized him from his photograph hanging in the waiting-room, and even expressed a wish to be introduced to him. Now Jones is the author of a monograph on the *Alptraum*—the nightmare. I did not know whether P. was acquainted with it; he avoided reading analytic literature.

I should like to begin by putting before you an investigation of what analytic understanding can be arrived at of the background of P.'s associations and of the motives for them. P. was placed similarly to me in relation to the name 'Forsyte' or 'Forsyth'; it meant the same to him, and it was entirely to him that I owed my acquaintance with the name. The remarkable fact was that he brought the name into the analysis unheralded, only the briefest time after it had become significant to me in another sense owing to a new event—the London doctor's arrival. But the manner in which the name emerged in his analytic session is perhaps not less interesting than the fact itself. He did not say, for instance: 'The name "Forsyte", out of the novels you are familiar with, has just occurred to me.' He was able, without any conscious relation to that source, to weave the name into his own experiences and to produce it thence—a

---

[1] ['People's University', providing what is known in England as 'Adult Education'.]

thing that might have happened long before but had not happened till then. What he *did* say now was: 'I'm a Forsyth too: that's what the girl calls me.' It is hard to mistake the mixture of jealous demand and melancholy self-deprecation which finds its expression in this remark. We shall not be going astray if we complete it in some such way as this: 'It's mortifying to me that your thoughts should be so intensely occupied with this new arrival. Do come back to me; after all I'm a Forsyth too—though it's true I'm only a Herr von Vorsicht [gentleman of foresight], as the girl says.' And thereupon his train of thought, passing along the associative threads of the element 'English' went back to two earlier events, which were able to stir up the same feelings of jealousy. 'A few days ago you paid a visit to my house—not, alas, to me but to a Herr von Freund.' This thought caused him to distort the name 'Freud' into 'Freund'. The 'Freud-Ottorego' from the lecture-syllabus must come in here because as a teacher of English she provided the manifest association. And now came the recollection of another visitor a few weeks before, of whom he was no doubt equally jealous, but for whom he also felt he was no match, for Dr. Jones was able to write a monograph on the nightmare whereas he was at best only able to produce such dreams himself. His mention of his mistake about the meaning of 'a mare's nest' comes into this connection, for it can only mean to say: 'After all I'm not a genuine Englishman any more than I'm a genuine Forsyth.'

Now I cannot describe his feelings of jealousy as either out of place or unintelligible. He had been warned that his analysis, and at the same time our contact, would come to an end as soon as foreign pupils and patients returned to Vienna; and that was in fact what happened shortly afterwards. What we have so far achieved, however, has been a piece of analytic work—the explanation of three associations brought up by him in the same session and nourished by the same motive: and this has not much to do with the other question of whether these associations could or could not have been made without thought-transference. This question arises in the case of each of the three associations and thus falls into three separate questions: Could P. have known that Dr. Forsyth had just paid me his first visit? Could he know the name of the person I had visited in his house? Did he know that Dr. Jones had written a monograph on the nightmare? Or was it only *my* knowledge about these things that was revealed in his associations? It will depend on the reply to these separate questions whether my observation allows of a conclusion favourable to thought-transference.

Let us leave the first question aside for a while; the other two

can be dealt with more easily. The case of my visit to his *pension*
makes a particularly convincing impression at first sight. I am
certain that in my short, joking reference to my visit to his house
I mentioned no name. I think it is most unlikely that P. made
enquiries at the *pension* as to the name of the person concerned;
I believe rather that the existence of that person remained entirely unknown to him. But the evidential value of this case is
totally destroyed by a chance circumstance. The man whom I
had visited at the *pension* was not only called 'Freund'; he was a
true friend to us all.[1] He was Dr. Anton von Freund whose
donation had made the foundation of our publishing house possible. His early death, together with that of our colleague Karl
Abraham a few years later, are the gravest misfortunes which
have befallen the growth of psycho-analysis. It is possible, therefore, that I had said to Herr P.: 'I visited a friend [*Freund*] in
your house' and with this possibility the occult interest of his
second association vanishes.

The impression made by the third association evaporates
equally quickly. Could P. know that Jones had published a
monograph on the nightmare if he never read any analytic literature? Yes, he could. He possessed books from our publishing
house and could in any case have seen the titles of the new publications advertised on the wrappers. This cannot be proved, but
neither can it be disproved. We can reach no decision, therefore,
along this path. To my regret, this observation of mine suffers
from the same weakness as so many similar ones: it was written
down too late and was discussed at a time when I was no longer
seeing Herr P. and could not question him further.

Let us go back to the first event, which even taken by itself
supports the apparent fact of thought-transference. Could P.
know that Dr. Forsyth had been with me a quarter of an hour
before him? Could he have any knowledge at all of his existence
or of his presence in Vienna? We must not give way to an inclination to deny both questions flatly. I can see a way that
leads to a partly affirmative answer. I may after all have told
Herr P. that I was expecting a doctor from England for instruction in analysis, as a first dove after the Deluge. This might
have happened in the summer of 1919, for Dr. Forsyth had
made arrangements with me by letter some months before his
arrival. I may even have mentioned his name, though that
seems to me most improbable. In view of the other connection
which the name carried for both of us, a discussion of it must

---

[1] ['*Freund*' is, of course, the German word for 'friend'. Freud had
written a moving obituary of him (1920*c*).]

inevitably have followed, of which something would have remained in my memory. Nevertheless such a discussion may have taken place and I may have totally forgotten it afterwards, so that it became possible for the emergence of 'Herr von Vorsicht' in the analytic session to strike me as a miracle. If one regards oneself as a sceptic, it is a good plan to have occasional doubts about one's scepticism too. It may be that I too have a secret inclination towards the miraculous which thus goes half way to meet the creation of occult facts.

If we have thus got one miraculous possibility out of the way, there is another waiting for us, and the most difficult of all. Assuming that Herr P. knew that there was a Dr. Forsyth and that he was expected in Vienna in the autumn, how is it to be explained that he became receptive to his presence on the very day of his arrival and immediately after his first visit? One might say it was chance—that is, leave it unexplained. But it was precisely in order to exclude chance that I discussed P.'s other two associations, in order to show you that he was really occupied with jealous thoughts about people who visited me. Or one might, not to neglect the most extreme possibility, experiment with the hypothesis that P. had observed a special excitement about me (which, to be sure, I myself knew nothing of) and drew his conclusion from it. Or Herr P. (though he arrived a quarter of an hour after the Englishman left) met him on the short stretch of street which they both had to pass along, recognized him by his characteristically English appearance and, being in a permanent state of jealous expectation, thought: 'Ah, so that's Dr. Forsyth with whose arrival my analysis is to come to an end! And he's probably just come straight from the Professor.' I cannot carry these rationalistic speculations any further. We are once again left with a *non liquet* [not proven]; but I must confess that I have a feeling that here too the scales weigh in favour of thought-transference. Moreover, I am certainly not alone in having been in the position of experiencing 'occult' events like this in the analytic situation. Helene Deutsch published some similar observations in 1926 and studied the question of their being determined by the transference relations between patient and analyst.

I am sure you will not feel very well satisfied with my attitude to this problem—with my not being entirely convinced but prepared to be convinced. You may perhaps say to yourselves: 'Here's another case of a man who has done honest work as a scientist all through his life and has grown feeble-minded, pious and credulous in his old age.' I am aware that a few great names must be included in this class, but you should not reckon me among them. At least I have not become pious, and I hope not credulous. It is only that, if one has gone about all one's life bending in order to avoid a painful collision with the facts, so too in one's old age one still keeps one's back ready to bow before new realities. No doubt you would like me to hold fast to a moderate theism and show myself relentless in my rejection of everything occult. But I am incapable of currying favour and I must urge you to have kindlier thoughts on the objective possibility of thought-transference and at the same time of telepathy as well.

You will not forget that here I am only treating these problems in so far as it is possible to approach them from the direction of psycho-analysis. When they first came into my range of vision more than ten years ago, I too felt a dread of a threat against our scientific *Weltanschauung*, which, I feared, was bound to give place to spiritualism or mysticism if portions of occultism were proved true.[1] To-day I think otherwise. In my opinion it shows no great confidence in science if one does not think it capable of assimilating and working over whatever may perhaps turn out to be true in the assertions of occultists. And particularly so far as thought-transference is concerned, it seems actually to favour the extension of the scientific—or, as our opponents say, the mechanistic—mode of thought to the mental phenomena which are so hard to lay hold of. The telepathic process is supposed to consist in a mental act in one person instigating the same mental act in another person. What lies between these two mental acts may easily be a physical process into which the mental one is transformed at one end and which is transformed back once more into the same mental one at the other end. The analogy with other transformations, such as occur in speaking and hearing by telephone, would then be unmistakable. And only think if one could get hold of this physical equivalent of the psychical act! It would seem to me that psycho-analysis, by inserting the unconscious between what is physical and what was previously called 'psychical', has paved the way for the assumption of such processes as telepathy. If only one accustoms oneself to the idea of telepathy, one can accomplish a great deal with it—for the time being, it is true, only in imagination. It is a familiar fact that we do not know how the common purpose comes about in the great insect communities: possibly it is done by means of a direct psychical

[1] [These thoughts were expressed by Freud at considerable length in the introductory portion of his posthumously published paper on 'Psycho-Analysis and Telepathy' (1941*d*).]

transference of this kind. One is led to a suspicion that this is the original, archaic method of communication between individuals and that in the course of phylogenetic evolution it has been replaced by the better method of giving information with the help of signals which are picked up by the sense organs. But the older method might have persisted in the background and still be able to put itself into effect under certain conditions—for instance, in passionately excited mobs. All this is still uncertain and full of unsolved riddles; but there is no reason to be frightened by it.

If there is such a thing as telepathy as a real process, we may suspect that, in spite of its being so hard to demonstrate, it is quite a common phenomenon. It would tally with our expectations if we were able to point to it particularly in the mental life of children. Here we are reminded of the frequent anxiety felt by children over the idea that their parents know all their thoughts without having to be told them—an exact counterpart and perhaps the source of the belief of adults in the omniscience of God. A short time ago Dorothy Burlingham, a trustworthy witness, in a paper on child analysis and the mother [1932] published some observations which, if they can be confirmed, would be bound to put an end to the remaining doubts on the reality of thought-transference. She made use of the situation, no longer a rare one, in which a mother and child are simultaneously in analysis, and reported some remarkable events such as the following. One day the mother spoke during her analytic session of a gold coin that had played a particular part in one of the scenes of her childhood. Immediately afterwards, after she had returned home, her little boy, about ten years old, came to her room and brought her a gold coin which he asked her to keep for him. She asked him in astonishment where he had got it from. He had been given it on his birthday; but his birthday had been several months earlier and there was no reason why the child should have remembered the gold coin precisely then. The mother reported the occurrence to the child's analyst and asked her to find out from the child the reason for his action. But the child's analysis threw no light on the matter; the action had forced its way that day into the child's life like a foreign body. A few weeks later the mother was sitting at her writing-desk to write down, as she had been told to do, an account of the experience, when in came the boy and asked for the gold coin back, as he wanted to take it with him to show in his analytic session. Once again the child's analysis could discover no explanation of his wish.

And this brings us back to psycho-analysis, which was what we started out from.

LECTURE XXXI

THE DISSECTION OF THE PSYCHICAL PERSONALITY[1]

LADIES AND GENTLEMEN,—I know you are aware in regard to your own relations, whether with people or things, of the importance of your starting-point. This was also the case with psycho-analysis. It has not been a matter of indifference for the course of its development or for the reception it met with that it began its work on what is, of all the contents of the mind, most foreign to the ego—on symptoms. Symptoms are derived from the repressed, they are, as it were, its representatives before the ego; but the repressed is foreign territory to the ego—internal foreign territory—just as reality (if you will forgive the unusual expression) is external foreign territory. The path led from symptoms to the unconscious, to the life of the instincts, to sexuality; and it was then that psycho-analysis was met by the brilliant objection that human beings are not merely sexual creatures but have nobler and higher impulses as well. It might have been added that, exalted by their consciousness of these higher impulses, they often assume the right to think nonsense and to neglect facts.

You know better. From the very first we have said that human beings fall ill of a conflict between the claims of instinctual life and the resistance which arises within them against it; and not for a moment have we forgotten this resisting, repelling, repressing agency, which we thought of as equipped with its special forces, the ego-instincts, and which coincides with the ego of popular psychology. The truth was merely that, in view of the laborious nature of the progress made by scientific work, even psycho-analysis was not able to study every field simultaneously and to express its views on every problem in a single breath. But at last the point was reached when it was possible for us to divert our attention from the repressed to the repressing forces, and we faced this ego, which had seemed so self-evident, with the secure expectation that here once again we should find things for which we could not have been prepared. It was not easy, however, to find a first approach; and that is what I intend to talk to you about to-day.

[1] [The greater part of the material in this lecture is derived (with some amplifications) from Chapters I, II, III and V of *The Ego and the Id* (1923b).]

I must, however, let you know of my suspicion that this account of mine of ego-psychology will affect you differently from the introduction into the psychical underworld which preceded it. I cannot say with certainty why this should be so. I thought first that you would discover that whereas what I reported to you previously were, in the main, facts, however strange and peculiar, now you will be listening principally to opinions—that is, to speculations. But that does not meet the position. After further consideration I must maintain that the amount of intellectual working-over of the factual material in our ego-psychology is not much greater than it was in the psychology of the neuroses. I have been obliged to reject other explanations as well of the result I anticipate: I now believe that it is somehow a question of the nature of the material itself and of our being unaccustomed to dealing with it. In any case, I shall not be surprised if you show yourselves even more reserved and cautious in your judgement than hitherto.

The situation in which we find ourselves at the beginning of our enquiry may be expected itself to point the way for us. We wish to make the ego the matter of our enquiry, our very own ego. But is that possible? After all, the ego is in its very essence a subject; how can it be made into an object? Well, there is no doubt that it can be. The ego can take itself as an object, can treat itself like other objects, can observe itself, criticize itself, and do Heaven knows what with itself. In this, one part of the ego is setting itself over against the rest. So the ego can be split; it splits itself during a number of its functions—temporarily at least. Its parts can come together again afterwards. That is not exactly a novelty, though it may perhaps be putting an unusual emphasis on what is generally known. On the other hand, we are familiar with the notion that pathology, by making things larger and coarser, can draw our attention to normal conditions which would otherwise have escaped us. Where it points to a breach or a rent, there may normally be an articulation present. If we throw a crystal to the floor, it breaks; but not into haphazard pieces. It comes apart along its lines of cleavage into fragments whose boundaries, though they were invisible, were predetermined by the crystal's structure. Mental patients are split and broken structures of this same kind. Even we cannot withhold from them something of the reverential awe which peoples of the past felt for the insane. They have turned away from external reality, but for that very reason they know more about internal, psychical reality and can reveal a number of things to us that would otherwise be inaccessible to us.

XXXI. DISSECTION OF THE PERSONALITY 53

We describe one group of these patients as suffering from delusions of being observed. They complain to us that perpetually, and down to their most intimate actions, they are being molested by the observation of unknown powers—presumably persons—and that in hallucinations they hear these persons reporting the outcome of their observation: 'now he's going to say this, now he's dressing to go out' and so on. Observation of this sort is not yet the same thing as persecution, but it is not far from it; it presupposes that people distrust them, and expect to catch them carrying out forbidden actions for which they would be punished. How would it be if these insane people were right, if in each of us there is present in his ego an agency like this which observes and threatens to punish, and which in them has merely become sharply divided from their ego and mistakenly displaced into external reality?

I cannot tell whether the same thing will happen to you as to me. Ever since, under the powerful impression of this clinical picture, I formed the idea that the separation of the observing agency from the rest of the ego might be a regular feature of the ego's structure, that idea has never left me, and I was driven to investigate the further characteristics and connections of the agency which was thus separated off. The next step is quickly taken. The content of the delusions of being observed already suggests that the observing is only a preparation for judging and punishing, and we accordingly guess that another function of this agency must be what we call our conscience. There is scarcely anything else in us that we so regularly separate from our ego and so easily set over against it as precisely our conscience. I feel an inclination to do something that I think will give me pleasure, but I abandon it on the ground that my conscience does not allow it. Or I have let myself be persuaded by too great an expectation of pleasure into doing something to which the voice of conscience has objected and after the deed my conscience punishes me with distressing reproaches and causes me to feel remorse for the deed. I might simply say that the special agency which I am beginning to distinguish in the ego is conscience. But it is more prudent to keep the agency as something independent and to suppose that conscience is one of its functions and that self-observation, which is an essential preliminary to the judging activity of conscience, is another of them. And since when we recognize that something has a separate existence we give it a name of its own, from this time forward I will describe this agency in the ego as the '*super-ego*'.

I am now prepared to hear you ask me scornfully whether our ego-psychology comes down to nothing more than taking commonly used abstractions literally and in a crude sense, and transforming them from concepts into things—by which not much would be gained. To this I would reply that in ego-psychology it will be difficult to escape what is universally known; it will rather be a question of new ways of looking at things and new ways of arranging them than of new discoveries. So hold to your contemptuous criticism for the time being and await further explanations. The facts of pathology give our efforts a background that you would look for in vain in popular psychology. So I will proceed.

Hardly have we familiarized ourselves with the idea of a super-ego like this which enjoys a certain degree of autonomy, follows its own intentions and is independent of the ego for its supply of energy, than a clinical picture forces itself on our notice which throws a striking light on the severity of this agency and indeed its cruelty, and on its changing relations to the ego. I am thinking of the condition of melancholia,[1] or, more precisely, of melancholic attacks, which you too will have heard plenty about, even if you are not psychiatrists. The most striking feature of this illness, of whose causation and mechanism we know much too little, is the way in which the super-ego —'conscience', you may call it, quietly—treats the ego. While a melancholic can, like other people, show a greater or lesser degree of severity to himself in his healthy periods, during a melancholic attack his super-ego becomes over-severe, abuses the poor ego, humiliates it and ill-treats it, threatens it with the direst punishments, reproaches it for actions in the remotest past which had been taken lightly at the time—as though it had spent the whole interval in collecting accusations and had only been waiting for its present access of strength in order to bring them up and make a condemnatory judgement on their basis. The super-ego applies the strictest moral standard to the help-less ego which is at its mercy; in general it represents the claims of morality, and we realize all at once that our moral sense of guilt is the expression of the tension between the ego and the super-ego. It is a most remarkable experience to see morality, which is supposed to have been given us by God and thus deeply implanted in us, functioning [in these patients] as a periodic phenomenon. For after a certain number of months the whole moral fuss is over, the criticism of the super-ego is silent, the ego is rehabilitated and again enjoys all the rights of man till the next attack. In some forms of the disease, indeed, something of a contrary sort occurs in the intervals; the ego finds itself in a

[1] [Modern terminology would probably speak of 'depression'.]

blissful state of intoxication, it celebrates a triumph, as though the super-ego had lost all its strength or had melted into the ego; and this liberated, manic ego permits itself a truly uninhibited satisfaction of all its appetites. Here are happenings rich in unsolved riddles!

No doubt you will expect me to give you more than a mere illustration when I inform you that we have found out all kinds of things about the formation of the super-ego—that is to say, about the origin of conscience. Following a well-known pronouncement of Kant's which couples the conscience within us with the starry Heavens, a pious man might well be tempted to honour these two things as the masterpieces of creation. The stars are indeed magnificent, but as regards conscience God has done an uneven and careless piece of work, for a large majority of men have brought along with them only a modest amount of it or scarcely enough to be worth mentioning. We are far from overlooking the portion of psychological truth that is contained in the assertion that conscience is of divine origin; but the thesis needs interpretation. Even if conscience is something 'within us', yet it is not so from the first. In this it is a real contrast to sexual life, which is in fact there from the beginning of life and not only a later addition. But, as is well known, young children are amoral and possess no internal inhibitions against their impulses striving for pleasure. The part which is later taken on by the super-ego is played to begin with by an external power, by parental authority. Parental influence governs the child by offering proofs of love and by threatening punishments which are signs to the child of loss of love and are bound to be feared on their own account. This realistic anxiety is the precursor of the later moral anxiety.[1] So long as it is dominant there is no need to talk of a super-ego and of a conscience. It is only subsequently that the secondary situation develops (which we are all too ready to regard as the normal one), where the external restraint is internalized and the super-ego takes the place of the parental agency and observes, directs and threatens the ego in exactly the same way as earlier the parents did with the child.

The super-ego, which thus takes over the power, function and even the methods of the parental agency, is however not merely its successor but actually the legitimate heir of its body. It proceeds directly out of it, we shall learn presently by what process. First, however, we must dwell upon a discrepancy between the two. The super-ego seems to have made a one-sided choice and to have picked out only the parents' strictness and

[1] ['*Gewissensangst*', literally 'conscience anxiety'.]

severity, their prohibiting and punitive function, whereas their loving care seems not to have been taken over and maintained. If the parents have really enforced their authority with severity we can easily understand the child's in turn developing a severe super-ego. But, contrary to our expectation, experience shows that the super-ego can acquire the same characteristic of relentless severity even if the upbringing had been mild and kindly and had so far as possible avoided threats and punishments. We shall come back later to this contradiction when we deal with the transformations of instinct during the formation of the super-ego.[1]

I cannot tell you as much as I should like about the metamorphosis of the parental relationship into the super-ego, partly because that process is so complicated that an account of it will not fit into the framework of an introductory course of lectures such as I am trying to give you, but partly also because we ourselves do not feel sure that we understand it completely. So you must be content with the sketch that follows.

The basis of the process is what is called an 'identification'—that is to say, the assimilation of one ego to another one,[2] as a result of which the first ego behaves like the second in certain respects, imitates it and in a sense takes it up into itself. Identification has been not unsuitably compared with the oral, cannibalistic incorporation of the other person. It is a very important form of attachment to someone else, probably the very first, and not the same thing as the choice of an object. The difference between the two can be expressed in some such way as this. If a boy identifies himself with his father, he wants to *be like* his father; if he makes him the object of his choice, he wants to *have* him, to possess him. In the first case his ego is altered on the model of his father; in the second case that is not necessary. Identification and object-choice are to a large extent independent of each other; it is however possible to identify oneself with someone whom, for instance, one has taken as a sexual object, and to alter one's ego on his model. It is said that the influencing of the ego by the sexual object occurs particularly often with women and is characteristic of femininity. I must already have spoken to you in my earlier lectures of what is by far the most instructive relation between identification and object-choice. It can be observed equally easily in children and adults, in normal as in sick people. If one has lost an object or has been obliged to give it up, one often compensates oneself by identifying oneself

[1] [See p. 97 below.]
[2] [I.e. one ego coming to resemble another one.]

with it and by setting it up once more in one's ego, so that here object-choice regresses, as it were, to identification.[1]

I myself am far from satisfied with these remarks on identification; but it will be enough if you can grant me that the installation of the super-ego can be described as a successful instance of identification with the parental agency. The fact that speaks decisively for this view is that this new creation of a superior agency within the ego is most intimately linked with the destiny of the Oedipus complex, so that the super-ego appears as the heir of that emotional attachment which is of such importance for childhood. With his abandonment of the Oedipus complex a child must, as we can see, renounce the intense object-cathexes which he has deposited with his parents, and it is as a compensation for this loss of objects that there is such a strong intensification of the identifications with his parents which have probably long been present in his ego. Identifications of this kind as precipitates of object-cathexes that have been given up will be repeated often enough later in the child's life; but it is entirely in accordance with the emotional importance of this first instance of such a transformation that a special place in the ego should be found for its outcome. Close investigation has shown us, too, that the super-ego is stunted in its strength and growth if the surmounting of the Oedipus complex is only incompletely successful. In the course of development the super-ego also takes on the influences of those who have stepped into the place of parents—educators, teachers, people chosen as ideal models. Normally it departs more and more from the original parental figures; it becomes, so to say, more impersonal. Nor must it be forgotten that a child has a different estimate of its parents at different periods of its life. At the time at which the Oedipus complex gives place to the super-ego they are something quite magnificent; but later they lose much of this. Identifications then come about with these later parents as well, and indeed they regularly make important contributions to the formation of character; but in that case they only affect the ego, they no longer influence the super-ego, which has been determined by the earliest parental imagos.[2]

I hope you have already formed an impression that the hypothesis of the super-ego really describes a structural relation

---

[1] [The matter is in fact only very briefly alluded to in the *Introductory Lectures* (see the later part of Lecture XXVI). Identification was the subject of Chapter VII of *Group Psychology* (1921c). The formation of the super-ego was discussed at length in Chapter III of *The Ego and the Id* (1923b), (Norton, 1961).]

[2] [This point was discussed by Freud in a paper on 'The Economic Problem of Masochism' (1924c).]

and is not merely a personification of some such abstraction as that of conscience. One more important function remains to be mentioned which we attribute to this super-ego. It is also the vehicle of the ego ideal by which the ego measures itself, which it emulates, and whose demand for ever greater perfection it strives to fulfil. There is no doubt that this ego ideal is the precipitate of the old picture of the parents, the expression of admiration for the perfection which the child then attributed to them.[1]

I am sure you have heard a great deal of the sense of inferiority which is supposed particularly to characterize neurotics. It especially haunts the pages of what are known as *belles lettres*. An author who uses the term 'inferiority complex' thinks that by so doing he has fulfilled all the demands of psycho-analysis and has raised his composition to a higher psychological plane. In fact 'inferiority complex' is a technical term that is scarcely used in psycho-analysis. For us it does not bear the meaning of anything simple, let alone elementary. To trace it back to the self-perception of possible organic defects, as the school of what are known as 'Individual Psychologists'[2] likes to do, seems to us a short-sighted error. The sense of inferiority has strong erotic roots. A child feels inferior if he notices that he is not loved, and so does an adult. The only bodily organ which is really regarded as inferior is the atrophied penis, a girl's clitoris.[3] But the major part of the sense of inferiority derives from the ego's relation to its super-ego; like the sense of guilt it is an expression of the tension between them. Altogether, it is hard to separate the sense of inferiority and the sense of guilt. It would perhaps be right to regard the former as the erotic complement to the moral sense

[1] [There is some obscurity in this passage, and in particular over the phrase '*der Träger des Ichideals*', here translated 'the vehicle of the ego ideal'. When Freud first introduced the concept in his paper on narcissism (1914c), he distinguished between the ego ideal itself and 'a special psychical agency which performs the task of seeing that narcissistic satisfaction from the ego ideal is ensured and which, with this end in view, constantly watches the actual ego and measures it by that ideal' Similarly, in Lecture XXVI of the *Introductory Lectures* (1916–17) he speaks of a person sensing 'an agency holding sway in his ego which measures his actual ego and each of its activities by an ideal ego that he has created for himself in the course of his development.' In some of Freud's later writings this distinction between the ideal and the agency enforcing it became blurred. It seems possible that it is revived here and that the super-ego is being identified with the enforcing agency. The use of the term '*Idealfunktion*' three paragraphs lower down (p. 59) raises the same question.]
[2] [Their views are discussed in Lecture XXXIV, p. 124 ff. below.]
[3] [Cf. a footnote of Freud's to his paper on the anatomical distinction between the sexes (1925j.]

of inferiority. Little attention has been given in psycho-analysis to the question of the delimitation of the two concepts.

If only because the inferiority complex has become so popular, I will venture to entertain you here with a short digression. A historical personality of our own days, who is still alive though at the moment he has retired into the background, suffers from a defect in one of his limbs owing to an injury at the time of his birth. A very well-known contemporary writer who is particularly fond of compiling the biographies of celebrities has dealt, among others, with the life of the man I am speaking of.[1] Now in writing a biography it may well be difficult to suppress a need to plumb the psychological depths. For this reason our author has ventured on an attempt to erect the whole of the development of his hero's character on the sense of inferiority which must have been called up by his physical defect. In doing so, he has overlooked one small but not insignificant fact. It is usual for mothers whom Fate has presented with a child who is sickly or otherwise at a disadvantage to try to compensate him for his unfair handicap by a superabundance of love. In the instance before us, the proud mother behaved otherwise; she withdrew her love from the child on account of his infirmity. When he had grown up into a man of great power, he proved unambiguously by his actions that he had never forgiven his mother. When you consider the importance of a mother's love for the mental life of a child, you will no doubt make a tacit correction of the biographer's inferiority theory.

But let us return to the super-ego. We have allotted it the functions of self-observation, of conscience and of [maintaining] the ideal.[2] It follows from what we have said about its origin that it presupposes an immensely important biological fact and a fateful psychological one: namely, the human child's long dependence on its parents and the Oedipus complex, both of which, again, are intimately interconnected. The super-ego is the representative for us of every moral restriction, the advocate of a striving towards perfection—it is, in short, as much as we have been able to grasp psychologically of what is described as the higher side of human life. Since it itself goes back to the influence of parents, educators and so on, we learn still more of its significance if we turn to those who are its sources. As a rule parents and authorities analogous to them follow the precepts of their own super-egos in educating children. Whatever understanding their ego may have come to with their super-ego, they

[1] [*Wilhelm II*, by Emil Ludwig (1926).]
[2] ['*Idealfunktion*.' Cf. footnote 1, p. 58 above.]

are severe and exacting in educating children. They have forgotten the difficulties of their own childhood and they are glad
to be able now to identify themselves fully with their own
parents who in the past laid such severe restrictions upon them.
Thus a child's super-ego is in fact constructed on the model not
of its parents but of its parents' super-ego; the contents which
fill it are the same and it becomes the vehicle of tradition and of
all the time-resisting judgements of value which have propa-
gated themselves in this manner from generation to generation.
You may easily guess what important assistance taking the
super-ego into account will give us in our understanding of the
social behaviour of mankind—in the problem of delinquency,
for instance—and perhaps even what practical hints on education. It seems likely that what are known as materialistic views
of history sin in under-estimating this factor. They brush it aside
with the remark that human 'ideologies' are nothing other than
the product and superstructure of their contemporary economic
conditions. That is true, but very probably not the whole truth.
Mankind never lives entirely in the present. The past, the tradition of the race and of the people, lives on in the ideologies of the
super-ego, and yields only slowly to the influences of the present
and to new changes; and so long as it operates through the
super-ego it plays a powerful part in human life, independently
of economic conditions. [Cf. p. 178 ff.]

In 1921 I endeavoured to make use of the differentiation between the ego and the super-ego in a study of group psychology.
I arrived at a formula such as this: a psychological group is a
collection of individuals who have introduced the same person
into their super-ego and, on the basis of this common element,
have identified themselves with one another in their ego.[1] This
applies, of course, only to groups that have a leader. If we possessed more applications of this kind, the hypothesis of the super-
ego would lose its last touch of strangeness for us, and we should
become completely free of the embarrassment that still comes
over us when, accustomed as we are to the atmosphere of the
underworld, we move in the more superficial, higher strata of
the mental apparatus. We do not suppose, of course, that with
the separation off of the super-ego we have said the last word on
the psychology of the ego. It is rather a first step; but in this case
it is not only the first step that is hard.

Now, however, another problem awaits us—at the opposite
end of the ego, as we might put it. It is presented to us by an

[1] [See the end of Chapter VIII of *Group Psychology* (1921*c*).]

observation during the work of analysis, an observation which is actually a very old one. As not infrequently happens, it has taken a long time to come to the point of appreciating its importance. The whole theory of psycho-analysis is, as you know, in fact built up on the perception of the resistance offered to us by the patient when we attempt to make his unconscious conscious to him. The objective sign of this resistance is that his associations fail or depart widely from the topic that is being dealt with. He may also recognize the resistance *subjectively* by the fact that he has distressing feelings when he approaches the topic. But this last sign may also be absent. We then say to the patient that we infer from his behaviour that he is now in a state of resistance; and he replies that he knows nothing of that, and is only aware that his associations have become more difficult. It turns out that we were right; but in that case his resistance was unconscious too, just as unconscious as the repressed, at the lifting of which we were working. We should long ago have asked the question: from what part of his mind does an unconscious resistance like this arise? The beginner in psycho-analysis will be ready at once with the answer: it is, of course, the resistance of the unconscious. An ambiguous and unserviceable answer! If it means that the resistance arises from the repressed, we must rejoin: certainly not! We must rather attribute to the repressed a strong upward drive, an impulsion to break through into consciousness. The resistance can only be a manifestation of the ego, which originally put the repression into force and now wishes to maintain it. That, moreover, is the view we always took. Since we have come to assume a special agency in the ego, the super-ego, which represents demands of a restrictive and rejecting character, we may say that repression is the work of this super-ego and that it is carried out either by itself or by the ego in obedience to its orders. If then we are met by the case of the resistance in analysis not being conscious to the patient, this means either that in quite important situations the super-ego and the ego can operate unconsciously, or—and this would be still more important—that portions of both of them, the ego and the super-ego themselves, are unconscious. In both cases we have to reckon with the disagreeable discovery that on the one hand (super-) ego and conscious and on the other hand repressed and unconscious are far from coinciding.

And here, Ladies and Gentlemen, I feel that I must make a pause to take breath—which you too will welcome as a relief—and, before I go on, to apologize to you. My intention is to give you some addenda to the introductory lectures on psycho-

analysis which I began fifteen years ago, and I am obliged to
behave as though you as well as I had in the interval done
nothing but practise psycho-analysis. I know that that assumption is out of place; but I am helpless, I cannot do otherwise.
This is no doubt related to the fact that it is in general so hard to
give anyone who is not himself a psycho-analyst an insight into
psycho-analysis. You can believe me when I tell you that we do
not enjoy giving an impression of being members of a secret
society and of practising a mystical science. Yet we have been
obliged to recognize and express as our conviction that no one
has a right to join in a discussion of psycho-analysis who has not
had particular experiences which can only be obtained by being
analysed oneself. When I gave you my lectures fifteen years ago
I tried to spare you certain speculative portions of our theory;
but it is precisely from them that are derived the new acquisitions of which I must speak to you to-day.

I return now to our topic. In face of the doubt whether the
ego and super-ego are themselves unconscious or merely produce unconscious effects, we have, for good reasons, decided in
favour of the former possibility. And it is indeed the case that
large portions of the ego and super-ego can remain unconscious
and are normally unconscious. That is to say, the individual
knows nothing of their contents and it requires an expenditure
of effort to make them conscious. It is a fact that ego and conscious, repressed and unconscious do not coincide. We feel a
need to make a fundamental revision of our attitude to the
problem of conscious–unconscious. At first we are inclined
greatly to reduce the value of the criterion of being conscious
since it has shown itself so untrustworthy. But we should be
doing it an injustice. As may be said of our life, it is not worth
much, but it is all we have. Without the illumination thrown by
the quality of consciousness, we should be lost in the obscurity
of depth-psychology; but we must attempt to find our bearings
afresh.

There is no need to discuss what is to be called conscious: it is
removed from all doubt. The oldest and best meaning of the
word 'unconscious' is the descriptive one; we call a psychical
process unconscious whose existence we are obliged to assume
—for some such reason as that we infer it from its effects—, but
of which we know nothing. In that case we have the same
relation to it as we have to a psychical process in another person, except that it is in fact one of our own. If we want to be
still more correct, we shall modify our assertion by saying that
we call a process unconscious if we are obliged to assume that it

is being activated *at the moment*, though *at the moment* we know nothing about it. This qualification makes us reflect that the majority of conscious processes are conscious only for a short time; very soon they become *latent*, but can easily become conscious again. We might also say that they had become unconscious, if it were at all certain that in the condition of latency they are still something psychical. So far we should have learnt nothing new; nor should we have acquired the right to introduce the concept of an unconscious into psychology. But then comes the new observation that we were already able to make in parapraxes. In order to explain a slip of the tongue, for instance, we find ourselves obliged to assume that the intention to make a particular remark was present in the subject. We infer it with certainty from the interference with his remark which has occurred; but the intention did not put itself through and was thus unconscious. If, when we subsequently put it before the speaker, he recognizes it as one familiar to him, then it was only temporarily unconscious to him; but if he repudiates it as something foreign to him, then it was permanently unconscious.[1] From this experience we retrospectively obtain the right also to pronounce as something unconscious what had been described as latent. A consideration of these dynamic relations permits us now to distinguish two kinds of unconscious—one which is easily, under frequently occurring circumstances, transformed into something conscious, and another with which this transformation is difficult and takes place only subject to a considerable expenditure of effort or possibly never at all. In order to escape the ambiguity as to whether we mean the one or the other unconscious, whether we are using the word in the descriptive or in the dynamic sense, we make use of a permissible and simple way out. We call the unconscious which is only latent, and thus easily becomes conscious, the 'preconscious' and retain the term 'unconscious' for the other. We now have three terms, 'conscious', 'preconscious' and 'unconscious', with which we can get along in our description of mental phenomena. Once again: the preconscious is also unconscious in the purely descriptive sense, but we do not give it that name, except in talking loosely or when we have to make a defence of the existence in mental life of unconscious processes in general.

You will admit, I hope, that so far that is not too bad and allows of convenient handling. Yes, but unluckily the work of psycho-analysis has found itself compelled to use the word 'unconscious' in yet another, third, sense, and this may, to be sure,

[1] [Cf. *Introductory Lectures*, IV.]

have led to confusion. Under the new and powerful impression of there being an extensive and important field of mental life which is normally withdrawn from the ego's knowledge so that the processes occurring in it have to be regarded as unconscious in the truly dynamic sense, we have come to understand the term 'unconscious' in a topographical or systematic sense as well; we have come to speak of a 'system' of the preconscious and a 'system' of the unconscious, of a conflict between the ego and the system *Ucs.*, and have used the word more and more to denote a mental province rather than a quality of what is mental. The discovery, actually an inconvenient one, that portions of the ego and super-ego as well are unconscious in the dynamic sense, operates at this point as a relief—it makes possible the removal of a complication. We perceive that we have no right to name the mental region that is foreign to the ego 'the system *Ucs.*', since the characteristic of being unconscious is not restricted to it. Very well; we will no longer use the term 'unconscious' in the systematic sense and we will give what we have hitherto so described a better name and one no longer open to misunderstanding. Following a verbal usage of Nietzsche's and taking up a suggestion by Georg Groddeck [1923],[1] we will in future call it the 'id'.[2] This impersonal pronoun seems particularly well suited for expressing the main characteristic of this province of the mind—the fact of its being alien to the ego. The super-ego, the ego and the id—these, then, are the three realms, regions, provinces, into which we divide an individual's mental apparatus, and with the mutual relations of which we shall be concerned in what follows.

But first a short interpolation. I suspect that you feel dissatisfied because the three qualities of the characteristic of consciousness and the three provinces of the mental apparatus do not fall together into three peaceable couples, and you may regard this as in some sense obscuring our findings. I do not think, however, that we should regret it, and we should tell ourselves that we had no right to expect any such smooth arrangement. Let me give you an analogy; analogies, it is true, decide nothing, but they can make one feel more at home. I am imagining a country with a landscape of varying configuration —hill-country, plains, and chains of lakes—, and with a mixed population: it is inhabited by Germans, Magyars and Slovaks,

---

[1] [A German physician by whose unconventional ideas Freud was much attracted.]

[2] [In German '*Es*', the ordinary word for 'it'.]

who carry on different activities. Now things might be parti-
tioned in such a way that the Germans, who breed cattle, live
in the hill-country, the Magyars, who grow cereals and wine,
live in the plains, and the Slovaks, who catch fish and plait
reeds, live by the lakes. If the partitioning could be neat and
clear-cut like this, a Woodrow Wilson would be delighted by
it;[1] it would also be convenient for a lecture in a geography
lesson. The probability is, however, that you will find less orderliness and more mixing, if you travel through the region. Germans, Magyars and Slovaks live interspersed all over it; in the
hill-country there is agricultural land as well, cattle are bred in
the plains too. A few things are naturally as you expected, for
fish cannot be caught in the mountains and wine does not grow
in the water. Indeed, the picture of the region that you brought
with you may on the whole fit the facts; but you will have to put
up with deviations in the details.

You will not expect me to have much to tell you that is new
about the id apart from its new name. It is the dark, inaccessible
part of our personality; what little we know of it we have learnt
from our study of the dream-work and of the construction of
neurotic symptoms, and most of that is of a negative character
and can be described only as a contrast to the ego. We approach
the id with analogies: we call it a chaos, a cauldron full of
seething excitations. We picture it as being open at its end to
somatic influences, and as there taking up into itself instinctual
needs which find their psychical expression in it,[2] but we cannot say in what substratum. It is filled with energy reaching it
from the instincts, but it has no organization, produces no col-
lective will, but only a striving to bring about the satisfaction of
the instinctual needs subject to the observance of the pleasure
principle. The logical laws of thought do not apply in the id,
and this is true above all of the law of contradiction. Contrary
impulses exist side by side, without cancelling each other out or
diminishing each other: at the most they may converge to form
compromises under the dominating economic pressure towards
the discharge of energy. There is nothing in the id that could be
compared with negation; and we perceive with surprise an ex-

[1] [It may be remarked that only a year or so before writing this
Freud had finished his collaboration with W. C. Bullitt (then American
Ambassador in Berlin) on a study of President Wilson, of whose political
judgement he was highly critical. The work has not hitherto (1965) been
published.]
[2] [Freud is here regarding instincts as something physical, of which
mental processes are the representatives.]

ception to the philosophical theorem that space and time are necessary forms of our mental acts.[1] There is nothing in the id that corresponds to the idea of time; there is no recognition of the passage of time, and—a thing that is most remarkable and awaits consideration in philosophical thought—no alteration in its mental processes is produced by the passage of time. Wishful impulses which have never passed beyond the id, but impressions, too, which have been sunk into the id by repression, are virtually immortal; after the passage of decades they behave as though they had just occurred. They can only be recognized as belonging to the past, can only lose their importance and be deprived of their cathexis of energy, when they have been made conscious by the work of analysis, and it is on this that the therapeutic effect of analytic treatment rests to no small extent.

Again and again I have had the impression that we have made too little theoretical use of this fact, established beyond any doubt, of the unalterability by time of the repressed. This seems to offer an approach to the most profound discoveries. Nor, unfortunately, have I myself made any progress here.

The id of course knows no judgements of value: no good and evil, no morality. The economic or, if you prefer, the quantitative factor, which is intimately linked to the pleasure principle, dominates all its processes. Instinctual cathexes seeking discharge—that, in our view, is all there is in the id. It even seems that the energy of these instinctual impulses is in a state different from that in the other regions of the mind, far more mobile and capable of discharge;[2] otherwise the displacements and condensations would not occur which are characteristic of the id and which so completely disregard the *quality* of what is cathected—what in the ego we should call an idea. We would give much to understand more about these things! You can see, incidentally, that we are in a position to attribute to the id characteristics other than that of its being unconscious, and you can recognize the possibility of portions of the ego and

---

[1] [The reference is to Kant.]

[2] [This difference was referred to by Freud in many passages. See, in particular, Section V of the metapsychological paper on 'The Unconscious' (1915e), and Chapter IV of *Beyond the Pleasure Principle* (1920g). In both these passages Freud attributes the distinction to Breuer, apparently having in mind a footnote to Section 2 (A) of Breuer's theoretical contribution to *Studies on Hysteria* (1895d).] In 'The Unconscious' he remarks that in his opinion this distinction represents the deepest insight we have gained up to the present into the nature of nervous energy. Cf. a further footnote on p. 79 below.]

super-ego being unconscious without possessing the same primitive and irrational characteristics.[1]

We can best arrive at the characteristics of the actual ego, in so far as it can be distinguished from the id and from the super-ego, by examining its relation to the outermost superficial portion of the mental apparatus, which we describe as the system *Pcpt.-Cs.*[2] This system is turned towards the external world, it is the medium for the perceptions arising thence, and during its functioning the phenomenon of consciousness arises in it. It is the sense-organ of the entire apparatus; moreover it is receptive not only to excitations from outside but also to those arising from the interior of the mind. We need scarcely look for a justification of the view that the ego is that portion of the id which was modified by the proximity and influence of the external world, which is adapted for the reception of stimuli and as a protective shield against stimuli, comparable to the cortical layer by which a small piece of living substance is surrounded. The relation to the external world has become the decisive factor for the ego; it has taken on the task of representing the external world to the id—fortunately for the id, which could not escape destruction if, in its blind efforts for the satisfaction of its instincts, it disregarded that supreme external power. In accomplishing this function, the ego must observe the external world, must lay down an accurate picture of it in the memory-traces of its perceptions, and by its exercise of the function of 'reality-testing'[3] must put aside whatever in this picture of the external world is an addition derived from internal sources of excitation. The ego controls the approaches to motility under the id's orders; but between a need and an action it has interposed a postponement in the form of the activity of thought,[4] during which it makes use of the mnemic residues of experience. In that way it has dethroned the pleasure principle which dominates the course of events in the id without any restriction and has replaced it by the reality principle, which promises more certainty and greater success.

The relation to time, which is so hard to describe, is also introduced into the ego by the perceptual system; it can scarcely be doubted that the mode of operation of that system is what provides the origin of the idea of time.[5] But what distinguishes the

[1] [This account of the id is in the main based on Section V of the paper on 'The Unconscious'.]

[2] [Perceptual-conscious.]   [3] [See footnote 1, p. 30 above.]

[4] [This is further discussed below, p. 79.]

[5] [Freud gave some indication of what he had in mind by this at the end of his paper on the 'Mystic Writing-Pad' (1925a).]

ego from the id quite especially is a tendency to synthesis in its contents, to a combination and unification in its mental processes which are totally lacking in the id. When presently we come to deal with the instincts in mental life we shall, I hope, succeed in tracing this essential characteristic of the ego back to its source.[1] It alone produces the high degree of organization which the ego needs for its best achievements. The ego develops from perceiving the instincts to controlling them; but this last is only achieved by the [psychical] representative of the instinct[2] being allotted its proper place in a considerable assemblage, by its being taken up into a coherent context. To adopt a popular mode of speaking, we might say that the ego stands for reason and good sense while the id stands for the untamed passions.

So far we have allowed ourselves to be impressed by the merits and capabilities of the ego; it is now time to consider the other side as well. The ego is after all only a portion of the id, a portion that has been expediently modified by the proximity of the external world with its threat of danger. From a dynamic point of view it is weak, it has borrowed its energies from the id, and we are not entirely without insight into the methods—we might .call them dodges—by which it extracts further amounts of energy from the id. One such method, for instance, is by identifying itself with actual or abandoned objects. The object-cathexes spring from the instinctual demands of the id. The ego has in the first instance to take note of them. But by identifying itself with the object it recommends itself to the id in place of the object and seeks to divert the id's libido on to itself. We have already seen [p. 57] that in the course of its life the ego takes into itself a large number of precipitates like this of former object-cathexes. The ego must on the whole carry out the id's intentions, it fulfils its task by finding out the circumstances in which those intentions can best be achieved. The ego's relation to the id might be compared with that of a rider to his horse. The horse supplies the locomotive energy, while the rider has

[1] [Freud does not seem, in fact, to have returned to the subject in these lectures.—He had discussed this characteristic of the ego at length in Chapter III of *Inhibitions, Symptoms and Anxiety* (1926d). Though he had stressed the synthetic tendency of the ego particularly in his later writings (e.g. among many others in Chapter II of *The Questions of Lay Analysis* (1926e), (Norton, 1950), the concept was implicit in his picture of the ego from the earliest times. See, for instance, the term he almost invariably used during the Breuer period for ideas that had to be repressed: 'incompatible'—i.e. that could not be synthesized by the ego. So in Section II of the first paper on the neuro-psychoses of defence (1894a).]

[2] [See footnote 2, p. 65 above.]

the privilege of deciding on the goal and of guiding the powerful animal's movement. But only too often there arises between
the ego and the id the not precisely ideal situation of the rider
being obliged to guide the horse along the path by which it
itself wants to go.

There is one portion of the id from which the ego has
separated itself by resistances due to repression. But the repression is not carried over into the id: the repressed merges into the
remainder of the id.

We are warned by a proverb against serving two masters at
the same time. The poor ego has things even worse: it serves
three severe masters and does what it can to bring their claims
and demands into harmony with one another. These claims are
always divergent and often seem incompatible. No wonder that
the ego so often fails in its task. Its three tyrannical masters are
the external world, the super-ego and the id. When we follow
the ego's efforts to satisfy them simultaneously—or rather, to
obey them simultaneously—we cannot feel any regret at having
personified this ego and having set it up as a separate organism.
It feels hemmed in on three sides, threatened by three kinds
of danger, to which, if it is hard pressed, it reacts by generating anxiety. Owing to its origin from the experiences of the
perceptual system, it is earmarked for representing the demands
of the external world, but it strives too to be a loyal servant of the
id, to remain on good terms with it, to recommend itself to it as
an object and to attract its libido to itself. In its attempts to
mediate between the id and reality, it is often obliged to cloak
the *Ucs.* commands of the id with its own *Pcs.* rationalizations,
to conceal the id's conflicts with reality, to profess, with diplo-
matic disingenuousness, to be taking notice of reality even when
the id has remained rigid and unyielding. On the other hand it
is observed at every step it takes by the strict super-ego, which
lays down definite standards for its conduct, without taking any
account of its difficulties from the direction of the id and the
external world, and which, if those standards are not obeyed,
punishes it with tense feelings of inferiority and of guilt. Thus the
ego, driven by the id, confined by the super-ego, repulsed by
reality, struggles to master its economic task of bringing about
harmony among the forces and influences working in and upon
it; and we can understand how it is that so often we cannot suppress a cry: 'Life is not easy!' If the ego is obliged to admit its
weakness, it breaks out in anxiety—realistic anxiety regarding the external world, moral anxiety regarding the super-ego
and neurotic anxiety regarding the strength of the passions in
the id.

I should like to portray the structural relations of the mental personality, as I have described them to you, in the unassuming sketch which I now present you with:

As you see here, the super-ego merges into the id; indeed, as heir to the Oedipus complex it has intimate relations with the id; it is more remote than the ego from the perceptual system.[1] The id has intercourse with the external world only through the ego—at least, according to this diagram. It is certainly hard to say to-day how far the drawing is correct. In one respect it is undoubtedly not. The space occupied by the unconscious id ought to have been incomparably greater than that of the ego or the preconscious. I must ask you to correct it in your thoughts.

And here is another warning, to conclude these remarks, which have certainly been exacting and not, perhaps, very illuminating. In thinking of this division of the personality into an ego, a super-ego and an id, you will not, of course, have pictured sharp frontiers like the artificial ones drawn in political geography. We cannot do justice to the characteristics of the mind by linear outlines like those in a drawing or in primitive painting, but rather by areas of colour melting into one another as they are presented by modern artists. After making the

[1] [If this diagram is compared with the similar one in Chapter II of *The Ego and the Id* (1923b), it will be seen that the earlier diagram differs principally from the present one in the fact that the super-ego is not indicated in it. Its absence is justified in a later passage in the same work. In the original edition of these lectures this picture was printed upright, like its predecessor in *The Ego and the Id*. For some reason, perhaps to economize space, it was turned over on to its side, though otherwise unchanged, in both *G.S.* and *G.W.*]

separation we must allow what we have separated to merge together once more. You must not judge too harshly a first attempt at giving a pictorial representation of something so intangible as psychical processes. It is highly probable that the development of these divisions is subject to great variations in different individuals; it is possible that in the course of actual functioning they may change and go through a temporary phase of involution. Particularly in the case of what is phylogenetically the last and most delicate of these divisions—the differentiation between the ego and the super-ego—something of the sort seems to be true. There is no question but that the same thing results from psychical illness. It is easy to imagine, too, that certain mystical practices may succeed in upsetting the normal relations between the different regions of the mind, so that, for instance, perception may be able to grasp happenings in the depths of the ego and in the id which were otherwise inaccessible to it. It may safely be doubted, however, whether this road will lead us to the ultimate truths from which salvation is to be expected. Nevertheless it may be admitted that the therapeutic efforts of psycho-analysis have chosen a similar line of approach. Its intention is, indeed, to strengthen the ego, to make it more independent of the super-ego, to widen its field of perception and enlarge its organization, so that it can appropriate fresh portions of the id.[1] Where id was, there ego shall be. It is a work of culture—not unlike the draining of the Zuider Zee.

[1] [Freud had said something similar in the last chapter of *The Ego and the Id.*]

LECTURE XXXII

ANXIETY AND INSTINCTUAL LIFE

LADIES AND GENTLEMEN,—You will not be surprised to hear that I have a number of novelties to report to you about our conception [*Auffassung*] of anxiety and of the basic instincts of mental life; nor will you be surprised to learn that none of these novelties can claim to offer a final solution of these still unsettled problems. I have a particular reason for using the word 'conception' here. These are the most difficult problems that are set to us, but their difficulty does not lie in any insufficiency of observations; what present us with these riddles are actually the commonest and most familiar of phenomena. Nor does the difficulty lie in the recondite nature of the speculations to which they give rise; speculative consideration plays little part in this sphere. But it is truly a matter of conceptions—that is to say, of introducing the right abstract ideas, whose application to the raw material of observation will produce order and clarity in it.

I devoted a lecture (the twenty-fifth) to anxiety in my previous series; and I must briefly recapitulate what I said in it. We described anxiety as an affective state—that is to say, a combination of certain feelings in the pleasure-unpleasure series with the corresponding innervations of discharge and a perception of them, but probably also the precipitate of a particular important event, incorporated by inheritance—something that may thus be likened to an individually acquired hysterical attack.[1] The event which we look upon as having left behind it an affective trace of this sort is the process of birth, at the time of which the effects upon the heart's action and upon respiration characteristic of anxiety were expedient ones. The very first anxiety would thus have been a toxic one. We then started off from a distinction between realistic anxiety and neurotic anxiety, of which the former was a reaction, which seemed intelligible to us, to a danger—that is, to an expected injury from outside—while the latter was completely enigmatic, and appeared to be pointless.

In an analysis of realistic anxiety we brought it down to the state of increased sensory attention and motor tension which we describe as 'preparedness for anxiety'. It is out of this that the

---

[1] [Cf. the clearer account in *Introductory Lectures*, XXV.]

anxiety reaction develops. Here two outcomes are possible. Either the generation of anxiety—the repetition of the old traumatic experience—is limited to a signal, in which case the remainder of the reaction can adapt itself to the new situation of danger and can proceed to flight or defence; or the old situation can retain the upper hand and the total reaction may consist in no more than a generation of anxiety, in which case the affective state becomes paralysing and will be inexpedient for present purposes.

We then turned to neurotic anxiety and pointed out that we observe it under three conditions. We find it first as a freely floating, general apprehensiveness, ready to attach itself temporarily, in the form of what is known as 'expectant anxiety', to any possibility that may freshly arise—as happens, for instance, in a typical anxiety neurosis. Secondly, we find it firmly attached to certain ideas in the so-called 'phobias', in which it is still possible to recognize a relation to external danger but in which we must judge the fear exaggerated out of all proportion. Thirdly and lastly, we find anxiety in hysteria and other forms of severe neurosis, where it either accompanies symptoms or emerges independently as an attack or more persistent state, but always without any visible basis in an external danger. We then asked ourselves two questions: 'What are people afraid of in neurotic anxiety?' and 'How are we to bring it into relation with realistic anxiety felt in the face of external dangers?'

Our investigations were far from remaining unsuccessful: we reached a few important conclusions. In regard to anxious expectation clinical experience revealed that it had a regular connection with the libidinal economics of sexual life. The commonest cause of anxiety neurosis is unconsummated excitation. Libidinal excitation is aroused but not satisfied, not employed; apprehensiveness then appears instead of this libido that has been diverted from its employment. I even thought I was justified in saying that this unsatisfied libido was directly changed into anxiety. This view found support in some quite regularly occurring phobias of small children. Many of these phobias are very puzzling to us, but others, such as the fear of being alone and the fear of strangers, can be explained with certainty. Loneliness as well as a strange face arouse the child's longing for his familiar mother; he is unable to control this libidinal excitation, he cannot hold it in suspense but changes it into anxiety. This infantile anxiety must therefore be regarded not as of the realistic but as of the neurotic kind. Infantile phobias and the expectation of anxiety in anxiety neurosis offer us two examples of one way in which neurotic anxiety originates: by a direct transformation of libido. We shall at once come to know of a second mechanism, but it will turn out not to be very different from the first.

For we consider that what is responsible for the anxiety in hysteria and other neuroses is the process of repression. We believe it is possible to give a more complete account of this than before, if we separate what happens to the idea that has to be repressed from what happens to the quota of libido attaching to it. It is the idea which is subjected to repression and which may be distorted to the point of being unrecognizable; but its quota of affect is regularly transformed into anxiety—and this is so whatever the nature of the affect may be, whether it is aggressiveness or love. It makes no essential difference, then, for what reason a quota of libido has become unemployable: whether it is on account of the infantile weakness of the ego, as in children's phobias, or on account of somatic processes in sexual life, as in anxiety neurosis, or owing to repression, as in hysteria. Thus in reality the two mechanisms that bring about neurotic anxiety coincide.

In the course of these investigations our attention was drawn to a highly significant relation between the generation of anxiety and the formation of symptoms—namely, that these two represent and replace each other. For instance, an agoraphobic patient may start his illness with an attack of anxiety in the street. This would be repeated every time he went into the street again. He will now develop the symptom of agoraphobia; this may also be described as an inhibition, a restriction of the ego's functioning, and by means of it he spares himself anxiety attacks. We can witness the converse of this if we interfere in the formation of symptoms, as is possible, for instance, with obsessions. If we prevent a patient from carrying out a washing ceremonial, he falls into a state of anxiety which he finds hard to tolerate and from which he had evidently been protected by his symptom. And it seems, indeed, that the generation of anxiety is the earlier and the formation of symptoms the later of the two, as though the symptoms are created in order to avoid the outbreak of the anxiety state. This is confirmed too by the fact that the first neuroses of childhood are phobias—states in which we see so clearly how an initial generation of anxiety is replaced by the later formation of a symptom; we get an impression that it is from these interrelations that we shall best obtain access to an understanding of neurotic anxiety. And at the same time we have also succeeded in answering the question of what it is that a person is afraid of in neurotic anxiety and so in establishing the connection between neurotic and realistic anxiety. What he is afraid of is evidently his own libido. The difference between this situation and that of realistic anxiety lies in two points: that the danger is an internal instead of an external one and that it is not consciously recognized.

In phobias it is very easy to observe the way in which this internal danger is transformed into an external one—that is to say, how a neurotic anxiety is changed into an apparently realistic one. In order to simplify what is often a very complicated business, let us suppose that the agoraphobic patient is invariably afraid of feelings of temptation that are aroused in him by meeting people in the street. In his phobia he brings about a displacement and henceforward is afraid of an external situation. What he gains by this is obviously that he thinks he will be able to protect himself better in that way. One can save oneself from an external danger by flight; fleeing from an internal danger is a difficult enterprise.

At the conclusion of my earlier lecture on anxiety I myself expressed the opinion that, although these various findings of our enquiry were not mutually contradictory, somehow they did not fit in with one another. Anxiety, it seems, in so far as it is an affective state, is the reproduction of an old event which brought a threat of danger; anxiety serves the purposes of self-preservation and is a signal of a new danger; it arises from libido that has in some way become unemployable and it also arises during the process of repression; it is replaced by the formation of a symptom, is, as it were, psychically bound—one has a feeling that something is missing here which would bring all these pieces together into a whole.

Ladies and Gentlemen, the dissection of the mental personality into a super-ego, an ego and an id, which I put before you in my last lecture, has obliged us to take our bearings afresh in the problem of anxiety as well. With the thesis that the ego is the sole seat of anxiety[1]—that the ego alone can produce and feel anxiety—we have established a new and stable position from which a number of things take on a new aspect. And indeed it is difficult to see what sense there would be in speaking of an 'anxiety of the id' or in attributing a capacity for apprehensiveness to the super-ego. On the other hand, we have welcomed a desirable element of correspondence in the fact that

---

[1] [This was first stated, in slightly different words, near the end of *The Ego and the Id* (1923b). It was discussed at several points in *Inhibitions, Symptoms and Anxiety* (1926d). The greater part of what follows on the subject of anxiety is derived from the latter work.]

the three main species of anxiety, realistic, neurotic and moral, can be so easily connected with the ego's three dependent relations—to the external world, to the id and to the super-ego [p. 69]. Along with this new view, moreover, the function of anxiety as a signal announcing a situation of danger (a notion, incidentally, not unfamiliar to us) comes into prominence, the question of what the material is out of which anxiety is made loses interest, and the relations between realistic and neurotic anxiety have become surprisingly clarified and simplified. It is also to be remarked that we now understand the apparently complicated cases of the generation of anxiety better than those which were considered simple.

For we have recently been examining the way in which anxiety is generated in certain phobias which we class as anxiety hysteria, and have chosen cases in which we were dealing with the typical repression of wishful impulses arising from the Oedipus complex. We should have expected to find that it was a libidinal cathexis of the boy's mother as object which, as a result of repression, had been changed into anxiety and which now emerged, expressed in symptomatic terms, attached to a substitute for his father. I cannot present you with the detailed steps of an investigation such as this; it will be enough to say that the surprising result was the opposite of what we expected. It was not the repression that created the anxiety; the anxiety was there earlier; it was the anxiety that made the repression.[1] But what sort of anxiety can it have been? Only anxiety in the face of a threatening external danger—that is to say, a realistic anxiety. It is true that the boy felt anxiety in the face of a demand by his libido—in this instance, anxiety at being in love with his mother; so the case was in fact one of neurotic anxiety. But this being in love only appeared to him as an internal danger, which he must avoid by renouncing that object, because it conjured up an external situation of danger. And in every case we examine we obtain the same result. It must be confessed that we were not prepared to find that internal instinctual danger would turn out to be a determinant and preparation for an external, real, situation of danger.

But we have not made any mention at all so far of what the real danger is that the child is afraid of as a result of being in love with his mother. The danger is the punishment of being castrated, of losing his genital organ. You will of course object that after all that is not a real danger. Our boys are not cas-

---

[1] [Cf. Chapter IV of *Inhibitions, Symptoms and Anxiety*. The cases examined there were those of 'Little Hans' and the 'Wolf Man'.]

trated because they are in love with their mothers during the phase of the Oedipus complex. But the matter cannot be dismissed so simply. Above all, it is not a question of whether castration is really carried out; what is decisive is that the danger is one that threatens from outside and that the child believes in it. He has some ground for this, for people threaten him often enough with cutting off his penis during the phallic phase,[1] at the time of his early masturbation, and hints at that punishment must regularly find a phylogenetic reinforcement in him. It is our suspicion that during the human family's primaeval period castration used actually to be carried out by a jealous and cruel father upon growing boys, and that circumcision, which so frequently plays a part in puberty rites among primitive peoples, is a clearly recognizable relic of it. We are aware that here we are diverging widely from the general opinion; but we must hold fast to the view that fear of castration is one of the commonest and strongest motives for repression and thus for the formation of neuroses. The analysis of cases in which circumcision, though not, it is true, castration, has been carried out on boys as a cure or punishment for masturbation (a far from rare occurrence in Anglo-American society) has given our conviction a last degree of certainty. It is very tempting at this point to go more deeply into the castration complex, but I will stick to our subject.

Fear of castration is not, of course, the only motive for repression: indeed, it finds no place in women, for though they have a castration complex they cannot have a fear of being castrated. Its place is taken in their sex by a fear of loss of love, which is evidently a later prolongation of the infant's anxiety if it finds its mother absent. You will realize how real a situation of danger is indicated by this anxiety. If a mother is absent or has withdrawn her love from her child, it is no longer sure of the satisfaction of its needs and is perhaps exposed to the most distressing feelings of tension. Do not reject the idea that these determinants of anxiety may at bottom repeat the situation of the original anxiety at birth, which, to be sure, also represented a separation from the mother. Indeed, if you follow a train of thought suggested by Ferenczi [1925], you may add the fear of castration to this series, for a loss of the male organ results in an inability to unite once more with the mother (or a substitute for her) in the sexual act. I may mention to you incidentally that the very frequent phantasy of returning into the mother's womb is a substitute for this wish to copulate. There

---

[1] [This phase is discussed later in this lecture, p. 87 f.]

would be many interesting things and surprising connections
to tell you at this point, but I cannot go outside the framework
of an introduction to psycho-analysis. I will only draw your
attention to the fact that here psychological researches trench
upon the facts of biology.

Otto Rank, to whom psycho-analysis is indebted for many
excellent contributions, also has the merit of having expressly
emphasized the significance of the act of birth and of separation
from the mother [Rank, 1924]. Nevertheless we have all found
it impossible to accept the extreme inferences which he has
drawn from this factor as bearing on the theory of the neuroses
and even on analytic therapy. The core of his theory—that the
experience of anxiety at birth is the model of all later situations
of danger—he found already there.[1] If we dwell on these
situations of danger for a moment, we can say that in fact a
particular determinant of anxiety (that is, situation of danger)
is allotted to every age of development as being appropriate to
it. The danger of psychical helplessness fits the stage of the
ego's early immaturity; the danger of loss of an object (or loss of
love) fits the lack of self-sufficiency in the first years of childhood; the danger of being castrated fits the phallic phase; and
finally fear of the super-ego, which assumes a special position, fits
the period of latency. In the course of development the old
determinants of anxiety should be dropped, since the situations
of danger corresponding to them have lost their importance
owing to the strengthening of the ego. But this only occurs most
incompletely. Many people are unable to surmount the fear
of loss of love; they never become sufficiently independent of
other people's love and in this respect carry on their behaviour
as infants. Fear of the super-ego should normally never cease,
since, in the form of moral anxiety, it is indispensable in social
relations, and only in the rarest cases can an individual become
independent of human society. A few of the old situations of
danger, too, succeed in surviving into later periods by making
contemporary modifications in their determinants of anxiety.
Thus, for instance, the danger of castration persists under the
mark of syphilidophobia. It is true that as an adult one knows
that castration is no longer customary as a punishment for the
indulgence of sexual desires, but on the other hand one has
learnt that instinctual liberty of that kind is threatened by

[1] [Freud had first published it in a footnote added to the second
(1909) edition of *The Interpretation of Dreams,* but there is reason
to believe that his theory had been known considerably earlier among
his adherents in Vienna. His criticism of Rank's birth theory occurs
chiefly in Chapters VIII and X of *Inhibitions, Symptoms and Anxiety.*]

serious diseases. There is no doubt that the people we describe as neurotics remain infantile in their attitude to danger and have not surmounted obsolete determinants of anxiety. We may take this as a factual contribution to the characterization of neurotics; it is not so easy to say why it should be so.

I hope you have not lost the thread of what I am saying and remember that we are investigating the relations between anxiety and repression. In the course of this we have learnt two new things: first, that anxiety makes repression and not, as we used to think, the other way round, and [secondly] that the instinctual situation which is feared goes back ultimately to an external situation of danger. The next question will be: how do we now picture the process of a repression under the influence of anxiety? The answer will, I think, be as follows. The ego notices that the satisfaction of an emerging instinctual demand would conjure up one of the well-remembered situations of danger. This instinctual cathexis must therefore be somehow suppressed, stopped, made powerless. We know that the ego succeeds in this task if it is strong and has drawn the instinctual impulse concerned into its organization. But what happens in the case of repression is that the instinctual impulse still belongs to the id and that the ego feels weak. The ego thereupon helps itself by a technique which is at bottom identical with normal thinking. Thinking is an experimental action carried out with small amounts of energy, in the same way as a general shifts small figures about on a map before setting his large bodies of troops in motion.[1] Thus the ego anticipates the satisfaction of the questionable instinctual impulse and permits it to bring about the reproduction of the unpleasurable feelings at the beginning of the feared situation of danger. With this the auto-

[1] [This postponing activity of thought has already been mentioned in the last lecture (p. 67) as one of the main functions of the ego. The conception of thinking as an experimental, small-scale kind of acting—an essential element in 'reality-testing'—is among the earliest and most fundamental of Freud's theories, closely related to his distinction between the primary and secondary psychical processes (cf. p. 66 and footnote 2). It appears first in Sections 16, 17 and 18 of Part I of the 'Project' of 1895 and is discussed again in Section 3 of Part III of the same work (1950a). There the discussion is in ostensibly neurological terms, but it reappears as pure psychology in Chapters VII (E) of *The Interpretation of Dreams* (1900a). It will be found again in Chapter VII of the book on jokes (1905c), p. 192, in the paper on the 'Two Principles of Mental Functioning' (1911b), in Section V of 'The Unconscious' (1915e), in Chapter V of *The Ego and the Id* (1923b), and in 'Negation' (1925h). It makes a final appearance in Chapter VIII of the *Outline of Psycho-Analysis* (1940 [1938]), Freud's last major work. (Norton, 1949).]

matism of the pleasure-unpleasure principle is brought into operation and now carries out the repression of the dangerous instinctual impulse.

'Stop a moment!' you will exclaim; 'we can't follow you any further there!' You are quite right; I must add a little more before it can seem acceptable to you. First, I must admit that I have tried to translate into the language of our normal thinking what must in fact be a process that is neither conscious nor preconscious, taking place between quotas of energy in some unimaginable substratum. But that is not a strong objection, for it cannot be done in any other way. What is more important is that we should distinguish clearly what happens in the ego and what happens in the id when there is a repression. We have just said what the ego does: it makes use of an experimental cathexis and starts up the pleasure-unpleasure automatism by means of a signal of anxiety. After that, several reactions are possible or a combination of them in varying proportions. Either the anxiety attack is fully generated and the ego withdraws entirely from the objectionable excitation; or, in place of the experimental cathexis it opposes the excitation with an anticathexis, and this combines with the energy of the repressed impulse to form a symptom; or the anticathexis is taken up into the ego as a reaction-formation, as an intensification of certain of the ego's dispositions, as a permanent alteration of it.[1] The more the generation of anxiety can be restricted to a mere signal, so much the more does the ego expend on actions of defence which amount to the psychical binding of the repressed [impulse], and so much the closer, too, does the process approximate to a normal working-over of it,[2] though no doubt without attaining to it.

Incidentally, here is a point on which we may dwell for a moment. You yourselves have no doubt assumed that what is known as 'character', a thing so hard to define, is to be ascribed

---

[1] [This idea of an alteration of the ego as a result of an anticathexis is already to be found in some of Freud's very early writings, e.g. at the end of the second paper on 'The Neuro-Psychoses of Defence' (1896b). It had occurred more recently in Chapter XI (A) of *Inhibitions, Symptoms and Anxiety* (1926d), and was to be discussed further in Sections II and V of the very late technical paper 'Analysis Terminable and Interminable' (1937c).]

[2] [The concept of 'working-over' as a normal method of dealing with a disagreeable mental event is an old one of Freud's. Thus, in a lecture on hysteria delivered at the date of the Breuer and Freud 'Preliminary Communication', he said: 'Incidentally, a healthy psychical mechanism has other methods of dealing with the effect of a psychical trauma . . .—namely by working it over associatively . . .' (1893h).]

entirely to the ego. We have already made out a little of what
it is that creates character. First and foremost there is the incorporation of the former parental agency as a super-ego, which is
no doubt its most important and decisive portion, and, further,
identifications with the two parents of the later period and with
other influential figures, and similar identifications formed as
precipitates of abandoned object-relations [cf. p. 57]. And we
may now add as contributions to the construction of character
which are never absent the reaction-formations which the ego
acquires—to begin with in making its repressions and later, by
a more normal method, when it rejects unwished-for instinctual
impulses.[1]

Now let us go back and turn to the id. It is not so easy to
guess what occurs during repression in connection with the
instinctual impulse that is being fought against. The main question which our interest raises is as to what happens to the
energy, to the libidinal charge, of that excitation—how is it
employed? You recollect that the earlier hypothesis was that it
is precisely this that is transformed by repression into anxiety.[2]
We no longer feel able to say that. The modest reply will rather
be that what happens to it is probably not always the same
thing. There is probably an intimate correspondence which
we ought to get to know about between what is occurring at
the time in the ego and in the id in connection with the repressed impulse. For since we have decided that the pleasure-
unpleasure principle, which is set in action by the signal of
anxiety, plays a part in repression, we must alter our expectations. That principle exercises an entirely unrestricted dominance over what happens in the id. We can rely on its bringing
about quite profound changes in the instinctual impulse in
question. We are prepared to find that repression will have
very various consequences, more or less far-reaching. In some
cases the repressed instinctual impulse may retain its libidinal
cathexis, and may persist in the id unchanged, although subject
to constant pressure from the ego. In other cases what seems to
happen is that it is totally destroyed, while its libido is permanently diverted along other paths. I expressed the view that
this is what happens when the Oedipus complex is dealt with
normally—in this desirable case, therefore, being not simply

[1] [The earlier part of this paragraph is derived from a discussion at
the beginning of Chapter III of *The Ego and the Id* (1923*b*). The
later part is based on Chapter XI (A) of *Inhibitions, Symptoms and
Anxiety*.]

[2] [Cf. the metapsychological paper on 'Repression' (1915*d*), and *Introductory Lectures*, XXV.]

repressed but destroyed in the id.[1] Clinical experience has
further shown us that in many cases, instead of the customary
result of repression, a degradation of the libido takes place—a
regression of the libidinal organization to an earlier stage. This
can, of course, only occur in the id, and if it occurs it will be
under the influence of the same conflict which was introduced
by the signal of anxiety. The most striking example of this kind
is provided by the obsessional neurosis, in which libidinal regression and repression operate together.

I fear, Ladies and Gentlemen, that you will find this exposition hard to follow, and you will guess that I have not
stated it exhaustively. I am sorry to have had to rouse your dis-
pleasure. But I can set myself no other aim than to give you an
impression of the nature of our findings and of the difficulties
involved in working them out. The deeper we penetrate into
the study of mental processes the more we recognize their abundance and complexity. A number of simple formulas which to
begin with seemed to meet our needs have later turned out to
be inadequate. We do not tire of altering and improving them.
In my lecture on the theory of dreams [the first in the present
series] I introduced you to a region in which for fifteen years
there has scarcely been a new discovery. Here, where we are
dealing with anxiety, you see everything in a state of flux and
change. These novelties, moreover, have not yet been thor-
oughly worked through and perhaps this too adds to the difficulties of demonstrating them. But have patience! We shall soon
be able to take leave of the subject of anxiety. I cannot promise
that it will have been settled to our satisfaction, but it is to be
hoped that we shall have made a little bit of progress. And in
the meantime we have made all sorts of new discoveries. Now,
for instance, our study of anxiety leads us to add a new feature
to our description of the ego. We have said that the ego is weak
in comparison with the id, that it is its loyal servant, eager to
carry out its orders and to fulfil its demands. We have no intention of withdrawing this statement. But on the other hand this
same ego is the better organized part of the id, with its face
turned towards reality. We must not exaggerate the separation
between the two of them too much, and we must not be surprised if the ego on its part can bring its influence to bear on the
processes in the id. I believe the ego exercises this influence by
putting into action the almost omnipotent pleasure-unpleasure
principle by means of the signal of anxiety. On the other hand,
it shows its weakness again immediately afterwards, for by the

[1] [Cf. 'The Dissolution of the Oedipus Complex' (1942d).]

act of repression it renounces a portion of its organization and has to allow the repressed instinctual impulse to remain permanently withdrawn from its influence.

And now, only one more remark on the problem of anxiety. Neurotic anxiety has changed in our hands into realistic anxiety, into fear of particular external situations of danger. But we cannot stop there, we must take another step—though it will be a step backward. We ask ourselves what it is that is actually dangerous and actually feared in a situation of danger of this kind. It is plainly not the injury to the subject as judged objectively, for this need be of no significance psychologically, but something brought about by it in the mind. Birth, for instance, our model for an anxiety state, can after all scarcely be regarded on its own account as an injury, although it may involve a danger of injuries. The essential thing about birth, as about every situation of danger, is that it calls up in mental experience a state of highly tense excitation, which is felt as unpleasure and which one is not able to master by discharging it. Let us call a state of this kind, before which the efforts of the pleasure principle break down, a 'traumatic' moment.[1] Then, if we take in succession neurotic anxiety, realistic anxiety and the situation of danger, we arrive at this simple proposition: what is feared, what is the object of the anxiety, is invariably the emergence of a traumatic moment, which cannot be dealt with by the normal rules of the pleasure principle. We understand at once that our endowment with the pleasure principle does not guarantee us against objective injuries but only against a particular injury to our psychical economics. It is a long step from the pleasure principle to the self-preservative instinct; the intentions of the two of them are very far from coinciding from the start. But we see something else besides; perhaps it is the solution we are in search of. Namely, that in all this it is a question of relative quantities. It is only the magnitude of the sum of excitation that turns an impression into a traumatic moment, paralyses the function of the pleasure principle and gives the situation of danger its significance. And if that is how things are, if these puzzles can be solved so prosaically, why should it not be possible for similar traumatic moments to arise in mental life without reference to hypothetical situations of danger—traumatic moments, then, in which anxiety is not aroused as a signal but is generated anew for a fresh reason.

[1] [This phrase, with its echo of Charcot, goes back to Freud's very earliest discussions of hysteria. See, for instance, Section I of his first paper on 'The Neuro-Psychoses of Defence' (1894a).]

Clinical experience declares decidedly that such is in fact the case. It is only the *later* repressions that exhibit the mechanism we have described, in which anxiety is awakened as a signal of an earlier situation of danger. The first and original repressions arise directly from traumatic moments, when the ego meets with an excessively great libidinal demand; they construct their anxiety afresh, although, it is true, on the model of birth. The same may apply to the generation of anxiety in anxiety neurosis owing to somatic damage to the sexual function. We shall no longer maintain that it is the libido itself that is turned into anxiety in such cases.[1] But I can see no objection to there being a twofold origin of anxiety—one as a direct consequence of the traumatic moment and the other as a signal threatening a repetition of such a moment.

I feel sure you are rejoicing, Ladies and Gentlemen, at not having to listen to any more about anxiety. But you have gained nothing by it: what follows is no better. It is my design to introduce you to-day as well to the field of the libido theory or theory of the instincts, where there have equally been a number of new developments. I will not claim that we have made great advances in it, so that it would be worth your taking any amount of trouble to learn about them. No. This is a region in which we are struggling laboriously to find our bearings and make discoveries; you will only be witnesses of our efforts. Here too I shall have to go back to some of the things I told you earlier.

The theory of the instincts is so to say our mythology. Instincts are mythical entities, magnificent in their indefiniteness. In our work we cannot for a moment disregard them, yet we are never sure that we are seeing them clearly. You know how popular thinking deals with the instincts. People assume as many and as various instincts as they happen to need at the moment—a self-assertive instinct, an imitative instinct, an instinct of play, a gregarious instinct and many others like them. People take them up, as it were, make each of them do its particular job, and then drop them again. We have always been moved by a suspicion that behind all these little *ad hoc* instincts there lay concealed something serious and powerful which we should like to approach cautiously. Our first step was modest

---

[1] [In Chapter VIII of *Inhibitions, Symptoms and Anxiety* Freud still maintained, at least as a possibility, that in anxiety neurosis 'what finds discharge in the generating of anxiety is precisely the surplus of unutilized libido'. With the present sentence the last trace of the old theory is abandoned.]

enough. We told ourselves we should probably not be going astray if we began by separating two main instincts or classes of instincts or groups of instincts in accordance with the two great needs—hunger and love. However jealously we usually defend the independence of psychology from every other science, here we stood in the shadow of the unshakable biological fact that the living individual organism is at the command of two intentions, self-preservation and the preservation of the species, which seem to be independent of each other, which, so far as we know at present, have no common origin and whose interests are often in conflict in animal life. Actually what we are talking now is biological psychology, we are studying the psychical accompaniments of biological processes. It was as representing this aspect of the subject that the 'ego-instincts' and the 'sexual instincts' were introduced into psycho-analysis. We included in the former everything that had to do with the preservation, assertion and magnification of the individual. To the latter we had to attribute the copiousness called for by infantile and perverse sexual life. In the course of investigating the neuroses we came to know the ego as the restricting and repressing power and the sexual trends as the restricted and repressed one; we therefore believed that we had clear evidence not only of the difference between the two groups of instincts but also of the conflict between them. The first object of our study was only the sexual instincts, whose energy we named 'libido'. It was in relation to them that we sought to clarify our ideas of what an instinct is and what is to be attributed to it. Here we have the libido theory.

An instinct, then, is distinguished from a stimulus by the fact that it arises from sources of stimulation within the body, that it operates as a constant force and that the subject cannot avoid it by flight, as is possible with an external stimulus. We can distinguish an instinct's source, object and aim. Its source is a state of excitation in the body, its aim is the removal of that excitation; on its path from its source to its aim the instinct becomes operative psychically. We picture it as a certain quota of energy which presses in a particular direction. It is from this pressing that it derives its name of 'Trieb'.[1] People speak of 'active' and 'passive' instincts, but it would be more correct to speak of instincts with active and passive aims: for an expenditure of activity is needed to achieve a passive aim as well. The

[1] [The German word is often translated 'drive' but 'instinct' has been used throughout the Standard Edition for reasons stated in the General Preface in Volume I.]

aim can be achieved in the subject's own body; as a rule an external object is brought in, in regard to which the instinct achieves its external aim; its internal aim invariably remains the bodily change which is felt as satisfaction. It has not become clear to us whether the relation of the instinct to its somatic source gives it a specific quality and if so what. The evidence of analytic experience shows that it is an undoubted fact that instinctual impulses from one source attach themselves to those from other sources and share their further vicissitudes and that in general one instinctual satisfaction can be replaced by another. But it must be admitted that we do not understand this very well. The relations of an instinct to its aim and object are also open to alterations; both can be exchanged for other ones, though its relation to its object is nevertheless the more easily loosened. A certain kind of modification of the aim and change of the object, in which our social valuation is taken into account, is described by us as 'sublimation'. Besides this, we have grounds for distinguishing instincts which are 'inhibited in their aim'—instinctual impulses from sources well known to us with an unambiguous aim, but which come to a stop on their way to satisfaction, so that a lasting object-cathexis comes about and a permanent trend [of feeling]. Such, for instance, is the relation of tenderness, which undoubtedly originates from the sources of sexual need and invariably renounces its satisfaction.[1]

You see how many of the characteristics and vicissitudes of the instincts still escape our comprehension. A further distinction should be mentioned here which is exhibited between the sexual and self-preservative instincts and which would be of the greatest theoretical importance if it applied to the groups as a whole. The sexual instincts are noticeable to us for their plasticity, their capacity for altering their aims, their replaceability, which admits of one instinctual satisfaction being replaced by another, and their readiness for being deferred, of which we have just given a good example in the aim-inhibited instincts. We should be glad to deny these characteristics to the self-preservative instincts, and to say of them that they are inflexible, admit of no delay, are imperative in a very different sense and have a quite other relation to repression and to anxiety. But a little reflection tells us that this exceptional position applies, not to all the ego-instincts, but only to hunger and thirst, and is evidently based on a peculiar character of the sources of those instincts. A good part of the confusing impression made by

[1] [The contents of this paragraph are largely repeated from the first portion of 'Instincts and their Vicissitudes' (1915c).]

all this is that we have not given separate consideration to the
alterations which the influence of the organized ego makes in the
instinctual impulses that belonged originally to the id.

We find ourselves on firmer ground when we investigate the
manner in which the life of the instincts serves the sexual function. Here we have acquired quite definite knowledge, with
which you too are already familiar. It is not the case, then, that
we recognize a sexual instinct which is from the first the vehicle
of an urge towards the aim of the sexual function—the union of
the two sex-cells. What we see is a great number of component
instincts arising from different areas and regions of the body,
which strive for satisfaction fairly independently of one another
and find that satisfaction in something that we may call 'organ-
pleasure'.[1] The genitals are the latest of these 'erotogenic zones'
and the name of 'sexual' pleasure cannot be withheld from their
organ-pleasure. These impulses which strive for pleasure are not
all taken up into the final organization of the sexual function.
A number of them are set aside as unserviceable, by repression
or some other means; a few of them are diverted from their aim
in the remarkable manner I have mentioned [p. 86] and used
to strengthen other impulses; yet others persist in minor roles,
and serve for the performance of introductory acts, for the pro-
duction of fore-pleasure.[2] You have heard how in the course of
this long-drawn-out development several phases of preliminary
organization can be recognized and also how this history of the
sexual function explains its aberrations and atrophies. The first
of these 'pregenital' phases is known to us as the *oral* one because, in conformity with the way in which an infant in arms is
nourished, the erotogenic zone of the mouth dominates what
may be called the sexual activity of that period of life. At a
second level the *sadistic* and *anal* impulses come to the fore, un
doubtedly in connection with the appearance of the teeth, the
strengthening of the muscular apparatus and the control of the
sphincter functions. We have learnt a number of interesting
details about this remarkable stage of development in particular.[3] Thirdly comes the *phallic* phase in which in both sexes
the male organ (and what corresponds to it in girls) attains

---

[1] [This term had been discussed by Freud at some length in *Introductory Lectures*, XXI. The same lecture covers the contents of much
of the first part of the present paragraph.]

[2] [A long discussion of fore-pleasure is given in Section I of the
third of Freud's *Three Essays on the Theory of Sexuality* (1905*d*). In
the book on jokes (1905*c*) p. 137 the subject recurs at several points.]

[3] [These are discussed below, pp. 88–91.]

an importance which can no longer be overlooked.[1] We have reserved the name of *genital* phase for the definitive sexual organization which is established after puberty and in which the female genital organ for the first time meets with the recognition which the male one acquired long before.

So far all this is trite repetition. And you must not suppose that the many things I have not mentioned this time no longer hold good. This repetition was necessary so that I might use it as the starting-point for a report on the advances in our knowledge. We can boast of having learnt much that is new, particularly about the early organizations of the libido, and of having obtained a clearer grasp of the significance of what is old; and I will give you at least a few examples to demonstrate this. Abraham showed in 1924 that two stages can be distinguished in the sadistic-anal phase. The earlier of these is dominated by the destructive trends of destroying and losing, the later one by trends friendly towards objects—those of keeping and possessing. It is in the middle of this phase, therefore, that consideration for the object makes its first appearance as a precursor of a later erotic cathexis. We are equally justified in making a similar subdivision in the first, oral phase. In the first sub-stage what is in question is only oral incorporation, there is no ambivalence at all in the relation to the object—the mother's breast. The second stage, characterized by the emergence of the biting activity, may be described as the 'oral-sadistic' one; it exhibits for the first time the phenomena of ambivalence, which become so much clearer afterwards, in the following sadistic-anal phase. The value of these new distinctions is to be seen especially if we look for the dispositional points in the development of the libido in the case of particular neuroses, such as obsessional neurosis or melancholia.[2] You must here recall to mind what we have learnt about the connection between fixation of the libido, disposition and regression.[3]

Our attitude to the phases of the organization of the libido has in general shifted a little. Whereas earlier we chiefly emphasized the way in which each of them passed away before the next, our attention now is directed to the facts that show us how much of each earlier phase persists alongside of and behind the later configurations and obtains a permanent representation in

[1] [See 'The Infantile Genital Organization' (1923e).]

[2] [I.e. the points in libidinal development at which a fixation lays down a disposition to some particular neurosis. Cf. 'The Disposition to Obsessional Neurosis' (1913i). The term 'dispositional point' occurs in Section III of the Schreber analysis (1911c).]

[3] [In *Introductory Lectures*, XXII.]

the libidinal economy and character of the subject. Still more significant have studies become which have taught us how frequently under pathological conditions regressions to earlier phases occur and that particular regressions are characteristic of particular forms of illness.[1] But I cannot go into that here, it forms part of the specialized psychology of the neuroses.

We have been able to study transformations of instinct and similar processes particularly in anal erotism, the excitations arising from the sources of the erotogenic anal zone, and we were surprised at the multiplicity of uses to which these instinctual impulses are put. It may not be easy, perhaps, to get free from the contempt into which this particular zone has fallen in the course of evolution. Let us therefore allow ourselves to be reminded by Abraham that embryologically the anus corresponds to the primitive mouth, which has migrated down to the end of the bowel.[2] We have learnt, then, that after a person's own faeces, his excrement, has lost its value for him, this instinctual interest derived from the anal source passes over on to objects that can be presented as *gifts*. And this is rightly so, for faeces were the first gift that an infant could make, something he could part with out of love for whoever was looking after him. After this, corresponding exactly to analogous changes of meaning that occur in linguistic development, this ancient interest in faeces is transformed into the high valuation of *gold* and *money* but also makes a contribution to the affective cathexis of *baby* and *penis*. It is a universal conviction among children, who long retain the cloaca theory, that babies are born from the bowel like a piece of faeces:[3] defaecation is the model of the act of birth. But the penis too has its fore-runner in the column of faeces which fills and stimulates the mucous membrane of the bowel. When a child, unwillingly enough, comes to realize that there are human creatures who do not possess a penis, that organ appears to him as something detachable from the body and becomes unmistakably analogous to the excrement, which was the first piece of bodily material that had to be renounced. A great part of anal erotism is thus carried over into a cathexis of the penis. But the interest in that part of the body has, in addition to its anal-erotic root, an oral one which is perhaps more powerful still: for when sucking has come to an end, the penis also becomes heir of the mother's nipple.

[1] [This is probably once again a reference to Abraham's important publication of 1924.]

[2] [Abraham, 1924; English translation, p. 500.]

[3] [Cf. Freud's early paper on 'The Sexual Theories of Children' (1908c).]

If one is not aware of these profound connections, it is impossible to find one's way about in the phantasies of human beings, in their associations, influenced as they are by the unconscious, and in their symptomatic language. Faeces—money —gift—baby—penis are treated there as though they meant the same thing, and they are represented too by the same symbols. Nor must you forget that I have only been able to give you very incomplete information. I may hurriedly add, perhaps, that interest in the vagina, which awakens later, is also essentially of anal-erotic origin. This is not to be wondered at, for the vagina itself, to borrow an apt phrase from Lou Andreas-Salomé [1916], is 'taken on lease' from the rectum:[1] in the life of homosexuals, who have failed to accomplish some part of normal sexual development, the vagina is once more represented by it. In dreams a locality often appears which was earlier a simple room but is now divided into two by a wall, or the other way round. This always means the relation of the vagina to the bowel.[2] It is also easy to follow the way in which in girls what is an entirely unfeminine wish to possess a penis is normally transformed into a wish for a baby, and then for a man as the bearer of the penis and giver of the baby; so that here we can see too how a portion of what was originally anal-erotic interest obtains admission into the later genital organization.[3]

During our studies of the pregenital phases of the libido we have also gained a few fresh insights into the formation of character. We noticed a triad of character-traits which are found together with fair regularity: orderliness, parsimoniousness and obstinacy; and we inferred from the analysis of people exhibiting these traits that they have arisen from their anal erotism becoming absorbed and employed in a different way. We therefore speak of an 'anal character' in which we find this remarkable combination and we draw a contrast to some extent between the anal character and unmodified anal erotism.[4] We also discovered a similar but perhaps still firmer link between ambition and urethral erotism. A striking allusion to this con-

[1] [Her paper was summarized by Freud in a footnote added in 1920 to the second of his *Three Essays* (1905*d*).]

[2] [This example had been added in 1919 to Chapter VI (E) of *The Interpretation of Dreams* (1900*a*).]

[3] [The greater part of the last two paragraphs is derived from 'Transformations of Instinct' (1917*c*), but there are a few additional points here. The subject had already been alluded to in *Introductory Lectures* XX.]

[4] [These connections had in fact been indicated in quite an early paper of Freud's, 'Character and Anal Erotism' (1908*b*).]

nection is to be seen in the legend that Alexander the Great was
born during the same night in which a certain Herostratus set
fire to the celebrated temple of Artemis at Ephesus out of a sheer
desire for fame. So the ancients would seem not to have been
unaware of the connection. You know, of course, how much
urination has to do with fire and extinguishing fire.[1] We naturally expect that other character traits as well will turn out
similarly to be precipitates or reaction-formations related to
particular pregenital libidinal structures; but we have not yet
been able to show this.

It is now time, however, for me to go back both in history and
in my subject-matter and once more to take up the most
general problems of instinctual life. To begin with, the opposition between the ego-instincts and the sexual instincts lay at the
base of our libido theory. When later on we began to study the
ego itself more closely and arrived at the conception of narcissism, this distinction itself lost its foundation. In rare cases one
can observe that the ego has taken itself as an object and is behaving as though it were in love with itself. Hence the term
'narcissism', borrowed from the Greek myth.[2] But that is only
an extreme exaggeration of a normal state of affairs. We came
to understand that the ego is always the main reservoir of libido,
from which libidinal cathexes of objects go out and into which
they return again, while the major part of this libido remains
permanently in the ego.[3] Thus ego libido is being constantly
changed into object libido and object libido into ego libido.
But in that case they could not be different in their nature
and it could have no sense to distinguish the energy of the
one from the energy of the other; we could either drop the
term 'libido' or use it as synonymous with psychical energy in
general.

We did not maintain this position for long. Our feeling of
their being a contrariety in instinctual life soon found another
and sharper expression. It is not my wish, however, to put before you the origin of this novelty in the theory of the instincts;
it too is based essentially on biological considerations. I shall
offer it to you as a ready-made product. Our hypothesis is that

[1] [Freud had very recently devoted a short paper to this subject
(1932a).]

[2] [Of Narcissus, who was in love with himself.]

[3] [But cf. the statement on p. 68 above that 'the object-cathexes
spring from the instinctual demands of the id'. See also, however, the
reference to a combined ego and id with regard to the destructive
instinct on p. 93 below.]

there are two essentially different classes of instincts: the sexual instincts, understood in the widest sense—Eros, if you prefer that name—and the aggressive instincts, whose aim is destruction. When it is put to you like this, you will scarcely regard it as a novelty. It looks like an attempt at a theoretical transfiguration of the commonplace opposition between loving and hating, which coincides, perhaps, with the other polarity, of attraction and repulsion, which physics assumes in the inorganic world. But it is a remarkable thing that this hypothesis is nevertheless felt by many people as an innovation and, indeed, as a most undesirable one which should be got rid of as quickly as possible. I presume that a strong affective factor is coming into effect in this rejection. Why have we ourselves needed such a long time before we decided to recognize an aggressive instinct? Why did we hesitate to make use, on behalf of our theory, of facts which were obvious and familiar to everyone? We should probably have met with little resistance if we had wanted to ascribe an instinct with such an aim to animals. But to include it in the human constitution appears sacrilegious; it contradicts too many religious presumptions and social conventions. No, man must be naturally good or at least good-natured. If he occasionally shows himself brutal, violent or cruel, these are only passing disturbances of his emotional life, for the most part provoked, or perhaps only consequences of the inexpedient social regulations which he has hitherto imposed on himself.

Unfortunately what history tells us and what we ourselves have experienced does not speak in this sense but rather justifies a judgement that belief in the 'goodness' of human nature is one of those evil illusions by which mankind expect their lives to be beautified and made easier while in reality they only cause damage. We need not continue this controversy, since we have argued in favour of a special aggressive and destructive instinct in men not on account of the teachings of history or of our experience in life but on the basis of general considerations to which we were led by examining the phenomena of sadism and masochism. As you know, we call it sadism when sexual satisfaction is linked to the condition of the sexual object's suffering pain, ill-treatment and humiliation, and masochism when the need is felt of being the ill-treated object oneself. As you know too, a certain admixture of these two trends is included in normal sexual relations, and we speak of perversions when they push the other sexual aims into the background and replace them by their own aims.[1] And you will scarcely have failed to

---

[1] [For this see *Introductory Lectures*, XX and XXI.]

notice that sadism has a more intimate relation with masculinity and masochism with femininity, as though there were a secret kinship present; though I must add that we have made no progress along that path. Both phenomena, sadism and masochism alike, but masochism quite especially, present a truly puzzling problem to the libido theory; and it is only proper if what was a stumbling-block for the one theory should become the cornerstone of the theory replacing it.

It is our opinion, then, that in sadism and in masochism we have before us two excellent examples of a mixture of the two classes of instinct, of Eros and aggressiveness; and we proceed to the hypothesis that this relation is a model one—that every instinctual impulse that we can examine consists of similar fusions or alloys of the two classes of instinct. These fusions, of course, would be in the most varied ratios. Thus the erotic instincts would introduce the multiplicity of their sexual aims into the fusion, while the others would only admit of mitigations or gradations in their monotonous trend. This hypothesis opens a prospect to us of investigations which may some day be of great importance for the understanding of pathological processes. For fusions may also come apart, and we may expect that functioning will be most gravely affected by defusions of such a kind. But these conceptions are still too new; no one has yet tried to apply them in our work.[1]

Let us go back to the special problem presented to us by masochism. If for a moment we leave its erotic components on one side, it affords us a guarantee of the existence of a trend that has self-destruction as its aim. If it is true of the destructive instinct as well [as of the libido] that the ego—but what we have in mind here is rather the id, the whole person[2]—originally includes all the instinctual impulses, we are led to the view that masochism is older than sadism, and that sadism is the destructive instinct directed outwards, thus acquiring the characteristic of aggressiveness. A certain amount of the original destructive instinct may still remain in the interior. It seems that we can only perceive it under two conditions: if it is combined with erotic instincts into masochism or if with a greater or lesser erotic addition—it is directed against the external world as aggressiveness. And now we are struck by the significance of the possibility that the aggressiveness may not be able to find satisfaction in the external world because it comes up against real obstacles. If this happens, it will perhaps re-

---

[1] [See for this question Chapter IV of *The Ego and the Id* (1923b).]
[2] [Cf. footnote 1, p. 91.]

treat and increase the amount of self-destructiveness holding sway in the interior. We shall hear how this is in fact what occurs and how important a process this is. Impeded aggressiveness seems to involve a grave injury. It really seems as though it is necessary for us to destroy some other thing or person in order not to destroy ourselves, in order to guard against the impulsion to self-destruction. A sad disclosure indeed for the moralist!

But the moralist will console himself for a long time to come with the improbability of our speculations. A queer instinct, indeed, directed to the destruction of its own organic home! Poets, it is true, talk of such things; but poets are irresponsible people and enjoy the privilege of poetic licence. Incidentally, such ideas are not foreign even to physiology: consider the notion, for instance, of the mucous membrane of the stomach digesting itself. It must be admitted, however, that our self-destructive instinct calls for support on a wider basis. One cannot, after all, venture on a hypothesis of such a wide range merely because a few poor fools have linked their sexual satisfaction to a peculiar condition. A more profound study of the instincts will, I believe, give us what we need. The instincts rule not only mental but also vegetative life, and these organic instincts exhibit a characteristic which deserves our deepest interest. (We shall not be able to judge until later whether it is a general characteristic of instincts.) For they reveal an effort to restore an earlier state of things. We may suppose that from the moment at which a state of things that has once been attained is upset, an instinct arises to create it afresh and brings about phenomena which we can describe as a 'compulsion to repeat'. Thus the whole of embryology is an example of the compulsion to repeat. A power of regenerating lost organs extends far up into the animal kingdom, and the instinct for recovery to which, alongside of therapeutic assistance, our cures are due must be the residue of this capacity which is so enormously developed in the lower animals. The spawning migrations of fishes, the migratory flights of birds, and possibly all that we describe as manifestations of instinct[1] in animals, take place under the orders of the compulsion to repeat, which expresses the *conservative nature* of the instincts. Nor have we far to look in the mental field for its manifestations. We have been struck by the fact that the forgotten and repressed experiences of childhood are reproduced during the work of analysis in dreams and reactions, particularly in those occurring in the transference, although their revival runs counter to the interest of the pleasure

---

[1] ['*Instinkt*' in the original; '*Triebe*' two lines below.]

principle; and we have explained this by supposing that in these cases a compulsion to repeat is overcoming even the pleasure principle. Outside analysis, too, something similar can be observed. There are people in whose lives the same reactions are perpetually being repeated uncorrected, to their own detriment, or others who seem to be pursued by a relentless fate, though closer investigation teaches us that they are unwittingly bringing this fate on themselves. In such cases we attribute a 'daemonic' character to the compulsion to repeat.

But how can this conservative characteristic of instincts help us to understand our self-destructiveness? What earlier state of things does an instinct such as this want to restore? Well, the answer is not far to seek and opens wide perspectives. If it is true that—at some immeasurably remote time and in a manner we cannot conceive—life once proceeded out of inorganic matter, then, according to our presumption, an instinct must have arisen which sought to do away with life once more and to re-establish the inorganic state. If we recognize in this instinct the self-destructiveness of our hypothesis, we may regard the self-destructiveness as an expression of a 'death instinct' which cannot fail to be present in every vital process. And now the instincts that we believe in divide themselves into two groups— the erotic instincts, which seek to combine more and more living substance into ever greater unities, and the death instincts, which oppose this effort and lead what is living back into an inorganic state. From the concurrent and opposing action of these two proceed the phenomena of life which are brought to an end by death.

You may perhaps shrug your shoulders and say: 'That isn't natural science, it's Schopenhauer's philosophy!' But, Ladies and Gentlemen, why should not a bold thinker have guessed something that is afterwards confirmed by sober and painstaking detailed research? Moreover, there is nothing that has not been said already, and similar things had been said by many people before Schopenhauer. Furthermore, what we are saying is not even genuine Schopenhauer. We are not asserting that death is the only aim of life; we are not overlooking the fact that there is life as well as death. We recognize two basic instincts and give each of them its own aim. How the two of them are mingled in the process of living, how the death instinct is made to serve the purposes of Eros, especially by being turned outwards as aggressiveness—these are tasks which are left to future investigation. We have not gone beyond the point at which this prospect lies open before us. The question, too, of whether the conservative character may not belong to all instincts without exception, whether the erotic instincts as well may not be seeking to bring back an earlier state of things when they strive to bring about a synthesis of living things into greater unities—this question, too, we must leave unanswered.[1]

We have travelled somewhat far from our basis. I will tell you in retrospect the starting-point of these reflections on the theory of the instincts. It was the same as that which led us to revise the relation between the ego and the unconscious—the impression derived from the work of analysis that the patient who puts up a resistance is so often unaware of that resistance. Not only the fact of the resistance is unconscious to him, however, but its motives as well. We were obliged to search out these motives or motive, and to our surprise we found them in a powerful need for punishment which we could only class with masochistic wishes. The practical significance of this discovery is not less than its theoretical one, for the need for punishment is the worst enemy of our therapeutic efforts. It is satisfied by the suffering which is linked to the neurosis, and for that reason holds fast to being ill. It seems that this factor, an unconscious need for punishment, has a share in every neurotic illness. And here those cases in which the neurotic suffering can be replaced by suffering of another kind are wholly convincing. I will report an experience of this kind.

I once succeeded in freeing an unmarried woman, no longer young, from the complex of symptoms which had condemned her for some fifteen years to an existence of torment and had excluded her from any participation in life. She now felt she was well, and she plunged into eager activity, in order to develop her by no means small talent and to snatch a little recognition, enjoyment, and success, late though the moment was. But every one of her attempts ended either with people letting her know or with herself recognizing that she was too old to accomplish anything in that field. After each outcome of this kind a relapse into illness would have been the obvious thing, but she was no longer able to bring that about. Instead, she met each time with an accident which put her out of action for a time and caused her suffering. She fell down and sprained her ankle or hurt her knee, or she injured her hand in something she was doing. When she was made aware of how great her own share might be in these apparent accidents, she, so to

---

[1] [This discussion of the compulsion to repeat and of the death instinct is almost wholly derived from *Beyond the Pleasure Principle* (1920g). A fuller account of masochism will be found in the rather later paper 'The Economic Problem of Masochism' (1924c).]

say, changed her technique. Instead of accidents, indispositions appeared on the same provocations—catarrhs, sore throats, influenzal conditions, rheumatic swellings—till at last she made up her mind to resign her attempts and the whole agitation came to an end.

There is, as we think, no doubt about the origin of this unconscious need for punishment. It behaves like a piece of conscience, like a prolongation of our conscience into the unconscious; and it must have the same origin as conscience and correspond, therefore, to a piece of aggressiveness that has been internalized and taken over by the super-ego. If only the words went together better, we should be justified for all practical purposes in calling it an 'unconscious sense of guilt'. Theoretically we are in fact in doubt whether we should suppose that all the aggressiveness that has returned from the external world is bound by the super-ego and accordingly turned against the ego, or that a part of it is carrying on its mute and uncanny activity as a free destructive instinct in the ego and the id. A distribution of the latter kind is the more probable; but we know nothing more about it. There is no doubt that, when the super-ego was first instituted, in equipping that agency use was made of the piece of the child's aggressiveness towards his parents for which he was unable to effect a discharge outwards on account of his erotic fixation as well as of external difficulties; and for that reason the severity of the super-ego need not simply correspond to the strictness of the upbringing [see p. 56 above]. It is very possible that, when there are later occasions for suppressing aggressiveness, the instinct may take the same path that was opened to it at that decisive point of time.

People in whom this unconscious sense of guilt is excessively strong betray themselves in analytic treatment by the negative therapeutic reaction which is so disagreeable from the prognostic point of view.[1] When one has given them the solution of a symptom, which should normally be followed by at least its temporary disappearance, what they produce instead is a momentary exacerbation of the symptom and of the illness. It is often enough to praise them for their behaviour in the treatment or to say a few hopeful words about the progress of the analysis in order to bring about an unmistakable worsening of their condition. A non-analyst would say that the 'will to recovery' was absent. If you follow the analytic way of thinking, you will see in this behaviour a manifestation of the unconscious sense of guilt, for which being ill, with its sufferings and

---

[1] [See a long footnote in Chapter V of *The Ego and the Id* (1923*b*).]

impediments, is just what is wanted. The problems which the unconscious sense of guilt has opened up, its connections with morality, education, crime and delinquency, are at present the preferred field of work for psycho-analysts.[1]

And here, at an unexpected point, we have emerged from the psychical underworld into the open market-place. I cannot lead you any further, but before I take leave of you for to-day I must detain you with one more train of thought. It has become our habit to say that our civilization has been built up at the cost of sexual trends which, being inhibited by society, are partly, it is true, repressed but have partly been made usable for other aims. We have admitted, too, that, in spite of all our pride in our cultural attainments, it is not easy for us to fulfil the requirements of this civilization or to feel comfortable in it, because the instinctual restrictions imposed on us constitute a heavy psychical burden. Well, what we have come to see about the sexual instincts, applies equally and perhaps still more to the other ones, the aggressive instincts. It is they above all that make human communal life difficult and threaten its survival. Restriction of the individual's aggressiveness is the first and perhaps the severest sacrifice which society requires of him. We have learnt the ingenious way in which the taming of this unruly thing has been achieved. The institution of the super-ego which takes over the dangerous aggressive impulses, introduces a garrison, as it were, into regions that are inclined to rebellion. But on the other hand, if we look at it purely psychologically, we must recognize that the ego does not feel happy in being thus sacrificed to the needs of society, in having to submit to the destructive trends of aggressiveness which it would have been glad to employ itself against others. It is like a prolongation in the mental sphere of the dilemma of 'eat or be eaten' which dominates the organic animate world. Luckily the aggressive instincts are never alone but always alloyed with the erotic ones. These latter have much to mitigate and much to avert under the conditions of the civilization which mankind has created.[1]

---

[1] [The main discussions of the sense of guilt will be found in Chapter V of *The Ego and the Id* (1923*b*), 'The Economic Problem of Masochism' (1924*c*) and Chapters VII and VIII of *Civilization and its Discontents* (1930*a*).]

[1] [The aggressive and destructive instincts had been discussed at length by Freud shortly before in *Civilization and its Discontents* (1930*a*) (Norton, 1962) particularly in Chapters V and VI.]

LECTURE XXXIII

FEMININITY[1]

LADIES AND GENTLEMEN,—All the while I am preparing to talk to you I am struggling with an internal difficulty. I feel uncertain, so to speak, of the extent of my licence. It is true that in the course of fifteen years of work psycho-analysis has changed and grown richer; but, in spite of that, an introduction to psycho-analysis might have been left without alteration or supplement. It is constantly in my mind that these lectures are without a *raison d'être*. For analysts I am saying too little and nothing at all that is new; but for you I am saying too much and saying things which you are not equipped to understand and which are not in your province. I have looked around for excuses and I have tried to justify each separate lecture on different grounds. The first one, on the theory of dreams, was supposed to put you back again at one blow into the analytic atmosphere and to show you how durable our views have turned out to be. I was led on to the second one, which followed the paths from dreams to what is called occultism, by the opportunity of speaking my mind without constraint on a department of work in which prejudiced expectations are fighting to-day against passionate resistances, and I could hope that your judgement, educated to tolerance on the example of psycho-analysis, would not refuse to accompany me on the excursion. The third lecture, on the dissection of the personality, certainly made the hardest demands upon you with its unfamiliar subject-matter; but it was impossible for me to keep this first beginning of an ego-psychology back from you, and if we had possessed it fifteen years ago I should have had to mention it to you then. My last lecture, finally, which you were probably able to follow only by great exertions, brought forward necessary corrections—fresh attempts at solving the most important conundrums; and my introduction would have been leading you astray if I had been silent about them. As you see, when one starts making excuses it turns out in the end that it was all in-

---

[1] [This lecture is mainly based on two earlier papers: 'Some Psychical Consequences of the Anatomical Distinction between the Sexes' (1925*j*) and 'Female Sexuality' (1931*b*). The last section, however, dealing with women in adult life, contains new material. Freud returned to the subject once again in Chapter VII of the posthumous *Outline of Psycho-Analysis* (1940*a* [1938]).]

100   NEW INTRODUCTORY LECTURES

evitable, all the work of destiny. I submit to it, and I beg you to
do the same.

To-day's lecture, too, should have no place in an introduction; but it may serve to give you an example of a detailed piece
of analytic work, and I can say two things to recommend it. It
brings forward nothing but observed facts, almost without any
speculative additions, and it deals with a subject which has
a claim on your interest second almost to no other. Throughout
history people have knocked their heads against the riddle of
the nature of femininity—

> Häupter in Hieroglyphenmützen,
> Häupter in Turban und schwarzem Barett,
> Perückenhäupter und tausend andre
> Arme, schwitzende Menschenhäupter. . . .[1]

Nor will *you* have escaped worrying over this problem—
those of you who are men; to those of you who are women this
will not apply—you are yourselves the problem. When you
meet a human being, the first distinction you make is 'male or
female?' and you are accustomed to make the distinction with
unhesitating certainty. Anatomical science shares your certainty at one point and not much further. The male sexual product, the spermatozoon, and its vehicle are male; the ovum and
the organism that harbours it are female. In both sexes organs
have been formed which serve exclusively for the sexual functions; they were probably developed from the same [innate]
disposition into two different forms. Besides this, in both sexes
the other organs, the bodily shapes and tissues, show the influence of the individual's sex, but this is inconstant and its
amount variable; these are what are known as the secondary
sexual characters. Science next tells you something that runs
counter to your expectations and is probably calculated to confuse your feelings. It draws your attention to the fact that portions of the male sexual apparatus also appear in women's
bodies, though in an atrophied state, and vice versa in the
alternative case. It regards their occurrence as indications of
bisexuality,[2] as though an individual is not a man or a woman
but always both—merely a certain amount more the one than

[1] Heads in hieroglyphic bonnets,
  Heads in turbans and black birettas,
  Heads in wigs and thousand other
  Wretched, sweating heads of humans. . . .
      (Heine, *Nordsee* [Second Cycle, VII, 'Fragen'].)

[2] [Bisexuality was discussed by Freud in the first edition of his *Three
Essays on the Theory of Sexuality* (1905d). The passage includes a long
footnote to which he made additions in later issues of the work.]

the other. You will then be asked to make yourselves familiar
with the idea that the proportion in which masculine and feminine are mixed in an individual is subject to quite considerable fluctuations. Since, however, apart from the very rarest
cases, only one kind of sexual product—ova or semen—is nevertheless present in one person, you are bound to have doubts
as to the decisive significance of those elements and must conclude that what constitutes masculinity or femininity is an unknown characteristic which anatomy cannot lay hold of.

Can psychology do so perhaps? We are accustomed to employ 'masculine' and 'feminine' as mental qualities as well, and
have in the same way transferred the notion of bisexuality to
mental life. Thus we speak of a person, whether male or female,
as behaving in a masculine way in one connection and in a
feminine way in another. But you will soon perceive that this
is only giving way to anatomy or to convention. You cannot
give the concepts of 'masculine' and 'feminine' *any* new conno-
tation. The distinction is not a psychological one; when you
say 'masculine', you usually mean 'active', and when you say
'feminine', you usually mean 'passive'. Now it is true that a relation of the kind exists. The male sex-cell is actively mobile and
searches out the female one, and the latter, the ovum, is im-
mobile and waits passively. This behaviour of the elementary
sexual organisms is indeed a model for the conduct of sexual
individuals during intercourse. The male pursues the female for
the purpose of sexual union, seizes hold of her and penetrates
into her. But by this you have precisely reduced the characteristic of masculinity to the factor of aggressiveness so far as psychology is concerned. You may well doubt whether you have gained
any real advantage from this when you reflect that in some classes
of animals the females are the stronger and more aggressive and
the male is active only in the single act of sexual union. This is
so, for instance, with the spiders. Even the functions of rearing
and caring for the young, which strike us as feminine *par excellence*, are not invariably attached to the female sex in animals. In
quite high species we find that the sexes share the task of caring
for the young between them or even that the male alone devotes
himself to it. Even in the sphere of human sexual life you soon
see how inadequate it is to make masculine behaviour coincide
with activity and feminine with passivity. A mother is active in
every sense towards her child; the act of lactation itself may
equally be described as the mother suckling the baby or as
her being sucked by it. The further you go from the narrow
sexual sphere the more obvious will the 'error of superimposi-

tion'[1] become. Women can display great activity in various directions, men are not able to live in company with their own kind unless they develop a large amount of passive adaptability. If you now tell me that these facts go to prove precisely that both men and women are bisexual in the psychological sense, I shall conclude that you have decided in your own minds to make 'active' coincide with 'masculine' and 'passive' with 'feminine'. But I advise you against it. It seems to me to serve no useful purpose and adds nothing to our knowledge.[2]

One might consider characterizing femininity psychologically as giving preference to passive aims. This is not, of course, the same thing as passivity; to achieve a passive aim may call for a large amount of activity. It is perhaps the case that in a woman, on the basis of her share in the sexual function, a preference for passive behaviour and passive aims is carried over into her life to a greater or lesser extent, in proportion to the limits, restricted or far-reaching, within which her sexual life thus serves as a model. But we must beware in this of underestimating the influence of social customs, which similarly force women into passive situations. All this is still far from being cleared up. There is one particularly constant relation between femininity and instinctual life which we do not want to overlook. The suppression of women's aggressiveness which is prescribed for them constitutionally and imposed on them socially favours the development of powerful masochistic impulses, which succeed, as we know, in binding erotically the destructive trends which have been diverted inwards. Thus masochism, as people say, is truly feminine. But if, as happens so often, you meet with masochism in men, what is left to you but to say that these men exhibit very plain feminine traits?

And now you are already prepared to hear that psychology too is unable to solve the riddle of femininity. The explanation must no doubt come from elsewhere, and cannot come till we have learnt how in general the differentiation of living organisms into two sexes came about. We know nothing about it, yet the existence of two sexes is a most striking characteristic of organic life which distinguishes it sharply from inanimate nature. However, we find enough to study in those human in-

[1] [I.e. mistaking two different things for a single one. The term was explained in *Introductory Lectures*, XX.]

[2] [The difficulty of finding a psychological meaning for 'masculine' and 'feminine' was discussed in a long footnote added in 1915 to Section 4 of the third of his *Three Essays* (1905*d*), and again at the beginning of a still longer footnote at the end of Chapter IV of *Civilization and its Discontents* (1930*a*).]

dividuals who, through the possession of female genitals, are characterized as manifestly or predominantly feminine. In conformity with its peculiar nature, psycho-analysis does not try to describe what a woman is—that would be a task it could scarcely perform—but sets about enquiring how she comes into being, how a woman develops out of a child with a bisexual disposition. In recent times we have begun to learn a little about this, thanks to the circumstance that several of our excellent women colleagues in analysis have begun to work at the question. The discussion of this has gained special attractiveness from the distinction between the sexes. For the ladies, whenever some comparison seemed to turn out unfavourable to their sex, were able to utter a suspicion that we, the male analysts, had been unable to overcome certain deeply-rooted prejudices against what was feminine, and that this was being paid for in the partiality of our researches. We, on the other hand, standing on the ground of bisexuality, had no difficulty in avoiding impoliteness. We had only to say: 'This doesn't apply to *you*. You're the exception; on this point you're more masculine than feminine.'

We approach the investigation of the sexual development of women with two expectations. The first is that here once more the constitution will not adapt itself to its function without a struggle. The second is that the decisive turning-points will already have been prepared for or completed before puberty. Both expectations are promptly confirmed. Furthermore, a comparison with what happens with boys tells us that the development of a little girl into a normal woman is more difficult and more complicated, since it includes two extra tasks, to which there is nothing corresponding in the development of a man. Let us follow the parallel lines from their beginning. Undoubtedly the material is different to start with in boys and girls: it did not need psycho-analysis to establish that. The difference in the structure of the genitals is accompanied by other bodily differences which are too well known to call for mention. Differences emerge too in the instinctual disposition which give a glimpse of the later nature of women. A little girl is as a rule less aggressive, defiant and self-sufficient; she seems to have a greater need for being shown affection and on that account to be more dependent and pliant. It is probably only as a result of this pliancy that she can be taught more easily and quicker to control her excretions: urine and faeces are the first gifts that children make to those who look after them [see p. 89 above], and controlling them is the first concession to which the instinctual life of children can be induced. One gets an impression, too, that little girls are more intelligent and livelier than boys of the same age; they go out more to meet the external world and at the same time form stronger object-cathexes. I cannot say whether this lead in development has been confirmed by exact observations, but in any case there is no question that girls cannot be described as intellectually backward. These sexual differences are not, however, of great consequence: they can be outweighed by individual variations. For our immediate purposes they can be disregarded.

Both sexes seem to pass through the early phases of libidinal development in the same manner. It might have been expected that in girls there would already have been some lag in aggressiveness in the sadistic-anal phase, but such is not the case. Analysis of children's play has shown our women analysts that the aggressive impulses of little girls leave nothing to be desired in the way of abundance and violence. With their entry into the phallic phase the differences between the sexes are completely eclipsed by their agreements. We are now obliged to recognize that the little girl is a little man. In boys, as we know, this phase is marked by the fact that they have learnt how to derive pleasurable sensations from their small penis and connect its excited state with their ideas of sexual intercourse. Little girls do the same thing with their still smaller clitoris. It seems that with them all their masturbatory acts are carried out on this penis-equivalent, and that the truly feminine vagina is still undiscovered by both sexes. It is true that there are a few isolated reports of early vaginal sensations as well, but it could not be easy to distinguish these from sensations in the anus or vestibulum; in any case they cannot play a great part. We are entitled to keep to our view that in the phallic phase of girls the clitoris is the leading erotogenic zone. But it is not, of course, going to remain so. With the change to femininity the clitoris should wholly or in part hand over its sensitivity, and at the same time its importance, to the vagina. This would be one of the two tasks which a woman has to perform in the course of her development, whereas the more fortunate man has only to continue at the time of his sexual maturity the activity that he has previously carried out at the period of the early efflorescence of his sexuality.

We shall return to the part played by the clitoris; let us now turn to the second task with which a girl's development is burdened. A boy's mother is the first object of his love, and she remains so too during the formation of his Oedipus complex and, in essence, all through his life. For a girl too her first object must be her mother (and the figures of wet-nurses and foster-mothers that merge into her). The first object-cathexes occur in attachment to the satisfaction of the major and simple vital needs,[1] and the circumstances of the care of children are the same for both sexes. But in the Oedipus situation the girl's father has become her love-object, and we expect that in the normal course of development she will find her way from this paternal object to her final choice of an object. In the course of time, therefore, a girl has to change her erotogenic zone and her object—both of which a boy retains. The question then arises of how this happens: in particular, how does a girl pass from her mother to an attachment to her father? or, in other words, how does she pass from her masculine phase to the feminine one to which she is biologically destined?

It would be a solution of ideal simplicity if we could suppose that from a particular age onwards the elementary influence of the mutual attraction between the sexes makes itself felt and impels the small woman towards men, while the same law allows the boy to continue with his mother. We might suppose in addition that in this the children are following the pointer given them by the sexual preference of their parents. But we are not going to find things so easy; we scarcely know whether we are to believe seriously in the power of which poets talk so much and with such enthusiasm but which cannot be further dissected analytically. We have found an answer of quite another sort by means of laborious investigations, the material for which at least was easy to arrive at. For you must know that the number of women who remain till a late age tenderly dependent on a paternal object, or indeed on their real father, is very great. We have established some surprising facts about these women with an intense attachment of long duration to their father. We knew, of course, that there had been a preliminary stage of attachment to the mother, but we did not know that it could be so rich in content and so long-lasting, and could leave behind so many opportunities for fixations and dispositions. During this time the girl's father is only a troublesome rival; in some cases the attachment to her mother lasts beyond the fourth year of life. Almost everything that we find later in her relation to her father was already present in this earlier attachment and has been transferred subsequently on to her father. In short, we get an impression that we cannot understand women unless we appreciate this phase of their pre-Oedipus attachment to their mother.

[1] [Cf. *Introductory Lectures*, XXI.]

We shall be glad, then, to know the nature of the girl's libidinal relations to her mother. The answer is that they are of very
many different kinds. Since they persist through all three phases
of infantile sexuality, they also take on the characteristics of the
different phases and express themselves by oral, sadistic-anal
and phallic wishes. These wishes represent active as well as
passive impulses; if we relate them to the differentiation of the
sexes which is to appear later—though we should avoid doing
so as far as possible—we may call them masculine and feminine.
Besides this, they are completely ambivalent, both affectionate
and of a hostile and aggressive nature. The latter often only
come to light after being changed into anxiety ideas. It is not
always easy to point to a formulation of these early sexual wishes;
what is most clearly expressed is a wish to get the mother with
child and the corresponding wish to bear her a child—both
belonging to the phallic period and sufficiently surprising, but
established beyond doubt by analytic observation. The attractiveness of these investigations lies in the surprising detailed
findings which they bring us. Thus, for instance, we discover
the fear of being murdered or poisoned, which may later form
the core of a paranoic illness, already present in this pre-
Oedipus period, in relation to the mother. Or another case: you
will recall an interesting episode in the history of analytic
research which caused me many distressing hours. In the period
in which the main interest was directed to discovering infantile
sexual traumas, almost all my women patients told me that
they had been seduced by their father. I was driven to recognize
in the end that these reports were untrue and so came to understand that hysterical symptoms are derived from phantasies and
not from real occurrences. It was only later that I was able to
recognize in this phantasy of being seduced by the father the
expression of the typical Oedipus complex in women. And now
we find the phantasy of seduction once more in the pre-Oedipus
prehistory of girls; but the seducer is regularly the mother.
Here, however, the phantasy touches the ground of reality, for
it was really the mother who by her activities over the child's
bodily hygiene inevitably stimulated, and perhaps even roused
for the first time, pleasurable sensations in her genitals.[1]

[1] [In his early discussions of the aetiology of hysteria Freud often
mentioned seduction by adults as among its commonest causes (see, for
instance, Section I of the second paper on the neuro-psychoses of
defence (1896c), and Section II (b) of 'The Aetiology of Hysteria'
(1896c). But nowhere in these early publications did he specifically
inculpate the girl's father. Indeed, in some additional footnotes written
in 1924 for the Gesammelte Schriften reprint of Studies on Hysteria, he

I have no doubt you are ready to suspect that this portrayal
of the abundance and strength of a little girl's sexual relations
with her mother is very much overdrawn. After all, one has
opportunities of seeing little girls and notices nothing of the sort.
But the objection is not to the point. Enough can be seen in
the children if one knows how to look. And besides, you should
consider how little of its sexual wishes a child can bring to preconscious expression or communicate at all. Accordingly we
are only within our rights if we study the residues and consequences of this emotional world in retrospect, in people in
whom these processes of development had attained a specially
clear and even excessive degree of expansion. Pathology has
always done us the service of making discernible by isolation
and exaggeration conditions which would remain concealed in
a normal state. And since our investigations have been carried
out on people who were by no means seriously abnormal, I
think we should regard their outcome as deserving belief.

We will now turn our interest on to the single question of
what it is that brings this powerful attachment of the girl to her
mother to an end. This, as we know, is its usual fate: it is destined to make room for an attachment to her father. Here we
come upon a fact which is a pointer to our further advance. This
step in development does not involve only a simple change of
object. The turning away from the mother is accompanied by
hostility; the attachment to the mother ends in hate. A hate of
that kind may become very striking and last all through life; it
may be carefully overcompensated later on; as a rule one part
of it is overcome while another part persists. Events of later
years naturally influence this greatly. We will restrict ourselves,
however, to studying it at the time at which the girl turns to her
father and to enquiring into the motives for it. We are then
given a long list of accusations and grievances against the

---

admitted to having on two occasions suppressed the fact of the father's
responsibility. He made this quite clear, however, in the letter to Fliess
of September 21, 1897 (Freud, 1950a, Letter 69), in which he first expressed his scepticism about these stories told by his patients. His first
published admission of his mistake was given several years later in a
hint in the second of the *Three Essays* (1905d), but a much fuller
account of the position followed in his contribution on the aetiology
of the neuroses to a volume by Löwenfeld (1906a). Later on he gave
two accounts of the effects that this discovery of his mistake had on
his own mind—in his 'History of the Psycho-Analytic Movement'
(1914d), and in his *Autobiographical Study* (1925d), (Norton, 1963). The
further discovery which is described in the present paragraph of the
text had already been indicated in the paper on 'Female Sexuality'
(1931b).]

mother which are supposed to justify the child's hostile feelings; they are of varying validity which we shall not fail to examine. A number of them are obvious rationalizations and the true sources of enmity remain to be found. I hope you will be interested if on this occasion I take you through all the details of a psycho-analytic investigation.

The reproach against the mother which goes back furthest is that she gave the child too little milk—which is construed against her as lack of love. Now there is some justification for this reproach in our families. Mothers often have insufficient nourishment to give their children and are content to suckle them for a few months, for half or three-quarters of a year. Among primitive peoples children are fed at their mother's breast for two or three years. The figure of the wet-nurse who suckles the child is as a rule merged into the mother; when this has not happened, the reproach is turned into another one— that the nurse, who fed the child so willingly, was sent away by the mother too early. But whatever the true state of affairs may have been, it is impossible that the child's reproach can be justified as often as it is met with. It seems, rather, that the child's avidity for its earliest nourishment is altogether insatiable, that it never gets over the pain of losing its mother's breast. I should not be surprised if the analysis of a primitive child, who could still suck at its mother's breast when it was already able to run about and talk, were to bring the same reproach to light. The fear of being poisoned is also probably connected with the withdrawal of the breast. Poison is nourishment that makes one ill. Perhaps children trace back their early illnesses too to this frustration. A fair amount of intellectual education is a prerequisite for believing in chance; primitive people and uneducated ones, and no doubt children as well, are able to assign a ground for everything that happens. Perhaps originally it was a reason on animistic lines. Even to-day in some strata of our population no one can die without having been killed by someone else—preferably by the doctor. And the regular reaction of a neurotic to the death of someone closely connected with him is to put the blame on himself for having caused the death.

The next accusation against the child's mother flares up when the next baby appears in the nursery. If possible the connection with oral frustration is preserved: the mother could not or would not give the child any more milk because she needed the nourishment for the new arrival. In cases in which the two children are so close in age that lactation is prejudiced by the second pregnancy, this reproach acquires a real basis,

and it is a remarkable fact that a child, even with an age difference of only 11 months, is not too young to take notice of what
is happening. But what the child grudges the unwanted intru-
der and rival is not only the suckling but all the other signs
of maternal care. It feels that it has been dethroned, despoiled,
prejudiced in its rights; it casts a jealous hatred upon the new
baby and develops a grievance against the faithless mother
which often finds expression in a disagreeable change in its
behaviour. It becomes 'naughty', perhaps, irritable and disobedient and goes back on the advances it has made towards
controlling its excretions. All of this has been very long familiar
and is accepted as self-evident; but we rarely form a correct
idea of the strength of these jealous impulses, of the tenacity
with which they persist and of the magnitude of their influence
on later development. Especially as this jealousy is constantly
receiving fresh nourishment in the later years of childhood
and the whole shock is repeated with the birth of each new
brother or sister. Nor does it make much difference if the child
happens to remain the mother's preferred favourite. A child's
demands for love are immoderate, they make exclusive claims
and tolerate no sharing.

An abundant source of a child's hostility to its mother is
provided by its multifarious sexual wishes, which alter according to the phase of the libido and which cannot for the most
part be satisfied. The strongest of these frustrations occur at the
phallic period, if the mother forbids pleasurable activity with
the genitals—often with severe threats and every sign of dis-
pleasure—activity to which, after all, she herself had introduced the child. One would think these were reasons enough
to account for a girl's turning away from her mother. One would
judge, if so, that the estrangement follows inevitably from the
nature of children's sexuality, from the immoderate character
of their demand for love and the impossibility of fulfilling their
sexual wishes. It might be thought indeed that this first love-
relation of the child's is doomed to dissolution for the very
reason that it is the first, for these early object-cathexes are
regularly ambivalent to a high degree. A powerful tendency to
aggressiveness is always present beside a powerful love, and the
more passionately a child loves its object the more sensitive
does it become to disappointments and frustrations from that
object; and in the end the love must succumb to the accumulated hostility. Or the idea that there is an original ambivalence
such as this in erotic cathexes may be rejected, and it may be
pointed out that it is the special nature of the mother-child
relation that leads, with equal inevitability, to the destruction

of the child's love; for even the mildest upbringing cannot avoid using compulsion and introducing restrictions, and any such intervention in the child's liberty must provoke as a reaction an inclination to rebelliousness and aggressiveness. A discussion of these possibilities might, I think, be most interesting; but an objection suddenly emerges which forces our interest in another direction. All these factors—the slights, the disappointments in love, the jealousy, the seduction followed by prohibition—are, after all, also in operation in the relation of a *boy* to his mother and are yet unable to alienate him from the maternal object. Unless we can find something that is specific for girls and is not present or not in the same way present in boys, we shall not have explained the termination of the attachment of girls to their mother.

I believe we have found this specific factor, and indeed where we expected to find it, even though in a surprising form. Where we expected to find it, I say, for it lies in the castration complex. After all, the anatomical distinction [between the sexes] must express itself in psychical consequences. It was, however, a surprise to learn from analyses that girls hold their mother responsible for their lack of a penis and do not forgive her for their being thus put at a disadvantage.

As you hear, then, we ascribe a castration complex to women as well. And for good reasons, though its content cannot be the same as with boys. In the latter the castration complex arises after they have learnt from the sight of the female genitals that the organ which they value so highly need not necessarily accompany the body. At this the boy recalls to mind the threats he brought on himself by his doings with that organ, he begins to give credence to them and falls under the influence of fear of castration, which will be the most powerful motive force in his subsequent development. The castration complex of girls is also started by the sight of the genitals of the other sex. They at once notice the difference and, it must be admitted, its significance too. They feel seriously wronged, often declare that they want to 'have something like it too', and fall a victim to 'envy for the penis', which will leave ineradicable traces on their development and the formation of their character and which will not be surmounted in even the most favourable cases without a severe expenditure of psychical energy. The girl's recognition of the fact of her being without a penis does not by any means imply that she submits to the fact easily. On the contrary, she continues to hold on for a long time to the wish to get something like it herself and she believes in that possibility for improbably long years; and analysis can show that,

at a period when knowledge of reality has long since rejected
the fulfilment of the wish as unattainable, it persists in the
unconscious and retains a considerable cathexis of energy.
The wish to get the longed-for penis eventually in spite of
everything may contribute to the motives that drive a mature
woman to analysis, and what she may reasonably expect from
analysis—a capacity, for instance, to carry on an intellectual
profession—may often be recognized as a sublimated modification of this repressed wish.

One cannot very well doubt the importance of envy for the
penis. You may take it as an instance of male injustice if I assert
that envy and jealousy play an even greater part in the mental
life of women than of men. It is not that I think these characteristics are absent in men or that I think they have no other
roots in women than envy for the penis; but I am inclined to
attribute their greater amount in women to this latter influence.
Some analysts, however, have shown an inclination to depre-
ciate the importance of this first instalment of penis-envy in the
phallic phase. They are of opinion that what we find of this
attitude in women is in the main a secondary structure which
has come about on the occasion of later conflicts by regression
to this early infantile impulse. This, however, is a general
problem of depth psychology. In many pathological—or even
unusual—instinctual attitudes (for instance, in all sexual perversions) the question arises of how much of their strength is to
be attributed to early infantile fixations and how much to the
influence of later experiences and developments. In such cases
it is almost always a matter of complemental series such as we
put forward in our discussion of the aetiology of the neuroses.[1]
Both factors play a part in varying amounts in the causation; a
less on the one side is balanced by a more on the other. The
infantile factor sets the pattern in all cases but does not always
determine the issue, though it often does. Precisely in the case
of penis-envy I should argue decidedly in favour of the prepon-
derance of the infantile factor.

The discovery that she is castrated is a turning-point in a
girl's growth. Three possible lines of development start from
it: one leads to sexual inhibition or to neurosis, the second to
change of character in the sense of a masculinity complex, the
third, finally, to normal femininity. We have learnt a fair
amount, though not everything, about all three.

The essential content of the first is as follows: the little girl
has hitherto lived in a masculine way, has been able to get

[1] [See *Introductory Lectures,* XXII and XXIII.]

pleasure by the excitation of her clitoris and has brought this
activity into relation with her sexual wishes directed towards
her mother, which are often active ones; now, owing to the
influence of her penis-envy, she loses her enjoyment in her
phallic sexuality. Her self-love is mortified by the comparison
with the boy's far superior equipment and in consequence she
renounces her masturbatory satisfaction from her clitoris, repudiates her love for her mother and at the same time not infrequently represses a good part of her sexual trends in general.
No doubt her turning away from her mother does not occur
all at once, for to begin with the girl regards her castration as an
individual misfortune, and only gradually extends it to other
females and finally to her mother as well. Her love was directed
to her *phallic* mother; with the discovery that her mother is
castrated it becomes possible to drop her as an object, so that
the motives for hostility, which have long been accumulating,
gain the upper hand. This means, therefore, that as a result
of the discovery of women's lack of a penis they are debased in
value for girls just as they are for boys and later perhaps for
men.

You all know the immense aetiological importance attributed
by our neurotic patients to their masturbation. They make it
responsible for all their troubles and we have the greatest
difficulty in persuading them that they are mistaken. In fact,
however, we ought to admit to them that they are right, for
masturbation is the executive agent of infantile sexuality, from
the faulty development of which they are indeed suffering.
But what neurotics mostly blame is the masturbation of the
period of puberty; they have mostly forgotten that of early
infancy, which is what is really in question. I wish I might
have an opportunity some time of explaining to you at length
how important all the factual details of early masturbation become for the individual's subsequent neurosis or character:
whether or not it was discovered, how the parents struggled
against it or permitted it, or whether he succeeded in suppressing it himself. All of this leaves permanent traces on his
development. But I am on the whole glad that I need not do
this. It would be a hard and tedious task and at the end of it you
would put me in an embarrassing situation by quite certainly
asking me to give you some practical advice as to how a parent
or educator should deal with the masturbation of small children.[1] From the development of girls, which is what my pre-

[1] [Freud's fullest discussion of masturbation was in his contributions
to a symposium on the subject in the Vienna Psycho-Analytical Society
(1912*f*).]

sent lecture is concerned with, I can give you the example
of a child herself trying to get free from masturbating. She does
not always succeed in this. If envy for the penis has provoked
a powerful impulse against clitoridal masturbation but this
nevertheless refuses to give way, a violent struggle for liberation
ensues in which the girl, as it were, herself takes over the role
of her deposed mother and gives expression to her entire
dissatisfaction with her inferior clitoris in her efforts against
obtaining satisfaction from it. Many years later, when her
masturbatory activity has long since been suppressed, an interest still persists which we must interpret as a defence against
a temptation that is still dreaded. It manifests inself in the
emergence of sympathy for those to whom similar difficulties
are attributed, it plays a part as a motive in contracting a
marriage and, indeed, it may determine the choice of a husband
or lover. Disposing of early infantile masturbation is truly no
easy or indifferent business.

Along with the abandonment of clitoridal masturbation a
certain amount of activity is renounced. Passivity now has the
upper hand, and the girl's turning to her father is accomplished
principally with the help of passive instinctual impulses. You
can see that a wave of development like this, which clears the
phallic activity out of the way, smooths the ground for femininity. If too much is not lost in the course of it through repression,
this femininity may turn out to be normal. The wish with
which the girl turns to her father is no doubt originally the
wish for the penis which her mother has refused her and which
she now expects from her father. The feminine situation is only
established, however, if the wish for a penis is replaced by one
for a baby, if, that is, a baby takes the place of a penis in accordance with an ancient symbolic equivalence [p. 89 f.]. It has not
escaped us that the girl has wished for a baby earlier, in the
undisturbed phallic phase: that, of course, was the meaning of
her playing with dolls. But that play was not in fact an expression of her femininity; it served as an identification with her
mother with the intention of substituting activity for passivity.
She was playing the part of her mother and the doll was herself:
now she could do with the baby everything that her mother
used to do with her. Not until the emergence of the wish for a
penis does the doll-baby become a baby from the girl's father,
and thereafter the aim of the most powerful feminine wish. Her
happiness is great if later on this wish for a baby finds fulfilment
in reality, and quite especially so if the baby is a little boy who
brings the longed-for penis with him.[1] Often enough in her

[1] [See p. 118 below.]

combined picture of 'a baby from her father' the emphasis is laid on the baby and her father left unstressed. In this way the ancient masculine wish for the possession of a penis is still faintly visible through the femininity now achieved. But perhaps we ought rather to recognize this wish for a penis as being *par excellence* a feminine one.

With the transference of the wish for a penis-baby on to her father, the girl has entered the situation of the Oedipus complex. Her hostility to her mother, which did not need to be freshly created, is now greatly intensified, for she becomes the girl's rival, who receives from her father everything that she desires from him. For a long time the girl's Oedipus complex concealed her pre-Oedipus attachment to her mother from our view, though it is nevertheless so important and leaves such lasting fixations behind it. For girls the Oedipus situation is the outcome of a long and difficult development; it is a kind of preliminary solution, a position of rest which is not soon abandoned, especially as the beginning of the latency period is not far distant. And we are now struck by a difference between the two sexes, which is probably momentous, in regard to the relation of the Oedipus complex to the castration complex. In a boy the Oedipus complex, in which he desires his mother and would like to get rid of his father as being a rival, develops naturally from the phase of his phallic sexuality. The threat of castration compels him, however, to give up that attitude. Under the impression of the danger of losing his penis, the Oedipus complex is abandoned, repressed and, in the most normal cases, entirely destroyed [see p. 81], and a severe super-ego is set up as its heir. What happens with a girl is almost the opposite. The castration complex prepares for the Oedipus complex instead of destroying it; the girl is driven out of her attachment to her mother through the influence of her envy for the penis and she enters the Oedipus situation as though into a haven of refuge. In the absence of fear of castration the chief motive is lacking which leads boys to surmount the Oedipus complex. Girls remain in it for an indeterminate length of time; they demolish it late and, even so, incompletely. In these circumstances the formation of the super-ego must suffer; it cannot attain the strength and independence which give it its cultural significance, and feminists are not pleased when we point out to them the effects of this factor upon the average feminine character.

To go back a little. We mentioned [p. 111] as the second possible reaction to the discovery of female castration the development of a powerful masculinity complex. By this we mean that the girl refuses, as it were, to recognize the unwelcome fact and,

defiantly rebellious, even exaggerates her previous masculinity, clings to her clitoridal activity and takes refuge in an
identification with her phallic mother or her father. What can
it be that decides in favour of this outcome? We can only suppose that it is a constitutional factor, a greater amount of
activity, such as is ordinarily characteristic of a male. However
that may be, the essence of this process is that at this point in
development the wave of passivity is avoided which opens the
way to the turn towards femininity. The extreme achievement
of such a masculinity complex would appear to be the influencing of the choice of an object in the sense of manifest homosexuality. Analytic experience teaches us, to be sure, that
female homosexuality is seldom or never a direct continuation
of infantile masculinity. Even for a girl of this kind it seems
necessary that she should take her father as an object for some
time and enter the Oedipus situation. But afterwards, as a
result of her inevitable disappointments from her father, she is
driven to regress into her early masculinity complex. The
significance of these disappointments must not be exaggerated;
a girl who is destined to become feminine is not spared them,
though they do not have the same effect. The predominance of
the constitutional factor seems indisputable; but the two phases
in the development of female homosexuality are well mirrored
in the practices of homosexuals, who play the parts of mother
and baby with each other as often and as clearly as those of
husband and wife.

What I have been telling you here may be described as the
prehistory of women. It is a product of the very last few years
and may have been of interest to you as an example of detailed
analytic work. Since its subject is woman, I will venture on
this occasion to mention by name a few of the women who have
made valuable contributions to this investigation. Dr. Ruth
Mack Brunswick [1928] was the first to describe a case of neurosis which went back to a fixation in the pre-Oedipus stage
and had never reached the Oedipus situation at all. The case
took the form of jealous paranoia and proved accessible to
therapy. Dr. Jeanne Lampl-de Groot [1927] has established the
incredible phallic activity of girls towards their mother by
some assured observations, and Dr. Helene Deutsch [1932] has
shown that the erotic actions of homosexual women reproduce
the relations between mother and baby.

It is not my intention to pursue the further behaviour of femininity through puberty to the period of maturity. Our knowledge, moreover, would be insufficient for the purpose. But

I will bring a few features together in what follows. Taking its prehistory as a starting-point, I will only emphasize here that the development of femininity remains exposed to disturbance by the residual phenomena of the early masculine period. Regressions to the fixations of the pre-Oedipus phases very frequently occur; in the course of some women's lives there is a repeated alternation between periods in which masculinity or femininity gains the upper hand. Some portion of what we men call 'the enigma of women' may perhaps be derived from this expression of bisexuality in women's lives. But another question seems to have become ripe for judgement in the course of these researches. We have called the motive force of sexual life 'the libido'. Sexual life is dominated by the polarity of masculine–feminine; thus the notion suggests itself of considering the relation of the libido to this antithesis. It would not be surprising if it were to turn out that each sexuality had its own special libido appropriated to it, so that one sort of libido would pursue the aims of a masculine sexual life and another sort those of a feminine one. But nothing of the kind is true. There is only one libido, which serves both the masculine and the feminine sexual functions. To it itself we cannot assign any sex; if, following the conventional equation of activity and masculinity, we are inclined to describe it as masculine, we must not forget that it also covers trends with a passive aim. Nevertheless the juxtaposition 'feminine libido' is without any justification. Furthermore, it is our impression that more constraint has been applied to the libido when it is pressed into the service of the feminine function, and that—to speak teleologically—Nature takes less careful account of its [that function's] demands than in the case of masculinity. And the reason for this may lie—thinking once again teleologically—in the fact that the accomplishment of the aim of biology has been entrusted to the aggressiveness of men and has been made to some extent independent of women's consent.

The sexual frigidity of women, the frequency of which appears to confirm this disregard, is a phenomenon that is still insufficiently understood. Sometimes it is psychogenic and in that case accessible to influence; but in other cases it suggests the hypothesis of its being constitutionally determined and even of there being a contributory anatomical factor.

I have promised to tell you of a few more psychical peculiarities of mature femininity, as we come across them in analytic observation. We do not lay claim to more than an average validity for these assertions; nor is it always easy to distinguish what should be ascribed to the influence of the sexual function

and what to social breeding. Thus, we attribute a larger amount
of narcissism to femininity, which also affects women's choice of
object, so that to be loved is a stronger need for them than to love.
The effect of penis-envy has a share, further, in the physical
vanity of women, since they are bound to value their charms
more highly as a late compensation for their original sexual
inferiority.[1] Shame, which is considered to be a feminine characteristic *par excellence* but is far more a matter of convention
than might be supposed, has as its purpose, we believe, con-
cealment of genital deficiency. We are not forgetting that at a
later time shame takes on other functions. It seems that women
have made few contributions to the discoveries and inventions
in the history of civilization; there is, however, one technique
which they may have invented—that of plaiting and weaving.
If that is so, we should be tempted to guess the unconscious
motive for the achievement. Nature herself would seem to have
given the model which this achievement imitates by causing
the growth at maturity of the pubic hair that conceals the
genitals. The step that remained to be taken lay in making the
threads adhere to one another, while on the body they stick
into the skin and are only matted together. If you reject this
idea as fantastic and regard my belief in the influence of lack
of a penis on the configuration of femininity as an *idée fixe*, I am
of course defenceless.

The determinants of women's choice of an object are often
made unrecognizable by social conditions. Where the choice
is able to show itself freely, it is often made in accordance with
the narcissistic ideal of the man whom the girl had wished to
become. If the girl has remained in her attachment to her father
—that is, in the Oedipus complex—her choice is made according to the paternal type. Since, when she turned from her
mother to her father, the hostility of her ambivalent relation
remained with her mother, a choice of this kind should guarantee a happy marriage. But very often the outcome is of a kind
that presents a general threat to such a settlement of the
conflict due to ambivalence. The hostility that has been left
behind follows in the train of the positive attachment and
spreads over on to the new object. The woman's husband, who
to begin with inherited from her father, becomes after a time
her mother's heir as well. So it may easily happen that the
second half of a woman's life may be filled by the struggle
against her husband, just as the shorter first half was filled by
her rebellion against her mother. When this reaction has been

---

[1] [Cf. Section II of 'On Narcissism' (1914*c*).]

lived through, a second marriage may easily turn out very much more satisfying.[1] Another alteration in a woman's nature, for which lovers are unprepared, may occur in a marriage after the first child is born. Under the influence of a woman's becoming a mother herself, an identification with her own mother may be revived, against which she had striven up till the time of her marriage, and this may attract all the available libido to itself, so that the compulsion to repeat reproduces an unhappy marriage between her parents. The difference in a mother's reaction to the birth of a son or a daughter shows that the old factor of lack of a penis has even now not lost its strength. A mother is only brought unlimited satisfaction by her relation to a son; this is altogether the most perfect, the most free from ambivalence of all human relationships.[2] A mother can transfer to her son the ambition which she has been obliged to suppress in herself, and she can expect from him the satisfaction of all that has been left over in her of her masculinity complex. Even a marriage is not made secure until the wife has succeeded in making her husband her child as well and in acting as a mother to him.

A woman's identification with her mother allows us to distinguish two strata: the pre-Oedipus one which rests on her affectionate attachment to her mother and takes her as a model, and the later one from the Oedipus complex which seeks to get rid of her mother and take her place with her father. We are no doubt justified in saying that much of both of them is left over for the future and that neither of them is adequately surmounted in the course of development. But the phase of the affectionate pre-Oedipus attachment is the decisive one for a woman's future: during it preparations are made for the acquisition of the characteristics with which she will later fulfil her role in the sexual function and perform her invaluable social tasks. It is in this identification too that she acquires her attractiveness to a man, whose Oedipus attachment to his mother it kindles into passion. How often it happens, however, that it is only his son who obtains what he himself aspired to! One gets an impression that a man's love and a woman's are a phase apart psychologically.

[1] [This had already been remarked upon earlier, in 'The Taboo of Virginity' (1918a).]

[2] [This point seems to have been made by Freud first in a footnote to Chapter VI of *Group Psychology* (1921c). He repeated it in the *Introductory Lectures*, XIII, and in Chapter V of *Civilization and its Discontents* (1930a). That exceptions may occur is shown by the example above. p. 59.]

The fact that women must be regarded as having little sense of justice is no doubt related to the predominance of envy in their mental life; for the demand for justice is a modification of envy and lays down the condition subject to which one can put envy aside. We also regard women as weaker in their social interests and as having less capacity for sublimating their instincts than men. The former is no doubt derived from the dissocial quality which unquestionably characterizes all sexual relations. Lovers find sufficiency in each other, and families too resist inclusion in more comprehensive associations.[1] The aptitude for sublimation is subject to the greatest individual variations. On the other hand I cannot help mentioning an impression that we are constantly receiving during analytic practice. A man of about thirty strikes us as a youthful, somewhat unformed individual, whom we expect to make powerful use of the possibilities for development opened up to him by analysis. A woman of the same age, however, oftens frightens us by her psychical rigidity and unchangeability. Her libido has taken up final positions and seems incapable of exchanging them for others. There are no paths open to further development; it is as though the whole process had already run its course and remains thenceforward insusceptible to influence—as though, indeed, the difficult development to femininity had exhausted the possibilities of the person concerned. As therapists we lament this state of things, even if we succeed in putting an end to our patient's ailment by doing away with her neurotic conflict.

That is all I had to say to you about femininity. It is certainly incomplete and fragmentary and does not always sound friendly. But do not forget that I have only been describing women in so far as their nature is determined by their sexual function. It is true that that influence extends very far; but we do not overlook the fact that an individual woman may be a human being in other respects as well. If you want to know more about femininity, enquire from your own experiences of life, or turn to the poets, or wait until science can give you deeper and more coherent information.

[1] [Cf. some remarks on this in Chapter XII (D) of *Group Psychology* (1921*c*).]

EXPLANATIONS, APPLICATIONS AND ORIENTATIONS

LADIES AND GENTLEMEN,—Perhaps you will allow me for once, as a relief from the dry tone of these lectures, to talk to you about some things which have very little theoretical significance but which concern you closely in so far as you are friendlily disposed to psycho-analysis. Let us imagine, for instance, that in your leisure hours you take up a German, English or American novel, in which you expect to find an account of contemporary people and society. After a few pages you come upon a first comment on psycho-analysis and soon afterwards upon others, even though the context does not seem to call for them. You must not imagine that it is a question of applying depth-psychology to a better understanding of the characters in the book or of their actions—though, incidentally, there are other and more serious works in which an attempt of that kind is in fact made. No, these are for the most part facetious remarks intended by the author to display his wide reading and intellectual superiority. Nor will you always form an impression that he really knows what he is talking about. Again, you may go as a recreation to a social gathering—and this need not necessarily happen in Vienna. After a short time the conversation turns upon psycho-analysis and you will hear the greatest variety of people passing their judgement on it, mostly in voices of unwavering certainty. It is quite usual for the judgement to be contemptuous or often slanderous or at least, once again, facetious. If you are so imprudent as to betray the fact that you know something about the subject, they fall upon you with one accord, ask for information and explanations and soon convince you that all these severe judgements had been arrived at without any basis of knowledge, that scarcely any of these critics had ever opened an analytic book or, if they had, had gone beyond the first resistance aroused by their contact with this new material.

You may perhaps expect an introduction to psycho-analysis to give you instructions, too, on what arguments you should use to correct these obvious errors about analysis, what books you should recommend to give more accurate information, or even what examples you should bring up in the discussion from your reading or experience in order to alter the company's attitude.

I must beg you to do none of this. It would be useless. The best plan would be for you to conceal your superior knowledge altogether. If that is no longer possible, limit yourself to saying that, so far as you can make out, psycho-analysis is a special branch of knowledge, very hard to understand and to form an opinion on, which is concerned with very serious things, so that a few jokes will not bring one to close quarters with it—and that it would be better to find some other plaything for social entertainment. Nor, of course, will you join in attempts at interpretation, if unwary people repeat their dreams; and you will resist the temptation to curry favour for analysis by retailing reports of its cures.

But you may raise the question of why these people—both the ones who write books and the conversationalists—behave so badly; and you may incline to the view that the responsibility for this lies not only on them but also on psycho-analysis. I think so too. What you come upon as prejudice in literature and society is an after-effect of an earlier judgement—the judgement, namely, that was formed upon the young psycho-analysis by the representatives of official science. I once complained of this in a historical account I wrote,[1] and I shall not do so again—perhaps that once was too often—but it is a fact that there was no violation of logic, and no violation of propriety and good taste, to which the scientific opponents of psycho-analysis did not give way at that time. The situation recalled what was actually put in practice in the Middle Ages when an evil-doer, or even a mere political opponent, was put in the pillory and given over to maltreatment by the mob. You may not realize clearly, perhaps, how far upwards in our society mob-characteristics extend, and what misconduct people will be guilty of when they feel themselves part of a crowd and relieved of personal responsibility. At the beginning of that time I was more or less alone and I soon saw that there was no future in polemics but that it was equally senseless to lament and to invoke the help of kindlier spirits, for there were not courts to which such appeals could be made. So I took another road. I made a first application of psycho-analysis by explaining to myself that this behaviour of the crowd was a manifestation of the same resistance which I had to struggle against in individual patients. I refrained from polemics myself and influenced my adherents, when little by little they appeared, in the same direction. This procedure was the right one. The interdict which lay upon psycho-analysis in those days has been lifted

---

[1] ['On the History of the Psycho-Analytic Movement' (1914d).]

since then. But, just as an abandoned faith survives as a super-stition, just as a theory which has been given up by science continues to exist as a popular belief, so the original outlaw-ing of psycho-analysis by scientific circles persists to-day in the facetious contempt of the laymen who write books or make conversation. So this will no longer surprise you.

But you must not expect to hear the glad tidings that the struggle about analysis is over and has ended in its recognition as a science and its admission as a subject for instruction at universities. There is no question of that. The struggle con-tinues, though in more polite forms. What is also new is that a sort of buffer-layer has formed in scientific society between analysis and its opponents. This consists of people who allow the validity of some portions of analysis and admit as much, subject to the most entertaining qualifications, but who on the other hand reject other portions of it, a fact which they cannot pro-claim too loudly. It is not easy to divine what determines their choice in this. It seems to depend on personal sympathies. One person will take objection to sexuality, another to the uncon-scious; what seems particularly unpopular is the fact of sym-bolism. Though the structure of psycho-analysis is unfinished, it nevertheless presents, even to-day, a unity from which elements cannot be broken off at the caprice of whoever comes along: but these eclectics seem to disregard this. I have never had the im-pression that these half- or quarter-adherents based their rejec-tion on an examination of the facts. Some distinguished men, too, are included in this category. They, to be sure, are excused by the fact that their time and their interest belong to other things—to those things, namely, in mastering which they have achieved so much. But in that case would they not do better to suspend their judgement instead of taking sides so decisively? With one of these great men I once succeeded in effecting a rapid conversion. He was a world-famous critic, who had fol-lowed the spiritual currents of the time with benevolent under-standing and prophetic penetration. I only came to know him when he was past his eightieth year; but he was still enchanting in his talk. You will easily guess whom I mean.[1] Nor was it I

---

[1] [It was Georg Brandes, the celebrated Danish scholar (1842–1927), for whom Freud had always had an admiration. Freud had heard him lecture in Vienna in March 1900. He was enthusiastic, and, on his wife's suggestion, sent a copy of *The Interpretation of Dreams* to Brandes at his hotel; but it is not known whether there was any reaction. See Letter 131 of the Fliess correspondence (Freud, 1950a). Ernest Jones mentions their meeting (which took place in 1925) in the third volume of his biography (1957, 120). Freud gave another account of it in a letter of April 19, 1927, to one of his nieces (Letter 229 in Freud, 1960a).]

who introduced the subject of psycho-analysis. It was he who did so, by comparing himself with me in the most modest fashion. 'I am only a literary man,' he said, 'but you are a natural scientist and discoverer. However, there is one thing I must say to you: I have never had sexual feelings towards my mother.' 'But there is no need at all for you to have known them,' was my reply; 'to grown-up people those are unconscious feelings.' 'Oh! so *that's* what you think!' he said with relief, and pressed my hand. We went on talking together on the best of terms for another few hours. I heard later that in the few remaining years of his life he often spoke of analysis in a friendly way and was pleased at being able to use a word that was new to him—'repression'.

There is a common saying that we should learn from our enemies. I confess I have never succeeded in doing so; but I thought all the same that it might be instructive for you if I undertook a review of all the reproaches and objections which the opponents of psycho-analysis have raised against it, and if I went on to point out the injustices and offences against logic which could so easily be revealed in them. But 'on second thoughts' [1] I told myself that it would not be at all interesting but would become tedious and distressing and would be precisely what I have been so carefully avoiding all these years. So you must forgive me if I pursue this path no further and if I spare you the judgements of our so-called scientific opponents. After all it is nearly always a question of people whose one qualification is the impartiality which they have preserved by keeping at a distance from the experiences of psycho-analysis. But I know there are other cases in which you will not let me off so lightly. 'Nevertheless', you will tell me, 'there are such a number of people to whom your last remark does not apply. They have not evaded analytic experience, they have analysed patients and have perhaps been analysed themselves; for a time they have even been your collaborators. Yet they have arrived at other views and theories on the basis of which they have seceded from you and founded independent schools of psycho-analysis. You ought to throw some light for us on the possibility and significance of these secessionist movements which have been so frequent in the history of analysis.'

Well, I will try to do so; but only in brief, since they contribute less to an understanding of analysis than you might expect. I feel sure you will be thinking in the first place of Adler's

---

[1] [In English in the original.]

'Individual Psychology', which, in America for instance, is regarded as a line of thought collateral with our psycho-analysis and on a par with it and which is regularly mentioned alongside of it. Actually, Individual Psychology has very little to do with psycho-analysis but, as a result of certain historical circumstances, leads a kind of parasitic existence at its expense. The determinants which we have attributed to this group of opponents apply to the founders of Individual Psychology only to a limited extent. Its very name is inappropriate and seems to have been the product of embarrassment. We cannot allow the legitimate use of the term as an antithesis to 'group psychology' to be interfered with; moreover, our own activity is concerned for the most part and primarily with the psychology of human individuals. I shall not enter to-day upon an objective criticism of Adler's Individual Psychology; there is no place for it in the plan of these introductory lectures. Besides, I have already attempted it once, and feel no temptation to change anything in what I said then.[1] I will, however, illustrate the impression his views produce by a small episode dating from the years before analysis.

In the neighbourhood of the little Moravian town in which I was born, and which I left when I was a three-year-old child,[2] there is a modest health-resort, prettily situated in the woods. During my schooldays I went there several times in the holidays. Some twenty years later the illness of a near relative was the occasion for my visiting the place again. In the course of a conversation with the physician attached to the spa, who had attended my relative, I enquired among other things about his relations with the peasants—Slovaks, I believe—who consti-tuted his whole *clientèle* during the winter. He told me that his medical practice proceeded as follows. In his consulting hours the patients came into his room and stood in a row. One after another stepped forward and described his complaint: he had back-ache or pains in his stomach or had tired legs, and so on. The doctor then examined him and, after satisfying himself as to what was the matter, called out the diagnosis, which was the same in every case. He translated the word to me; it meant

---

[1] [Freud's main criticism of Adler's views was made in his 'History of the Psycho-Analytic Movement' (1914d). It will perhaps seem sur-prising that Jung's defection is not alluded to in the present lecture, apart from the short unidentified reference on p. 126 below, and that Freud expected Adler's views to be given first place by his readers. This is in agreement with some remarks in the 'History' in which he says that 'of the two movements under discussion Adler's is in-dubitably the more important'.]

[2] [Freiberg, afterwards re-named Příbor.]

approximately 'bewitched'. I asked in astonishment whether the peasants made no objection to his verdict being the same with every patient. 'Oh, no!' he replied, 'they are very pleased with it: it is what they expected. Each of them, as he went back to his place in the row, showed the others by looks and gestures that I was a fellow who understood things.' Little did I guess at the time in what circumstances I should come across an analogous situation once again.

For, whether a man is a homosexual or a necrophilic, a hysteric suffering from anxiety, an obsessional neurotic cut off from society, or a raving lunatic, the 'Individual Psychologist' of the Adlerian school will declare that the impelling motive of his condition is that he wishes to assert himself, to overcompensate for his inferiority, to remain 'on top', to pass from the feminine to the masculine line. In my young student days we used to hear something very much the same in the out-patients' department when a case of hysteria was introduced: hysterical patients, we were told, produce their symptoms to make themselves interesting, to draw attention to themselves. It is a remarkable thing how these ancient pieces of wisdom keep on cropping up. But even at that time this fragment of psychology did not seem to cover the riddle of hysteria. It left unexplained, for instance, why the patients used no other methods for attaining their purpose. There must, of course, be *something* correct in this theory of the 'Individual Psychologists': a small particle is taken for the whole. The self-preservative instinct will try to profit by every situation; the ego will seek to turn even illness to its advantage. In psycho-analysis this is known as the 'secondary gain from illness'.[1] Though, indeed, when we think of the facts of masochism, of the unconscious need for punishment and of neurotic self-injury, which make plausible the hypothesis of there being instinctual impulses that run contrary to self-preservation, we even feel shaken in our belief in the general validity of the commonplace truth on which the theoretical structure of Individual Psychology is erected. But a theory such as this is bound to be very welcome to the great mass of the people, a theory which recognizes no complications, which introduces no new concepts that are hard to grasp, which knows nothing of the unconscious, which gets rid at a single blow of the universally oppressive problem of sexuality and which restricts itself to the discovery of the artifices by which people seek to make life easy. For the mass of the people themselves take things easily: they call for no more than a single reason by way of ex-

[1] [Cf. *Introductory Lectures*, XXIV.]

planation, they do not thank science for its diffuseness, they want to have simple solutions and to know that problems are solved. When we consider how very far Individual Psychology goes in meeting these demands, we cannot suppress the recollection of a sentence in *Wallenstein*:

> Wär' der Gedank' nicht so verwünscht gescheidt,
> Man wär' versucht, ihn herzlich dumm zu nennen.[1]

Criticism from specialist circles, which is so relentless against psycho-analysis, has in general handled Individual Psychology with kid gloves. It is true that in America one of the most highly respected psychiatrists published a paper against Adler under the title 'Enough', in which he gave energetic expression to his boredom at the 'compulsion to repeat' of Individual Psychology. If others have treated it far more amiably, no doubt their antagonism to analysis has had much to do with it.

I need not say much about other schools which have branched off from our psycho-analysis. The fact that they have done so cannot be used either for or against the validity of psycho-analytic theories. You have only to think of the strong emotional factors that make it hard for many people to fit themselves in with others or to subordinate themselves, and of the still greater difficulty justly insisted on by the dictum 'Quot capita tot sensus'.[2] When the differences of opinion had gone beyond a certain point, the most sensible thing was to part and thereafter to proceed along our different ways—especially when the theoretical divergence involved a change in practical procedure. Suppose, for instance, that an analyst[3] attaches little value to the influence of the patient's personal past and looks for the causation of neuroses exclusively in present-day motives and in expectations of the future. In that case he will also neglect the analysis of childhood; he will have to adopt an entirely different technique and will have to make up for the omission of the events from the analysis of childhood by increasing his didactic influence and by directly indicating certain particular aims in life. We for our part will then say: 'This may be a school of wisdom; but it is no longer analysis.' Or someone else[4] may arrive at the view that the experience of anxiety at birth sows the seed of all later neurotic disturbances.

---

[1] [Were the idea not so confounded clever,
    I'd be inclined to call it really stupid.
                    Schiller, *Die Piccolomini*, II, 7.]
[2] [More usually given in the form (derived from Terence, *Phormio*, II, 4) 'Quot homines tot sententiae (As many men, so many opinions)'.]
[3] [The allusion is to Jung.]   [4] [Here Rank is referred to.]

It may thereupon seem to him legitimate to restrict analysis to the consequences of this single impression and to promise therapeutic success from a treatment lasting from three to four months. As you will observe, I have chosen two examples which start from diametrically opposite premisses. It is an almost universal characteristic of these 'secessionist movements' that each of them takes hold of one fragment out of the wealth of themes in psycho-analysis and makes itself independent on the basis of this seizure—selecting the instinct for mastery, for instance, or ethical conflict, or the [importance of the] mother, or genitality, and so on. If it appears to you that secessions of this sort are already more numerous to-day in the history of psycho-analysis than in other intellectual movements, I am not sure that I should agree with you. If it is the case, the responsibility must be laid on the intimate relations which exist in psycho-analysis between theoretical views and therapeutic treatment. Mere differences of opinion would be tolerable for far longer. People like accusing us psycho-analysts of intolerance. The only manifestation of this ugly characteristic has been precisely our parting from those who think differently from us. No other harm has been done to them. On the contrary, they have fallen on their feet, and are better off than they were before. For by their separation they have usually freed themselves of one of the burdens which weigh us down—the odium of infantile sexuality, perhaps, or the absurdity of symbolism—and are regarded by their environment as passably respectable, which is still not true of those of us who are left behind. Moreover, apart from one notable exception, it was they who excluded themselves.[1]

What further claims do you make in the name of tolerance? That when someone has uttered an opinion which we regard as completely false we should say to him: 'Thank you very much for having given voice to this contradiction. You are guarding us against the danger of complacency and are giving us an opportunity of showing the Americans that we are really as "broad-minded" [2] as they always wish. To be sure, we do not believe a word of what you are saying, but that makes no difference. Probably you are just as right as we are. After all, who can possibly know who is right? In spite of our antagonism, pray allow us to represent your point of view in our publications. We hope that you will be kind enough in exchange to find a place for our views which you deny.' In the future, when the misuse of Einstein's relativity has been entirely achieved, this will obviously become the regular custom in scientific affairs. For the moment,

[1] [This may possibly refer to Stekel.]   [2] [In English in the original.]

it is true, we have not gone quite so far. We restrict ourselves, in the old fashion, to putting forward only our own convictions, we expose ourselves to the risk of error because it cannot be guarded against, and we reject what is in contradiction to us. We have made plentiful use in psycho-analysis of the right to change our opinions if we think we have found something better.

One of the first applications of psycho-analysis was to teach us to understand the opposition offered to us by our contemporaries because we practised psycho-analysis. Other applications, of an objective nature, may claim a more general interest. Our first purpose, of course, was to understand the disorders of the human mind, because a remarkable experience had shown that here understanding and cure almost coincide, that a traversable road leads from the one to the other.[1] And for a long time it was our only purpose. Then, however, we perceived the close relations, the internal identity indeed, between pathological processes and what are known as normal ones. Psycho-analysis became a depth-psychology; and, since nothing that men make or do is understandable without the co-operation of psychology, the applications of psycho-analysis to numerous fields of knowledge, in particular to those of the mental sciences, came about of their own accord, pushed their way to the front and called for ventilation. These tasks unluckily came up against obstacles which, rooted as they were in the circumstances, have not yet been overcome even to-day. An application of this kind presupposes specialized knowledge which an analyst does not possess, while those who possess it, the specialists, know nothing of analysis and perhaps want to know nothing. The result has been that analysts, as amateurs with an equipment of greater or less adequacy, often hastily scraped together, have made excursions into such fields of knowledge as mythology, the history of civilization, ethnology, the science of religion and so on. They were no better treated by the experts resident in those fields than are trespassers in general: their methods and their findings, in so far as they attracted attention, were in the first instance rejected. But these conditions are constantly improving, and in every region there is a growing number of people who study psycho-analysis in order to make use of it in their special subject, and in order, as colonists, to replace the pioneers. Here we may expect a rich harvest of new discoveries. Applications of analysis are always confirmations of it as well. There, too, where scientific work is further removed

[1] [Breuer's treatment of his first patient. See *Introductory Lectures,* XVIII.]

from practical activity, the inevitable differences of opinion will no doubt take a less embittered form.

I feel a strong temptation to conduct you through all the applications of psycho-analysis to the mental sciences. They are things worth knowing by anyone with intellectual interests; and not to hear about abnormality and illness for a time would be a well-deserved relaxation. But I must renounce the idea: it would once more carry us outside the framework of these lectures and, I must honestly admit, I should not be equal to the task. It is true that in a few of these regions I myself took the first step; but to-day I no longer embrace the whole field, and I should have to do a great deal of studying in order to master what has been accomplished since my beginnings. Any of you who are disappointed by my refusal may make up for it in the pages of our periodical *Imago*, which is designed to cover the non-medical applications of analysis.[1]

But there is one topic which I cannot pass over so easily—not, however, because I understand particularly much about it or have contributed very much to it. Quite the contrary: I have scarcely concerned myself with it at all.[2] I must mention it because it is so exceedingly important, so rich in hopes for the future, perhaps the most important of all the activities of analysis. What I am thinking of is the application of psycho-analysis to education, to the upbringing of the next generation. I am glad that I am at least able to say that my daughter, Anna Freud, has made this study her life-work and has in that way compensated for my neglect.

The road that led to this application is easily traced. When in the treatment of an adult neurotic we followed up the determinants of his symptoms, we were regularly led back to his early childhood. A knowledge of the later aetiological factors was not

---

[1] [See *Introductory Lectures*, X, *Standard Ed.*]

[2] [Though this is perhaps the longest of Freud's discussions on the relations between analysis and education, it is in fact far from being the only one. Apart from numerous incidental references, the question was considered by him at some length in Section III of Chapter III of the 'Little Hans' case history (1909*b*); and he dealt with it again in his prefaces to two books, one by Pfister (1913*b*), and the other by Aichhorn (1925*f*). The special problems connected with sex education were the theme of an early paper on 'The Sexual Enlightenment of Children' (1907*c*) and were touched on again thirty years later in the last paragraph of Section IV of 'Analysis Terminable and Interminable' (1937*c*). Lastly it may be mentioned that the question of religious education had come up at several points in Chapters IX and X of *The Future of an Illusion* (1927*c*).]

sufficient either for understanding the case or for producing a
therapeutic effect. We were therefore compelled to make ourselves acquainted with the psychical peculiarities of childhood;
we learnt a quantity of things which could not have been learnt
except through analysis, and we were able to put right many
opinions that were generally held about childhood. We recognized that particular importance attached to the first years of
childhood—up to the age of five, perhaps—for several reasons.
Firstly, because those years include the early efflorescence of
sexuality which leaves behind it decisive instigating factors for
the sexual life of maturity. Secondly, because the impressions of
this period impinge upon an immature and feeble ego, and act
upon it like traumas. The ego cannot fend off the emotional
storms which they provoke in any way except by repression and
in this manner acquires in childhood all its dispositions to later
illnesses and functional disturbances. We realized that the
difficulty of childhood lies in the fact that in a short span of time
a child has to appropriate the results of a cultural evolution
which stretches over thousands of years, including the acquisition of control over his instincts and adaptation to society—or
at least the first beginnings of these two. He can only achieve a
part of this modification through his own development; much
must be imposed on him by education.[1] We are not surprised
that children often carry out this task very imperfectly. During
these early times many of them pass through states that may be
put on a par with neuroses—and this is certainly so in the case
of all those who produce manifest illnesses later on. In some
children the neurotic illness does not wait till maturity but
breaks out already in childhood and gives parents and doctors
plenty of trouble.

We had no misgivings over applying analytic treatment to
children who either exhibited unambiguous neurotic symptoms
or who were on the road to an unfavourable development of
character. The apprehension expressed by opponents of analysis that the child would be injured by it proved unfounded.
What we gained from these undertakings was that we were
able to confirm on the living subject what we had inferred (from
historical documents, as it were) in the case of adults. But the
gain for the children was also very satisfactory. It turned out
that a child is a very favourable subject for analytic therapy; the
results are thorough and lasting. The technique of treatment

---

[1] [The German word 'Erziehung', which is here and elsewhere in this
discussion translated 'education', has a much wider meaning than the
English word and includes 'upbringing' in a general sense.]

worked out for adults must, of course, be largely altered for children. A child is psychologically a different object from an adult. As yet he possesses no super-ego, the method of free association does not carry far with him, transference (since the real parents are still on the spot) plays a different part. The internal resistances against which we struggle in adults are replaced for the most part in children by external difficulties. If the parents make themselves vehicles of the resistance, the aim of the analysis—and even the analysis itself—is often imperilled. Hence it is often necessary to combine with a child's analysis a certain amount of analytic influencing of his parents. On the other hand, the inevitable deviations of analyses of children from those of adults are diminished by the circumstance that some of our patients have retained so many infantile character-traits that the analyst (once again adapting himself to his subject) cannot avoid making use with them of certain of the techniques of child-analysis. It has automatically happened that child-analysis has become the domain of women analysts, and no doubt this will remain true.

The recognition that most of our children pass through a neurotic phase in the course of their development carries with it the germ of a hygienic challenge. The question may be raised whether it would not be expedient to come to a child's help with an analysis even if he shows no signs of a disturbance, as a measure for safeguarding his health, just as to-day we inoculate healthy children against diphtheria without waiting to see if they fall ill of it. The discussion of this question has only an academic interest at present, but I may venture to consider it here. The mere suggestion would seem to the great bulk of our contemporaries to be a monstrous outrage, and in view of the attitude towards analysis of most people in a parental position any hope of putting through such an idea must be abandoned for the time being. Prophylaxis such as this against neurotic illness, which would probably be very effective, also presupposes a quite other constitution of society. The watchword for the application of psycho-analysis to education is to be found to-day elsewhere. Let us make ourselves clear as to what the first task of education is. The child must learn to control his instincts. It is impossible to give him liberty to carry out all his impulses without restriction. To do so would be a very instructive experiment for child-psychologists; but life would be impossible for the parents and the children themselves would suffer grave damage, which would show itself partly at once and partly in later years. Accordingly, education must inhibit, forbid and suppress, and this it has abundantly seen to in all periods of history. But we have learnt from analysis that precisely this suppression of instincts involves the risk of neurotic illness. As you will remember, we have examined in detail how this occurs.[1] Thus education has to find its way between the Scylla of non-interference and the Charybdis of frustration. Unless this problem is entirely insoluble, an optimum must be discovered which will enable education to achieve the most and damage the least. It will therefore be a matter of deciding how much to forbid, at what times and by what means. And in addition we have to take into account the fact that the objects of our educational influence have very different innate constitutional dispositions, so that it is quite impossible that the same educational procedure can be equally good for all children. A moment's reflection tells us that hitherto education has fulfilled its task very badly and has done children great damage. If it discovers the optimum and carries out its task ideally, it can hope to wipe out one of the factors in the aetiology of falling ill—the influence of the accidental traumas of childhood. It cannot in any case get rid of the other factor—the power of an insubordinate instinctual constitution. If now we consider the difficult problems that confront the educator—how he has to recognize the child's constitutional individuality, to infer from small indications what is going on in his immature mind, to give him the right amount of love and yet to maintain an effective degree of authority—we shall tell ourselves that the only appropriate preparation for the profession of educator is a thorough psycho-analytic training. It would be best that he should have been analysed himself, for, when all is said and done, it is impossible to assimilate analysis without experiencing it personally. The analysis of teachers and educators seems to be a more efficacious prophylactic measure than the analysis of children themselves, and there are less difficulties in the way of putting it into practice.

We may mention, though only as an incidental consideration, an indirect way in which the upbringing of children may be helped by analysis and which may with time acquire a greater influence. Parents who have themselves experienced an analysis and owe much to it, including an insight into the faults of their own upbringing, will treat their children with better understanding and will spare them much of what they themselves were not spared.

Parallel with the efforts of analysts to influence education,

[1] [See *Introductory Lectures,* in particular Lectures XXII and XXIII.]

other investigations are being made into the origin and prevention of delinquency and crime. Here again I am only opening
the door for you and showing you the rooms that lie beyond it,
without leading you inside.[1] I am certain that if you remain
loyal to your interest in psycho-analysis you will be able to
learn much that is new and valuable on these subjects. I must
not, however, leave the topic of education without referring to
one particular aspect of it. It has been said—and no doubt
justly—that every education has a partisan aim, that it endeavours to bring the child into line with the established order
of society, without considering how valuable or how stable that
order may be in itself. If [it is argued] one is convinced of the
defects in our present social arrangements, education with a
psycho-analytic alignment cannot justifiably be put at their service as well: it must be given another and higher aim, liberated
from the prevailing demands of society. In my opinion, however,
this argument is out of place here. Such a demand goes beyond
the legitimate function of analysis. In the same way, it is not the
business of a doctor who is called in to treat a case of pneu-
monia to concern himself with whether the patient is an honest
man or a suicide or a criminal, whether he deserves to remain
alive or whether one ought to wish him to. This other aim
which it is desired to give to education will also be a partisan
one, and it is not the affair of an analyst to decide between the
parties. I am leaving entirely on one side the fact that psycho-
analysis would be refused any influence on education if it
admitted to intentions inconsistent with the established social
order. Psycho-analytic education will be taking an uninvited
responsibility on itself if it proposes to mould its pupils into
rebels. It will have played its part if it sends them away as
healthy and efficient as possible. It itself contains enough
revolutionary factors to ensure that no one educated by it will
in later life take the side of reaction and suppression. It is
even my opinion that revolutionary children are not desirable
from any point of view.

I propose further, Ladies and Gentlemen, to say a few words
to you about psycho-analysis as a form of therapy. I discussed
the theoretical side of this question fifteen years ago[2] and I cannot formulate it in any other manner to-day; I have now to tell
you of our experience during this interval. As you know, psycho-
analysis originated as a method of treatment; it has far out-

[1] [See, in this connection, Freud's preface to Aichhorn's *Wayward
Youth* (Freud, 1925f).]
[2] [In *Introductory Lectures*, XXVII and XXVIII.]

grown this, but it has not abandoned its home-ground and it is still linked to its contact with patients for increasing its depth and for its further development. The accumulated impressions from which we derive our theories could be arrived at in no other way. The failures we meet with as therapists are constantly setting us new tasks and the demands of real life are an effective guard against an overgrowth of the speculation which we cannot after all do without in our work. I have already discussed long ago the means used by psycho-analysis in helping patients, when it does help them, and the method by which it does so;[1] to-day I shall enquire how much it achieves.

You are perhaps aware that I have never been a therapeutic enthusiast; there is no danger of my misusing this lecture by indulging in eulogies. I would rather say too little than too much. During the period at which I was the only analyst, people who were ostensibly friendly to my ideas used to say to me: 'That's all very nice and clever; but show me a case that you have cured by analysis.' This was one of the many formulas which in the course of time have succeeded one another in performing the function of pushing the uncomfortable novelty aside. To-day it is as out of date as many others: the analyst, too, has a heap of letters in his files from grateful patients who have been cured. The analogy does not stop at that. Psycho-analysis is really a method of treatment like others. It has its triumphs and its defeats, its difficulties, its limitations, its indications. At one time a complaint was made against analysis that it was not to be taken seriously as a treatment since it did not dare to issue any statistics of its successes. Since then, the Psycho-Analytic Institute in Berlin, which was founded by Dr. Max Eitingon, has published a statement of its results during its first ten years.[2] Its therapeutic successes give grounds neither for boasting nor for being ashamed. But statistics of that kind are in general uninstructive; the material worked upon is so heterogeneous that only very large numbers would show anything. It is wiser to examine one's individual experiences. And here I should like to add that I do not think our cures can compete with those of Lourdes. There are so many more people who believe in the miracles of the Blessed Virgin than in the existence of the unconscious. If we turn to mundane competitors, we must compare psycho-analytic treatment with other kinds of psychotherapy. To-day organic physical methods of treating neurotic states need scarcely be mentioned. Analysis as

---

[1] [See last footnote and the papers on technique in Volume XII of the *Standard Edition*.]

[2] [Freud contributed a preface to this (1930*b*).]

a psycho-therapeutic procedure does not stand in opposition to other methods used in this specialized branch of medicine; it does not diminish their value nor exclude them. There is no theoretical inconsistency in a doctor who likes to call himself a psychotherapist using analysis on his patients alongside of any other method of treatment according to the peculiarities of the case and the favourable or unfavourable external circumstances. It is in fact technique that necessitates the specialization in medical practice. Thus in the same way surgery and orthopaedics were obliged to separate. Psycho-analytic activity is arduous and exacting; it cannot well be handled like a pair of glasses that one puts on for reading and takes off when one goes for a walk. As a rule psycho-analysis possesses a doctor either entirely or not at all. Those psychotherapists who make use of analysis among other methods, occasionally, do not to my knowledge stand on firm analytic ground; they have not accepted the whole of analysis but have watered it down—have drawn its fangs, perhaps; they cannot be counted as analysts. This is, I think, to be regretted. But co-operation in medical practice between an analyst and a psychotherapist who restricts himself to other techniques would serve quite a useful purpose.

Compared with the other psychotherapeutic procedures psycho-analysis is beyond any doubt the most powerful. It is just and fair, too, that this should be so for it is also the most laborious and time-consuming; it would not be used on slight cases. In suitable cases it is possible by its means to get rid of disturbances and bring about changes for which in pre-analytic times one would not have ventured to hope. But it has its very appreciable limits. The therapeutic ambition of some of my adherents has made the greatest efforts to overcome these obstacles so that every sort of neurotic disorder might be curable by psycho-analysis. They have endeavoured to compress the work of analysis into a shorter duration, to intensify transference so that it may be able to overcome any resistance, to unite other forms of influence with it so as to compel a cure. These efforts are certainly praiseworthy, but, in my opinion, they are vain. They bring with them, too, a danger of being oneself forced away from analysis and drawn into a boundless course of experimentation.[1] The expectation that every neurotic phenomenon can be cured may, I suspect, be derived from the layman's belief that the neuroses are something quite un-

[1] [It may well be that in writing these sentences Freud had his friend Ferenczi in mind, whose obituary, which he was to write a few months later, contains an echo of these ideas.]

necessary which have no right whatever to exist. Whereas in fact they are severe, constitutionally fixed illnesses, which rarely restrict themselves to only a few attacks but persist as a rule over long periods or throughout life. Our analytic experience that they can be extensively influenced, if the historical precipitating causes and accidental auxiliary factors of the illness can be dealt with, has led us to neglect the constitutional factor in our therapeutic practice, and in any case we can do nothing about it; but in theory we ought always to bear it in mind. The radical inaccessibility of the psychoses to analytic treatment should, in view of their close relationship to the neuroses, restrict our pretensions in regard to these latter. The therapeutic effectiveness of psycho-analysis remains cramped by a number of weighty and scarcely assailable factors. In the case of children, where one might count on the greatest successes, the difficulties are the external ones connected with their relation to their parents, though these difficulties are after all a necessary part of being a child. In the case of adults the difficulties arise in the first instance from two factors: the amount of psychical rigidity present and the form of the illness with all that that covers in the way of deeper determinants.

The first of these factors is often unjustly overlooked. However great may be the plasticity of mental life and the possibility of reviving old conditions, not everything can be brought to life again. Some changes seem to be definitive and correspond to scars formed when a process has run its course. On other occasions one has an impression of a general stiffening of mental life; the psychical processes, to which one could very well indicate other paths, seem incapable of abandoning the old ones. But perhaps this is the same thing as what I mentioned just now, only looked at differently. All too often one seems to see that it is only the treatment's lack of the necessary motive force that prevents one from bringing the change about. One particular dependent relation, one special instinctual component, is too powerful in comparison with the opposing forces that we are able to mobilize. This is quite generally true with the psychoses. We understand them well enough to know the point at which the levers should be applied, but they would not be able to move the weight. It is here, indeed, that hope for the future lies: the possibility that our knowledge of the operation of the hormones (you know what they are) may give us the means of successfully combating the quantitative factors of the illnesses: but we are far from that to-day. I realize that the uncertainty in all these matters is a constant instigation towards perfecting analysis and in particular the transference. Beginners in analysis especially are left in doubt in case of a failure whether they should blame the peculiarities of the case or their own clumsy handling of the therapeutic procedure. But, as I have said already, I do not think much can be achieved by efforts in this direction.

The second limitation upon analytic successes is given by the form of the illness. You know already that the field of application of analytic therapy lies in the transference neuroses—phobias, hysteria, obsessional neurosis—and further, abnormalities of character which have been developed in place of these illnesses. Everything differing from these, narcissistic and psychotic conditions, is unsuitable to a greater or less extent. It would be entirely legitimate to guard against failures by carefully excluding such cases. This precaution would lead to a great improvement in the statistics of analysis. There is, however, a pitfall here. Our diagnoses are very often made only after the event. They resemble the Scottish King's test for identifying witches that I read about in Victor Hugo.[1] This king declared that he was in possession of an infallible method of recognizing a witch. He had the women stewed in a cauldron of boiling water and then tasted the broth. Afterwards he was able to say: 'That was a witch', or 'No, that was not one.' It is the same with us, except that *we* are the sufferers. We cannot judge the patient who comes for treatment (or, in the same way, the candidate who comes for training) till we have studied him analytically for a few weeks or months. We are in fact buying a pig in a poke. The patient brings along indefinite general ailments which do not admit of a conclusive diagnosis. After this period of testing it may turn out that the case is an unsuitable one. If so we send him away if he is a candidate, or continue the trial a little longer if he is a patient on the chance that we may yet see things in a more favourable light. The patient has his revenge by adding to our list of failures, and the rejected candidate does so perhaps, if he is paranoid, by writing books on psycho-analysis himself. As you see, our precautions have been of no avail.

I am afraid these detailed discussions are exhausting your interest. But I should be still more sorry if you were to think it is my intention to lower your opinion of psycho-analysis as a therapy. Perhaps I really made a clumsy start. For I wanted to do the opposite: to excuse the therapeutic limitations of analysis by pointing out their inevitability. With the same aim in view I

---

[1] [The origin of this anecdote has not been found. Freud had already used it in his contribution to a discussion on masturbation (1912*f*).]

turn to another point: the reproach against analytic treatment that it takes a disproportionately long time. On this it must be said that psychical changes do in fact only take place slowly; if they occur rapidly, suddenly, that is a bad sign. It is true that the treatment of a fairly severe neurosis may easily extend over several years; but consider, in case of success, how long the illness would have lasted. A decade, probably, for every year of treatment: the illness, that is to say (as we see so often in untreated cases), would not have ended at all. In some cases we have reasons for resuming an analysis many years afterwards. Life had developed fresh pathological reactions to fresh precipitating causes; but in the meantime our patient had been well. The first analysis had not in fact brought to light all his pathological dispositions, and it was natural for the analysis to have been stopped when success was achieved. There are also severely handicapped people who are kept under analytic supervision all through their lives and are taken back into analysis from time to time. But these people would otherwise have been altogether incapable of existence and we must feel glad that they can be kept on their feet by this piecemeal and recurrent treatment. The analysis of character disorders also calls for long periods of treatment; but it is often successful; and do you know of any other therapy with which such a task could even be approached? Therapeutic ambition may feel unsatisfied by such results; but we have learnt from the example of tuberculosis and lupus that success can only be obtained when the treatment has been adapted to the characteristics of the illness.[1]

I have told you that psycho-analysis began as a method of treatment; but I did not want to commend it to your interest as a method of treatment but on account of the truths it contains, on account of the information it gives us about what concerns human beings most of all—their own nature—and on account of the connections it discloses between the most different of their activities. As a method of treatment it is one among many, though, to be sure, *primus inter pares*. If it was without therapeutic value it would not have been discovered, as it was, in connection with sick people and would not have gone on developing for more than thirty years.

---

[1] [One of the very last of Freud's writings, 'Analysis Terminable and Interminable' (1937c), is devoted to a long discussion of the limitations of psycho-analytic therapy.]

LECTURE XXXV

THE QUESTION
OF A WELTANSCHAUUNG[1]

LADIES AND GENTLEMEN,—At our last meeting we were occupied with little everyday concerns—putting our own modest house in order, as it were. I propose that we should now take a bold leap and venture upon answering a question which is constantly being asked in other quarters: does psycho-analysis lead to a particular *Weltanschauung* and, if so, to which?

'*Weltanschauung*' is, I am afraid, a specifically German concept, the translation of which into foreign languages might well raise difficulties. If I try to give you a definition of it, it is bound to seem clumsy to you. In my opinion, then, a *Weltanschauung* is an intellectual construction which solves all the problems of our existence uniformly on the basis of one overriding hypothesis, which, accordingly, leaves no question unanswered and in which everything that interests us finds its fixed place. It will easily be understood that the possession of a *Weltanschauung* of this kind is among the ideal wishes of human beings. Believing in it one can feel secure in life, one can know what to strive for, and how one can deal most expediently with one's emotions and interests.

If that is the nature of a *Weltanschauung*, the answer as regards psycho-analysis is made easy. As a specialist science, a branch of psychology—a depth-psychology or psychology of the unconscious—it is quite unfit to construct a *Weltanschauung* of its own: it must accept the scientific one. But the *Weltanschauung* of science already departs noticeably from our definition. It is true that it too assumes the *uniformity* of the explanation of the universe; but it does so only as a programme, the fulfilment of which is relegated to the future. Apart from this it is marked by negative characteristics, by its limitation to what is at the moment knowable and by its sharp rejection of certain elements that are alien to it. It asserts that there are no sources of know-

---

[1] [This word might be translated 'A View of the Universe', but Freud himself explains its meaning in the second paragraph below. As it appears more than thirty times in the course of this lecture, the simplest plan seems to be to leave it in German; and in any case it has almost naturalized itself in our language. Freud had already approached the topic of this lecture in a passage at the end of Chapter II of *Inhibitions, Symptoms and Anxiety* (1926d).]

ledge of the universe other than the intellectual working-over
of carefully scrutinized observations—in other words, what we
call research—and alongside of it no knowledge derived from
revelation, intuition or divination. It seems as though this view
came very near to being generally recognized in the course of
the last few centuries that have passed; and it has been left to
our century to discover the presumptuous objection that a *Weltanschauung* like this is alike paltry and cheerless, that it over-
looks the claims of the human intellect and the needs of the
human mind.

This objection cannot be too energetically repudiated. It is
quite without a basis, since the intellect and the mind are objects for scientific research in exactly the same way as any non-
human things. Psycho-analysis has a special right to speak for
the scientific *Weltanschauung* at this point, since it cannot be
reproached with having neglected what is mental in the picture
of the universe. Its contribution to science lies precisely in having extended research to the mental field. And, incidentally,
without such a psychology science would be very incomplete.
If, however, the investigation of the intellectual and emotional
functions of men (and of animals) is included in science, then it
will be seen that nothing is altered in the attitude of science
as a whole, that no new sources of knowledge or methods of
research have come into being. Intuition and divination would
be such, if they existed; but they may safely be reckoned as
illusions, the fulfilments of wishful impulses. It is easy to see, too,
that these demands upon a *Weltanschauung* are only based on
emotion. Science takes notice of the fact that the human mind
produces these demands and is ready to examine their sources;
but it has not the slightest reason to regard them as justified.
On the contrary it sees this as a warning carefully to separate
from knowledge everything that is illusion and an outcome of
emotional demands like these.

This does not in the least mean that these wishes are to be
pushed contemptuously on one side or their value for human life
under-estimated. We are ready to trace out the fulfilments of
them which they have created for themselves in the products of
art and in the systems of religion and philosophy; but we cannot nevertheless overlook the fact that it would be illegitimate
and highly inexpedient to allow these demands to be transferred
to the sphere of knowledge. For this would be to lay open the
paths which lead to psychosis, whether to individual or group
psychosis, and would withdraw valuable amounts of energy
from endeavours which are directed towards reality in order, so
far as possible, to find satisfaction in it for wishes and needs.

From the standpoint of science one cannot avoid exercising one's critical faculty here and proceeding with rejections and dismissals. It is not permissible to declare that science is one field of human mental activity and that religion and philosophy are others, at least its equal in value, and that science has no business to interfere with the other two: that they all have an equal claim to be true and that everyone is at liberty to choose from which he will draw his convictions and in which he will place his belief. A view of this kind is regarded as particularly superior, tolerant, broad-minded and free from illiberal prejudices. Unfortunately it is not tenable and shares all the pernicious features of an entirely unscientific *Weltanschauung* and is equivalent to one in practice. It is simply a fact that the truth cannot be tolerant, that it admits of no compromises or limitations, that research regards every sphere of human activity as belonging to it and that it must be relentlessly critical if any other power tries to take over any part of it.

Of the three powers which may dispute the basic position of science, religion alone is to be taken seriously as an enemy. Art is almost always harmless and beneficent; it does not seek to be anything but an illusion. Except for a few people who are spoken of as being 'possessed' by art, it makes no attempt at invading the realm of reality. Philosophy is not opposed to science, it behaves like a science and works in part by the same methods; it departs from it, however, by clinging to the illusion of being able to present a picture of the universe which is without gaps and is coherent, though one which is bound to collapse with every fresh advance in our knowledge. It goes astray in its method by over-estimating the epistemological value of our logical operations and by accepting other sources of knowledge such as intuition. And it often seems that the poet's derisive comment is not unjustified when he says of the philosopher:

Mit seinen Nachtmützen und Schlafrockfetzen
Stopft er die Lücken des Weltenbaus.[1]

[1] Heine, ['Die Heimkehr', LVIII. Literally: 'With his nightcaps and the tatters of his dressing-gown he patches up the gaps in the structure of the universe.' The lines were favourite ones with Freud. He alluded to them in connection with the secondary revision of dreams in Chapter VI (I) of *The Interpretation of Dreams* (1900a), and again in a letter to Jung of February 25, 1908 (Jones, 1955, 488). Many years earlier he had quoted them in full in a letter to his future wife, apparently in 1883 (Jones, 1953, 214).]

But philosophy has no direct influence on the great mass of mankind; it is of interest to only a small number even of the top layer of intellectuals and is scarcely intelligible to anyone else. On the other hand, religion is an immense power which has the strongest emotions of human beings at its service. It is well known that at an earlier date it comprised everything that played an intellectual part in men's lives, that it took the place of science when there was scarcely yet such a thing as science, and that it constructed a *Weltanschauung*, consistent and self-contained to an unparalleled degree, which, although it has been profoundly shaken, persists to this day.

If we are to give an account of the grandiose nature of religion, we must bear in mind what it undertakes to do for human beings. It gives them information about the origin and coming into existence of the universe, it assures them of its protection and of ultimate happiness in the ups and downs of life and it directs their thoughts and actions by precepts which it lays down with its whole authority. Thus it fulfils three functions. With the first of them it satisfies the human thirst for knowledge; it does the same thing that science attempts to do with *its* means, and at that point enters into rivalry with it. It is to its second function that it no doubt owes the greatest part of its influence. Science can be no match for it when it soothes the fear that men feel of the dangers and vicissitudes of life, when it assures them of a happy ending and offers them comfort in unhappiness. It is true that science can teach us how to avoid certain dangers and that there are some sufferings which it can successfully combat; it would be most unjust to deny that it is a powerful helper to men; but there are many situations in which it must leave a man to his suffering and can only advise him to submit to it. In its third function, in which it issues precepts and lays down prohibitions and restrictions, religion is furthest away from science. For science is content to investigate and to establish facts, though it is true that from its applications rules and advice are derived on the conduct of life. In some circumstances these are the same as those offered by religion, but, when this is so, the reasons for them are different.

The convergence between these three aspects of religion is not entirely clear. What has an explanation of the origin of the universe to do with the inculcation of certain particular ethical precepts? The assurances of protection and happiness are more intimately linked with the ethical requirements. They are the reward for fulfilling these commands; only those who obey them may count upon these benefits, punishment awaits the disobedient. Incidentally, something similar is true of science.

Those who disregard its lessons, so it tells us, expose themselves to injury.

The remarkable combination in religion of instruction, consolation and requirements can only be understood if it is subjected to a genetic analysis. This may be approached from the most striking point of the aggregate, from its instruction on the origin of the universe; for why, we may ask, should a cosmogony be a regular component of religious systems? The doctrine is, then, that the universe was created by a being resembling a man, but magnified in every respect, in power, wisdom, and the strength of his passions—an idealized super-man. Animals as creators of the universe point to the influence of totemism, upon which we shall have a few words at least to say presently. It is an interesting fact that this creator is always only a single being, even when there are believed to be many gods. It is interesting, too, that the creator is usually a man, though there is far from being a lack of indications of female deities; and some mythologies actually make the creation begin with a male god getting rid of a female deity,[1] who is degraded into being a monster. Here the most interesting problems of detail open out; but we must hurry on. Our further path is made easy to recognize, for this god-creator is undisguisedly called 'father'. Psycho-analysis infers that he really is the father, with all the magnificence in which he once appeared to the small child. A religious man pictures the creation of the universe just as he pictures his own origin.

This being so, it is easy to explain how it is that consoling assurances and strict ethical demands are combined with a cosmogony. For the same person to whom the child owed his existence, the father (or more correctly, no doubt, the parental agency compounded of the father and mother), also protected and watched over him in his feeble and helpless state, exposed as he was to all the dangers lying in wait in the external world; under his father's protection he felt safe. When a human being has himself grown up, he knows, to be sure, that he is in possession of greater strength, but his insight into the perils of life has also grown greater, and he rightly concludes that fundamentally he still remains just as helpless and unprotected as he was in his childhood, that faced by the world he is still a child. Even now, therefore, he cannot do without the protection which he enjoyed as a child. But he has long since recognized, too, that his father is a being of narrowly restricted power, and not

---

[1] [Freud had considerably more to say about female deities in Essay III, Part I, Section D, of *Moses and Monotheism* (1939a).]

equipped with every excellence. He therefore harks back to the mnemic image of the father whom in his childhood he so greatly overvalued. He exalts the image into a deity and makes it into something contemporary and real. The effective strength of this mnemic image and the persistence of his need for protection jointly sustain his belief in God.

The third main item in the religious programme, the ethical demand, also fits into this childhood situation with ease. I may remind you of Kant's famous pronouncement in which he names, in a single breath, the starry heavens and the moral law within us [see p. 55 above].[1] However strange this juxtaposition may sound—for what have the heavenly bodies to do with the question of whether one human creature loves another or kills him?—it nevertheless touches on a great psychological truth. The same father (or parental agency) which gave the child life and guarded him against its perils, taught him as well what he might do and what he must leave undone, instructed him that he must adapt himself to certain restrictions on his instinctual wishes, and made him understand what regard he was expected to have for his parents and brothers and sisters, if he wanted to become a tolerated and welcome member of the family circle and later on of larger associations. The child is brought up to a knowledge of his social duties by a system of loving rewards and punishments, he is taught that his security in life depends on his parents (and afterwards other people) loving him and on their being able to believe that he loves them. All these relations are afterwards introduced by men unaltered into their religion. Their parents' prohibitions and demands persist within them as a moral conscience. With the help of this same system of rewards and punishments, God rules the world of men. The amount of protection and happy satisfaction assigned to an individual depends on his fulfilment of the ethical demands; his love of God and his consciousness of being loved by God are the foundations of the security with which he is armed against the dangers of the external world and of his human environment. Finally, in prayer he has assured himself a direct influence on the divine will and with it a share in the divine omnipotence.

[1] [In the original edition the present sentence read: 'In a famous pronouncement the philosopher Kant named the existence of the starry heavens and that of the moral law within us as the most powerful witnesses to the greatness of God.' It was changed to the form translated above in *G.S.* (1934)—the earlier quotation of the same passage having no doubt been previously overlooked.]

I feel sure that while you have been listening to me you have been bothered by a number of questions which you would be glad to hear answered. I cannot undertake to do so here and now, but I feel confident that none of these detailed enquiries would upset our thesis that the religious *Weltanschauung* is determined by the situation of our childhood. That being so, it is all the more remarkable that, in spite of its infantile nature, it nevertheless had a precursor. There is no doubt that there was a time without religion, without gods. This is known as the stage of animism. At that time, too, the world was peopled with spiritual beings resembling men—we call them demons. All the objects in the external world were their habitation, or perhaps were identical with them; but there was no superior power which had created them all and afterwards ruled them and to which one could turn for protection and help. The demons of animism were for the most part hostile in their attitude to human beings, but it appears that human beings had more self-confidence then than later on. They were certainly in a constant state of the most acute fear of these evil spirits; but they defended themselves against them by certain actions to which they ascribed the power to drive them away. Nor apart from this did they regard themselves as defenceless. If they desired something from Nature—if they wished for rain, for instance—they did not direct a prayer to the weather-god, but they performed a magical act which they expected to influence Nature directly: they themselves did something which resembled rain. In their struggle against the powers of the world around them their first weapon was *magic*, the earliest fore-runner of the technology of to-day. Their reliance on magic was, as we suppose, derived from their overvaluation of their own intellectual operations, from their belief in the 'omnipotence of thoughts', which, incidentally, we come upon again in our obsessional neurotic patients.[1] We may suppose that human beings at that period were particularly proud of their acquisitions in the way of language, which must have been accompanied by a great facilitation of thinking. They attributed magical power to words. This feature was later taken over by religion. 'And God said "Let there be light!" and there was light.' Moreover the fact of their magical actions shows that animistic men did not simply rely on the power of their wishes. They expected results, rather, from the performance of an action which would induce Nature to imitate it. If they wanted rain, they themselves poured out

[1] [For all of this see the third essay in *Totem and Taboo* (1912–13), (Norton, 1952), particularly Section 3.]

water; if they wanted to encourage the earth to be fruitful, they demonstrated a dramatic performance of sexual intercourse to it in the fields.

You know how hard it is for anything to die away when once it has achieved psychical expression. So you will not be surprised to hear that many of the utterances of animism have persisted to this day, for the most part as what we call superstition, alongside of and behind religion. But more than this, you will scarcely be able to reject a judgement that the philosophy of today has retained some essential features of the animistic mode of thought—the overvaluation of the magic of words and the belief that the real events in the world take the course which our thinking seeks to impose on them. It would seem, it is true, to be an animism without magical actions. On the other hand, we may suppose that even in those days there were ethics of some sort, precepts upon the mutual relations of men; but nothing suggests that they had any intimate connection with animistic beliefs. They were probably the direct expression of men's relative powers and of their practical needs.

It would be well worth knowing what brought about the transition from animism to religion, but you may imagine the obscurity which to-day still veils these primaeval ages of the evolution of the human spirit. It appears to be a fact that the first form assumed by religion was the remarkable phenomenon of totemism, the worship of animals, in whose train the first ethical commandments, the taboos, made their appearance. In a volume called *Totem and Taboo* [1912–13], I once elaborated a notion which traced this transformation back to a revolution in the circumstances of the human family. The main achievement of religion as compared with animism lies in the psychical binding of the fear of demons. Nevertheless a vestige of this primaeval age, the Evil Spirit, has kept a place in the religious system.

This being the prehistory of the religious *Weltanschauung*, let us turn now to what has happened since then and to what is still going on before our eyes. The scientific spirit, strengthened by the observation of natural processes, has begun, in the course of time, to treat religion as a human affair and to submit it to a critical examination. Religion was not able to stand up to this. What first gave rise to suspicion and scepticism were its tales of miracles, for they contradicted everything that had been taught by sober observation and betrayed too clearly the influence of the activity of the human imagination. After this its doctrines explaining the origin of the universe met with rejection, for they gave evidence of an ignorance which bore the stamp of ancient times and to which, thanks to their increased familiarity with the laws of nature, people knew they were superior. The idea that the universe came into existence through acts of copulation or creation analogous to the origin of individual people had ceased to be the most obvious and self-evident hypothesis since the distinction between animate creatures with a mind and an inanimate Nature had impressed itself on human thought—a distinction which made it impossible to retain belief in the original animism. Nor must we overlook the influence of the comparative study of different religious systems and the impression of their mutual exclusiveness and intolerance.

Strengthened by these preliminary exercises, the scientific spirit gained enough courage at last to venture on an examination of the most important and emotionally valuable elements of the religious *Weltanschauung*. People may always have seen, though it was long before they dared to say so openly, that the pronouncements of religion promising men protection and happiness if they would only fulfil certain ethical requirements had also shown themselves unworthy of belief. It seems not to be the case that there is a Power in the universe which watches over the well-being of individuals with parental care and brings all their affairs to a happy ending. On the contrary, the destinies of mankind can be brought into harmony neither with the hypothesis of a Universal Benevolence nor with the partly contradictory one of a Universal Justice. Earthquakes, tidal waves, conflagrations, make no distinction between the virtuous and pious and the scoundrel or unbeliever. Even where what is in question is not inanimate Nature but where an individual's fate depends on his relations to other people, it is by no means the rule that virtue is rewarded and that evil finds its punishment. Often enough the violent, cunning or ruthless man seizes the envied good things of the world and the pious man goes away empty. Obscure, unfeeling and unloving powers determine men's fate; the system of rewards and punishments which religion ascribes to the government of the universe seems not to exist. Here once again is a reason for dropping a portion of the animistic theory which had been rescued from animism by religion.

The last contribution to the criticism of the religious *Weltanschauung* was effected by psycho-analysis, by showing how religion originated from the helplessness of children and by tracing its contents to the survival into maturity of the wishes and needs of childhood. This did not precisely mean a contradiction of religion, but it was nevertheless a necessary rounding-off of our

knowledge about it, and in one respect at least it was a contradiction, for religion itself lays claim to a divine origin. And, to
be sure, it is not wrong in this, provided that our interpretation
of God is accepted.

In summary, therefore, the judgement of science on the
religious *Weltanschauung* is this. While the different religions
wrangle with one another as to which of them is in possession of
the truth, our view is that the question of the truth of religious
beliefs may be left altogether on one side. Religion is an attempt
to master the sensory world in which we are situated by means
of the wishful world which we have developed within us as a
result of biological and psychological necessities. But religion
cannot achieve this. Its doctrines bear the imprint of the times
in which they arose, the ignorant times of the childhood of
humanity. Its consolations deserve no trust. Experience teaches
us that the world is no nursery. The ethical demands on which
religion seeks to lay stress need, rather, to be given another
basis; for they are indispensable to human society and it is
dangerous to link obedience to them with religious faith. If we
attempt to assign the place of religion in the evolution of mankind, it appears not as a permanent acquisition but as a counterpart to the neurosis which individual civilized men have to go
through in their passage from childhood to maturity.[1]

You are of course free to criticize this description of mine; I
will even go half way to meet you on this. What I told you about
the gradual crumbling away of the religious *Weltanschauung* was
certainly incomplete in its abbreviated form. The order of the
different processes was not given quite correctly; the co-operation of various forces in the awakening of the scientific spirit was
not followed out. I also left out of account the alterations which
took place in the religious *Weltanschauung* itself during the period
of its undisputed sway and afterwards under the influence
of growing criticism. Finally, I restricted my remarks, strictly
speaking, to one single form taken by religion, that of the
Western peoples. I constructed an anatomical model, so to
speak, for the purpose of a hurried demonstration which was to
be as impressive as possible. Let us leave on one side the question of whether my knowledge would in any case have been

---

[1] [The possibility of society suffering from neuroses analogous to individual ones was mentioned by Freud in Chapter VIII of *The Future
of an Illusion* (1927c), and near the end of *Civilization and its Discontents* (1930a). He discussed it at much greater length in Essay III,
Part I, Section C of *Moses and Monotheism* (1939a). The analogy
between religious practices and obsessive actions had been pointed out
much earlier (Freud, 1907b).]

sufficient to do the thing better and more completely. I am
aware that you can find everything I said to you said better
elsewhere. Nothing in it is new. But let me express a conviction that the most careful working-over of the material of the
problems of religion would not shake our conclusions.

The struggle of the scientific spirit against the religious
Weltanschauung is, as you know, not at an end: it is still going on
to-day under our eyes. Though as a rule psycho-analysis makes
little use of the weapon of controversy, I will not hold back from
looking into this dispute. In doing so I may perhaps throw some
further light on our attitude to *Weltanschauungen*. You will see
how easily some of the arguments brought forward by the
supporters of religion can be answered, though it is true that
others may evade refutation.

The first objection we meet with is to the effect that it is an
impertinence on the part of science to make religion a subject
for its investigations, for religion is something sublime, superior
to any operation of the human intellect, something which may
not be approached with hair-splitting criticisms. In other words,
science is not qualified to judge religion: it is quite serviceable
and estimable otherwise, so long as it keeps to its own sphere.
But religion is not its sphere, and it has no business there. If we
do not let ourselves be put off by this brusque repulse and enquire further what is the basis of this claim to a position exceptional among all human concerns, the reply we receive (if we
are thought worthy of any reply) is that religion cannot be
measured by human measurements, for it is of divine origin and
was given us as a revelation by a Spirit which the human spirit
cannot comprehend. One would have thought that there was
nothing easier than the refutation of this argument: it is a clear
case of *petitio principii*, of 'begging the question' [1]—I know of no
good German equivalent expression. The actual question raised
is whether there *is* a divine spirit and a revelation by it; and the
matter is certainly not decided by saying that this question
cannot be asked, since the deity may not be put in question.
The position here is what it occasionally is during the work of
analysis. If a usually sensible patient rejects some particular
suggestion on specially foolish grounds, this logical weakness is
evidence of the existence of a specially strong motive for the
denial—a motive which can only be of an affective nature, an
emotional tie.

We may also be given another answer, in which a motive of
this kind is openly admitted: religion may not be critically

---

[1] [In English in the original.]

examined because it is the highest, most precious, and most sublime thing that the human spirit has produced, because it gives expression to the deepest feelings and alone makes the world tolerable and life worthy of men. We need not reply by disputing this estimate of religion but by drawing attention to another matter. What we do is to emphasize the fact that what is in question is not in the least an invasion of the field of religion by the scientific spirit, but on the contrary an invasion by religion of the sphere of scientific thought. Whatever may be the value and importance of religion, it has no right in any way to restrict thought—no right, therefore, to exclude itself from having thought applied to it.

Scientific thinking does not differ in its nature from the normal activity of thought, which all of us, believers and un-believers, employ in looking after our affairs in ordinary life. It has only developed certain features: it takes an interest in things even if they have no immediate, tangible use; it is concerned carefully to avoid individual factors and affective influences; it examines more strictly the trustworthiness of the sense-perceptions on which it bases its conclusions; it provides itself with new perceptions which cannot be obtained by everyday means and it isolates the determinants of these new experiences in experiments which are deliberately varied. Its endeavour is to arrive at correspondence with reality—that is to say, with what exists outside us and independently of us and, as experience has taught us, is decisive for the fulfilment or disappointment of our wishes. This correspondence with the real external world we call 'truth'. It remains the aim of scientific work even if we leave the practical value of that work out of account. When, there-fore, religion asserts that it can take the place of science, that, because it is beneficent and elevating, it must also be true, that is in fact an invasion which must be repulsed in the most general interest. It is asking a great deal of a person who has learnt to conduct his ordinary affairs in accordance with the rules of experience and with a regard to reality, to suggest that he shall hand over the care of what are precisely his most in-timate interests to an agency which claims as its privilege free-dom from the precepts of rational thinking. And as regards the protection which religion promises its believers, I think none of us would be so much as prepared to enter a motor-car if its driver announced that he drove, unperturbed by traffic regu-lations, in accordance with the impulses of his soaring imagina-tion.

The prohibition against thought issued by religion to assist in its self-preservation is also far from being free from danger

XXXV. A WELTANSCHAUUNG?   151

either for the individual or for human society. Analytic experience has taught us that a prohibition like this, even if it is originally limited to a particular field, tends to widen out and
thereafter to become the cause of severe inhibitions in the subject's conduct of life. This result may be observed, too, in the
female sex, following from their being forbidden to have anything to do with their sexuality even in thought.[1] Biography is
able to point to the damage done by the religious inhibition of
thought in the life stories of nearly all eminent individuals in the
past. On the other hand intellect—or let us call it by the name
that is familiar to us, reason—is among the powers which we
may most expect to exercise a unifying influence on men—on
men who are held together with such difficulty and whom it is
therefore scarcely possible to rule. It may be imagined how
impossible human society would be, merely if everyone had his
own multiplication table and his own private units of length
and weight. Our best hope for the future is that intellect—the
scientific spirit, reason—may in process of time establish a
dictatorship in the mental life of man. The nature of reason is a
guarantee that afterwards it will not fail to give man's emotional impulses and what is determined by them the position
they deserve. But the common compulsion exercised by such a
dominance of reason will prove to be the strongest uniting bond
among men and lead the way to further unions. Whatever, like
religion's prohibition against thought, opposes such a development, is a danger for the future of mankind.

It may then be asked why religion does not put an end to
this dispute which is so hopeless for it by frankly declaring: 'It is
a fact that I cannot give you what is commonly called "truth";
if you want that, you must keep to science. But what I have to
offer you is something incomparably more beautiful, more consoling and more uplifting than anything you could get from
science. And because of that, I say to you that it is true in another, higher sense.' It is easy to find the answer to this. Religion cannot make this admission because it would involve its
forfeiting all its influence on the mass of mankind. The ordinary
man only knows one kind of truth, in the ordinary sense of the
word. He cannot imagine what a higher or a highest truth may
be. Truth seems to him no more capable of comparative degrees
than death; and he cannot join in the leap from the beautiful
to the true. Perhaps you will think as I do that he is right in
this.

---

[1] [This had been considered in Chapter IX of *The Future of an
Illusion* (1927c).]

So the struggle is not at an end. The supporters of the religious *Weltanschauung* act upon the ancient dictum: the best defence is attack. 'What', they ask, 'is this science which presumes to disparage our religion—our religion which has brought salvation and consolation to millions of people over many thousands of years? What has it accomplished so far? What can we expect from it in the future? On its own admission it is incapable of bringing consolation and exaltation. Let us leave them on one side then, though that is no light renunciation. But what about its theories? Can it tell us how the universe came about and what fate lies before it? Can it even draw us a coherent picture of the universe, or show us where we are to look for the unexplained phenomena of life or how the forces of the mind are able to act upon inert matter? If it could do this we should not refuse it our respect. But none of these, no problem of this kind, has been solved by it hitherto. It gives us fragments of alleged discovery, which it cannot bring into harmony with one another; it collects observations of uniformities in the course of events which it dignifies with the name of laws and submits to its risky interpretations. And consider the small degree of certainty which it attaches to its findings! Everything it teaches is only provisionally true: what is praised to-day as the highest wisdom will be rejected to-morrow and replaced by something else, though once more only tentatively. The latest error is then described as the truth. And for this truth we are to sacrifice our highest good!'

I expect, Ladies and Gentlemen, that, in so far as you yourselves are supporters of the scientific *Weltanschauung* which is attacked in these words, you will not be too profoundly shaken by this criticism. And here I should like to recall to you a remark that once went the rounds in Imperial Austria. The old gentleman[1] once shouted at the Committee of a parliamentary party that was troublesome to him: 'This isn't ordinary opposition any more! It's *factious* opposition!' Similarly, as you will recognize, the reproaches against science for not having yet solved the problems of the universe are exaggerated in an unjust and malicious manner; it has truly not had time enough yet for these great achievements. Science is very young—a human activity which developed late. Let us bear in mind, to select only a few dates, that only some three hundred years have passed since Kepler discovered the laws of planetary movement, that the life of Newton, who analysed light into the colours of the spectrum and laid down the theory of gravitation,

---

[1] [The Emperor Francis Joseph was popularly so named.]

ended in 1727—that is to say, little more than two hundred years ago—and that Lavoisier discovered oxygen shortly before the French Revolution. The life of an individual is very short in comparison with the duration of human evolution; I may be a very old man to-day,[1] but nevertheless I was already alive when Darwin published his book on the origin of species. In the same year as that, 1859, Pierre Curie, the discoverer of radium, was born. And if you go further back, to the beginnings of exact science among the Greeks, to Archimedes, to Aristarchus of Samos (about 250 B.C.) who was the fore-runner of Copernicus, or even to the first beginnings of astronomy among the Babylonians, you will only have covered a small fraction of the length of time which anthropologists require for the evolution of man from an ape-like ancestral form, and which certainly comprises more than a hundred thousand years. And we must not forget that the last century has brought such a wealth of new discoveries, such a great acceleration of scientific advance that we have every reason to view the future of science with confidence.

We must admit to some extent the correctness of the other criticisms. The path of science is indeed slow, hesitating, laborious. This fact cannot be denied or altered. No wonder the gentlemen in the other camp are dissatisfied. They are spoilt: revelation gave them an easier time. Progress in scientific work is just as it is in an analysis. We bring expectations with us into the work, but they must be forcibly held back. By observation, now at one point and now at another, we come upon something new; but to begin with the pieces do not fit together. We put forward conjectures, we construct hypotheses, which we withdraw if they are not confirmed, we need much patience and readiness for any eventuality, we renounce early convictions so as not to be led by them into overlooking unexpected factors, and in the end our whole expenditure of effort is rewarded, the scattered findings fit themselves together, we get an insight into a whole section of mental events, we have completed our task and now we are free for the next one. In analysis, however, we have to do without the assistance afforded to research by experiment.

Moreover, there is a good deal of exaggeration in this criticism of science. It is not true that it staggers blindly from one experiment to another, that it replaces one error by another. It works as a rule like a sculptor at his clay model, who tirelessly alters his rough sketch, adds to it and takes away from it, till he

[1] [Freud was 76 when he wrote this.]

has arrived at what he feels is a satisfactory degree of resemblance to the object he sees or imagines. Besides, at least in the older and more mature sciences, there is even to-day a solid ground-work which is only modified and improved but no longer demolished. Things are not looking so bad in the business of science.

And what, finally, is the aim of these passionate disparagements of science? In spite of its present incompleteness and of the difficulties attaching to it, it remains indispensable to us and nothing can take its place. It is capable of undreamt-of improvements, whereas the religious *Weltanschauung* is not. This is complete in all essential respects; if it was a mistake, it must remain one for ever. No belittlement of science can in any way alter the fact that it is attempting to take account of our dependence on the real external world, while religion is an illusion and it derives its strength from its readiness to fit in with our instinctual wishful impulses.[1]

I am under an obligation to go on to consider other *Weltanschauungen* which are in opposition to the scientific one; but I do so unwillingly, for I know that I am not properly competent to judge them. So you must bear this proviso in mind in listening to the following remarks, and if your interest has been aroused you should seek better instruction elsewhere.

And here I must first mention the various systems of philosophy which have ventured to draw a picture of the universe as it is reflected in the mind of thinkers who were for the most part turned away from the world. But I have already attempted to give a general account of the characteristics of philosophy [p. 141 f. above] and I am probably as unqualified as few people have ever been to form an estimate of the different systems. So I will invite you to join me in turning to a consideration of two other phenomena which, particularly in our days, it is impossible to disregard.

The first of these *Weltanschauungen* is as it were a counterpart to political anarchism, and is perhaps a derivative of it. There have certainly been intellectual nihilists of this kind in the past, but just now the relativity theory of modern physics seems to have gone to their head. They start out from science, indeed, but they contrive to force it into self-abrogation, into suicide; they set it the task of getting itself out of the way by refuting its

[1] [Freud's most elaborate evaluation of religion had been made in *The Future of an Illusion* (1927c).]

own claims. One often has an impression in this connection that this nihilism is only a temporary attitude which is to be retained until this task has been performed. Once science has been disposed of, the space vacated may be filled by some kind of mysticism or, indeed, by the old religious *Weltanschauung*. According to the anarchist theory there is no such thing as truth, no assured knowledge of the external world. What we give out as being scientific truth is only the product of our own needs as they are bound to find utterance under changing external conditions: once again, they are illusion. Fundamentally, we find only what we need and see only what we want to see. We have no other possibility. Since the criterion of truth—correspondence with the external world—is absent, it is entirely a matter of indifference what opinions we adopt. All of them are equally true and equally false. And no one has a right to accuse anyone else of error.

A person of an epistemological bent might find it tempting to follow the paths—the sophistries—by which the anarchists succeed in enticing such conclusions from science. No doubt we should come upon situations similar to those derived from the familiar paradox of the Cretan who says that all Cretans are liars.[1] But I have neither the desire nor the capacity for going into this more deeply. All I can say is that the anarchist theory sounds wonderfully superior so long as it relates to opinions about abstract things: it breaks down with its first step into practical life. Now the actions of men are governed by their opinions, their knowledge; and it is the same scientific spirit that speculates about the structure of atoms or the origin of man and that plans the construction of a bridge capable of bearing a load. If what we believe were really a matter of indifference, if there were no such thing as knowledge distinguished among our opinions by corresponding to reality, we might build bridges just as well out of cardboard as out of stone, we might inject our patients with a decagram of morphine instead of a centigram, and might use tear-gas as a narcotic instead of ether. But even the intellectual anarchists would violently repudiate such practical applications of their theory.

The other opposition has to be taken far more seriously, and in this instance I feel the liveliest regret at the inadequacy of my information. I suspect that you know more about this business than I do and that you took up your position long ago in favour

[1] [The simplest form of this paradox (known as the 'Epimenides') is provided by a man who says 'I am lying'. If he is lying, he is speaking the truth; and if he is speaking the truth, he is lying.]

of Marxism or against it. Karl Marx's investigations into the
economic structure of society and into the influence of different
economic systems upon every department of human life have in
our days acquired an undeniable authority. How far his views
in detail are correct or go astray, I cannot of course tell. I understand that this is not an easy matter even for others better
instructed than I am. There are assertions contained in Marx's
theory which have struck me as strange: such as that the development of forms of society is a process of natural history, or that
the changes in social stratification arise from one another in
the manner of a dialectical process. I am far from sure that I
understand these assertions aright; nor do they sound to me
'materialistic' but, rather, like a precipitate of the obscure
Hegelian philosophy in whose school Marx graduated. I do not
know how I can shake off my lay opinion that the class structure of society goes back to the struggles which, from the beginning of history, took place between human hordes[1] only
slightly differing from each other. Social distinctions, so I
thought, were originally distinctions between clans or races.
Victory was decided by psychological factors, such as the
amount of constitutional aggressiveness, but also by the firm-
ness of the organization within the horde, and by material
factors, such as the possession of superior weapons. Living together in the same area, the victors became the masters and the
vanquished the slaves. There is no sign to be seen in this of a
natural law or of a conceptual [dialectical] evolution. On the
other hand the influence exercised upon the social relations of
mankind by progressive control over the forces of Nature is
unmistakable. For men always put their newly acquired instruments of power at the service of their aggressiveness and use
them against one another. The introduction of metals—bronze
and iron—made an end to whole epochs of civilization and
their social institutions. I really believe that it was gunpowder
and fire-arms that abolished chivalry and aristocratic rule, and
that the Russian despotism was already doomed before it lost
the War, because no amount of inbreeding among the ruling
families of Europe could have produced a race of Tsars capable
of withstanding the explosive force of dynamite.

It is possible, indeed, that with our present economic crisis,
following after the Great War, we are only paying the price of
our latest tremendous victory over nature, the conquest of the
air. That does not sound very illuminating, but the first links
at least in the chain are clearly recognizable. English politics

[1] [Freud always uses the term 'horde' to mean comparatively *small*
groups.]

were based on the security which was guaranteed by the seas that washed her coasts. In the moment at which Blériot flew across the Channel in his aeroplane this protective isolation was breached; and in the night during which (in peace-time and on an exercise) a German Zeppelin cruised over London the war against Germany was no doubt a foregone conclusion.[1] Nor must the U-boat threat be forgotten in this connection.

I am almost ashamed to comment to you on a subject of such importance and complexity with these few inadequate remarks, and I know too that I have told you nothing that is new to you. I merely want to draw your attention to the fact that the relation of mankind to their control over Nature, from which they derive their weapons for fighting their fellow-men, must necessarily also affect their economic arrangements. We seem to have come a long way from the problem of a *Weltanschauung*, but we shall very soon be back to it. The strength of Marxism clearly lies, not in its view of history or the prophecies of the future that are based on it, but in its sagacious indication of the decisive influence which the economic circumstances of men have upon their intellectual, ethical and artistic attitudes. A number of connections and implications were thus uncovered, which had previously been almost totally overlooked. But it cannot be assumed that economic motives are the only ones that determine the behaviour of human beings in society. The undoubted fact that different individuals, races and nations behave differently under the same economic conditions is alone enough to show that economic motives are not the sole dominating factors. It is altogether incomprehensible how psychological factors can be overlooked where what is in question are the reactions of living human beings; for not only were these reactions concerned in establishing the economic conditions, but even under the domination of those conditions men can only bring their original instinctual impulses into play—their self-preservative instinct, their aggressiveness, their need to be loved, their drive towards obtaining pleasure and avoiding unpleasure. In an earlier enquiry I also pointed out the important claims made by the super-ego, which represents tradition and the ideals of the past and will for a time resist the incentives of a new economic situation.[2] And finally we must not forget that the mass of human beings who are subjected to economic necessities also undergo the process of cultural development—of civilization as

---

[1] I was told of this from trustworthy sources during the first year of the war.

[2] [See above, p. 60.]

other people may say[1]—which, though no doubt influenced by all the other factors, is certainly independent of them in its origin, being comparable to an organic process and very well able on its part to exercise an influence on the other factors.[2] It displaces instinctual aims and brings it about that people become antagonistic to what they had previously tolerated. Moreover, the progressive strengthening of the scientific spirit seems to form an essential part of it. If anyone were in a position to show in detail the way in which these different factors—the general inherited human disposition, its racial variations and its cultural transformations—inhibit and promote one another under the conditions of social rank, profession and earning capacity—if anyone were able to do this, he would have supplemented Marxism so that it was made into a genuine social science. For sociology too, dealing as it does with the behaviour of people in society, cannot be anything but applied psychology. Strictly speaking there are only two sciences: psychology, pure and applied, and natural science.

The newly achieved discovery of the far-reaching importance of economic relations brought with it a temptation not to leave alterations in them to the course of historical development but to put them into effect oneself by revolutionary action. Theoretical Marxism, as realized in Russian Bolshevism, has acquired the energy and the self-contained and exclusive character of a *Weltanschauung*, but at the same time an uncanny likeness to what it is fighting against. Though originally a portion of science and built up, in its implementation, upon science and technology, it has created a prohibition of thought which is just as ruthless as was that of religion in the past. Any critical examination of Marxist theory is forbidden, doubts of its correctness are punished in the same way as heresy was once punished by the Catholic Church. The writings of Marx have taken the place of the Bible and the Koran as a source of revelation, though they would seem to be no more free from contradictions and obscurities than those older sacred books.

[1] [Cf. a parallel passage in *Why War?* (1933*b*), and Freud's sweeping comment on this verbal point in *The Future of an Illusion* (1927*c*): 'I scorn to distinguish between culture and civilization.']

[2] [The notion of a 'process of civilization' was very much in Freud's mind at this time. He had discussed it at several points in *Civilization and its Discontents* (1930*a*); and he mentioned it again in *Why War?* (1933*b*). But the idea was closely linked with one of much longer standing—the hypothesis, namely, of *repression* as an organic process. He himself brought out the connection fully in the two long footnotes at the beginning and end of Chapter IV of *Civilization and its Discontents*.]

And although practical Marxism has mercilessly cleared away all idealistic systems and illusions, it has itself developed illusions which are no less questionable and unprovable than the earlier ones. It hopes in the course of a few generations so to alter human nature that people will live together almost without friction in the new order of society, and that they will undertake the duties of work without any compulsion. Meanwhile it shifts elsewhere the instinctual restrictions which are essential in society; it diverts the aggressive tendencies which threaten all human communities to the outside and finds support in the hostility of the poor against the rich and of the hitherto powerless against the former rulers. But a transformation of human nature such as this is highly improbable. The enthusiasm with which the mass of the people follow the Bolshevist instigation at present, so long as the new order is incomplete and is threatened from outside, gives no certainty for a future in which it would be fully built up and in no danger. In just the same way as religion, Bolshevism too must compensate its believers for the sufferings and deprivations of their present life by promises of a better future in which there will no longer be any unsatisfied need. This Paradise, however, is to be in this life, instituted on earth and thrown open within a foreseeable time. But we must remember that the Jews as well, whose religion knows nothing of an after-life, expected the arrival of a Messiah on earth, and that the Christian Middle Ages at many times believed that the Kingdom of God was at hand.

There is no doubt of how Bolshevism will reply to these objections. It will say that so long as men's nature has not yet been transformed it is necessary to make use of the means which affect them to-day. It is impossible to do without compulsion in their education, without the prohibition of thought and without the employment of force to the point of bloodshed; and if the illusions were not awakened in them, they could not be brought to acquiesce in this compulsion. And we should be politely asked to say how things could be managed differently. This would defeat us. I could think of no advice to give. I should admit that the conditions of this experiment would have deterred me and those like me from undertaking it; but we are not the only people concerned. There are men of action, unshakable in their convictions, inaccessible to doubt, without feeling for the sufferings of others if they stand in the way of their intentions. We have to thank men of this kind for the fact that the tremendous experiment of producing a new order of this kind is now actually being carried out in Russia. At a time when the great nations announce that they expect salvation only from the maintenance of Christian piety, the revolution in Russia—in spite of all its disagreeable details—seems none the less like the message of a better future. Unluckily neither our scepticism nor the fanatical faith of the other side gives a hint as to how the experiment will turn out. The future will tell us; perhaps it will show that the experiment was undertaken prematurely, that a sweeping alteration of the social order has little prospect of success until new discoveries have increased our control over the forces of Nature and so made easier the satisfaction of our needs. Only then perhaps may it become possible for a new social order not only to put an end to the material need of the masses but also to give a hearing to the cultural demands of the individual. Even then, to be sure, we shall still have to struggle for an incalculable time with the difficulties which the untameable character of human nature presents to every kind of social community.

Ladies and Gentlemen,—Allow me in conclusion to sum up what I had to say of the relation of psycho-analysis to the question of a *Weltanschauung*. Psycho-analysis, in my opinion, is incapable of creating a *Weltanschauung* of its own. It does not need one; it is a part of science and can adhere to the scientific *Weltanschauung*. This, however, scarcely deserves such a grandiloquent title, for it is not all-comprehensive, it is too incomplete and makes no claim to being self-contained and to the construction of systems. Scientific thought is still very young among human beings; there are too many of the great problems which it has not yet been able to solve. A *Weltanschauung* erected upon science has, apart from its emphasis on the real external world, mainly negative traits, such as submission to the truth and rejection of illusions. Any of our fellow-men who is dissatisfied with this state of things, who calls for more than this for his momentary consolation, may look for it where he can find it. We shall not grudge it him, we cannot help him, but nor can we on his account think differently.

BIBLIOGRAPHY
AND AUTHOR INDEX

[Titles of books and periodicals are in italics; titles of papers are in inverted commas. Abbreviations are in accordance with the *World List of Scientific Periodicals* (London, 1952). Further abbreviations used in this volume will be found in the List at the end of this bibliography. Numerals in thick type refer to volumes; ordinary numerals refer to pages. The figures in round brackets at the end of each entry indicate the page or pages of this volume on which the work in question is mentioned. In the case of the Freud entries, the letters attached to the dates of publication are in accordance with the corresponding entries in the complete bibliography of Freud's writings to be included in the last volume of the *Standard Edition*.

For non-technical authors, and for technical authors where no specific work is mentioned, see the General Index.]

ABRAHAM, K. (1922) 'Die Spinne als Traumsymbol', *Int. Z. Psychoan.*, **8**, 470. (22)

[*Trans.*: 'The Spider as a Dream Symbol', *Selected Papers on Psycho-Analysis*, London, 1927, Chap. XIX.]

—— (1924) *Versuch einer Entwicklungsgeschichte der Libido*, Leipzig, Vienna, Zurich. (88, 89)

[*Trans.*: 'A Short Study of the Development of the Libido', *Selected Papers on Psycho-Analysis*, London, 1927, Chap. XXVI.]

AICHHORN, A. (1925) *Verwahrloste Jugend*, Vienna. (129, 133)

[*Trans.*: *Wayward Youth*, New York, 1935; London, 1936; revised reprint, London, 1951.]

ALEXANDER, F. (1925) 'Über Traumpaare und Traumreihen', *Int. Z. Psychoan.*, **11**, 80. (24)

[*Trans.*: 'Dreams in Pairs and Series', *Int. J. Psycho-Anal.*, **6**, 446.]

ANDREAS-SALOMÉ, L. (1916) ' "Anal" und "Sexual" ', *Imago*, **4**, 249. (90)

BETLHEIM, S., and HARTMANN, H. (1924) 'Über Fehlreaktionen des Gedächtnisses bei Korsakoffschen Psychose', *Arch. Psychiat. Nervenkr.*, **72**, 278. (21)

BREUER, J., and FREUD, S. (1895) *See* FREUD, S. (1895d)

BRUNSWICK, R. MACK (1928) 'Die Analyse eines Eifersuchtswahnes', *Int. Z. Psychoan.*, **14**, 458. (115)

[*English Text:* 'The Analysis of a Case of Paranoia', *J. nerv. ment. Dis.*, **70** (1929), 177.]

BURLINGHAM, D. (1932) 'Kinderanalyse und Mutter', *Psychoan. Päd.*, **6**, 269. (50)

BURLINGHAM, D. (cont.)
> [*English Text:* 'Child Analysis and the Mother', *Psychoanal. Quart.*, 4 (1935), 69.]

DEUTSCH, H. (1926) 'Okkulte Vorgänge während der Psychoanalyse', *Imago*, 12, 418. (48)
> (1932) 'Über die weibliche Homosexualität', *Int. Z. Psychoan.*, 18, 219. (115)
> [*Trans.:* 'Homosexuality in Women', *Int. J. Psycho-Anal*, 14 (1933), 34.]

DEVEREUX, G. (1953) *Psychoanalysis and the Occult*, New York. (3)

EISLER, M. J. (1919) 'Beiträge zur Traumdeutung', *Int. Z. (ärztl.) Psychoanal.*, 5, 295.
> [*Trans.:* in *The Psychoanalytic Reader* (ed. R. Fliess), New York, 1948, 378.]

EISLER, R. (1910) *Weltenmantel und Himmelszelt* (2 vols.), Munich. (22)

FERENCZI, S. (1921) 'Die Symbolik der Brücke', *Int. Z. Psychoan*, 7, 211. (22)
> [*Trans.:* 'The Symbolism of the Bridge', *Further Contributions to the Theory and Technique of Psycho-Analysis*, London, 1926, Chap. LXI.]
> (1922) 'Die Brückensymbolik und die Don Juan-Legende', *Int. Z. Psychoan.*, 8, 77. (22)
> [*Trans.:* 'Bridge Symbolism and the Don Juan Legend', *Further Contributions to the Theory and Technique of Psycho-Analysis*, London, 1926, Chap. LXII.]
> (1925) 'Zur Psychoanalyse von Sexualgewohnheiten', *Int. Z. Psychoan.*, 11, 6. (77)
> [*Trans.:* 'Psycho-Analysis of Sexual Habits', *Further Contributions to the Theory and Technique of Psycho-Analysis*, London, 1926, Chap. XXXII.]

FREUD, S. (1893h) Vortrag 'Über den psychischen Mechanismus hysterischer Phänomene' [shorthand report revised by lecturer], *Wien. med. Pr.*, 34, Nr. 4, 121, and 5, 165. (81)
> [*Trans.:* Lecture 'On the Psychical Mechanism of Hysterical Phenomena', *Int. J. Psycho-Anal.*, 37, 8; *Standard Ed.*, 3, 27.]
> (1894a) 'Die Abwehr-Neuropsychosen', *G.S.*, 1, 290; *G.W.*, 1, 59. (15, 68, 83)
> [*Trans.:* 'The Neuro-Psychoses of Defence', *C.P.*, 1, 59; *Standard Ed.*, 3, 43.]
> (1895d) With BREUER, J., *Studien über Hysterie*, Vienna. *G.S.*, 1, 3; *G.W.*, 1, 77 (omitting Breuer's contributions). (36, 66, 106–7)
> [*Trans.: Studies on Hysteria*, London, 1956; *Standard Ed.*, 2. Including Breuer's contributions.]
> (1896b) 'Weitere Bemerkungen über die Abwehr-Neuropsychosen', *G.S.*, 1, 363; *G.W.*, 1, 379. (80, 106)
> [*Trans.:* 'Further Remarks on the Neuro-Psychoses of Defence',

FREUD, S. (*cont.*)
    C.P., 1, 155; *Standard Ed.*, 3, 159.]
  (1896c) 'Zur Ätiologie der Hysterie', *G.S.*, 1, 404; *G.W.*, 1, 425.
    (106)
    [*Trans.*: 'The Aetiology of Hysteria', *C.P.*, 1, 183; *Standard Ed.*,
    3, 189.]
  (1900a) *Die Traumdeutung*, Vienna. *G.S.*, 2–3; *G.W.*, 2–3. (3, 8,
    10, 13, 15, 21, 24, 78, 79, 90, 122, 141)
    [*Trans.*: *The Interpretation of Dreams*, London and New York,
    1955; *Standard Ed.*, 4–5.]
  (1901b) *Zur Psychopathologie des Alltagslebens*, Berlin, 1904. *G.S.*,
    4, 3; *G.W.*, 4. (36)
    [*Trans.*: *The Psychopathology of Everyday Life*, *Standard Ed.*, 6.]
  (1905c) *Der Witz und seine Beziehung zum Unbewussten*, Vienna,
    G.S., 9, 5; *G.W.*, 6. (30, 36, 79, 87)
    [*Trans.*: *Jokes and their Relation to the Unconscious*, London,
    1960; *Standard Ed.*, 8.]
  (1905d) *Drei Abhandlungen zur Sexualtheorie*, Vienna. *G.S.*, 5, 3;
    G.W., 5, 29. (87, 90, 100, 102, 107)
    [*Trans.*: *Three Essays on the Theory of Sexuality*, London,
    1962; *Standard Ed.*, 7, 125.]
  (1906a) 'Meine Ansichten über die Rolle der Sexualität in der
    Ätiologie der Neurosen', *G.S.*, 5, 123; *G.W.*, 5, 149. (107)
    [*Trans.*: 'My Views on the Part played by Sexuality in the
    Aetiology of the Neuroses', *C.P.*, 1, 272; *Standard Ed.*, 7, 271.]
  (1907b) 'Zwangshandlungen und Religionsübung', *G.S.*, 10, 210;
    G.W., 7, 129. (148)
    [*Trans.*: 'Obsessive Actions and Religious Practices', *C.P.*, 2, 25;
    Standard Ed., 9, 116.]
  (1907c) 'Zur sexuellen Aufklärung der Kinder', *G.S.*, 5, 134; *G.W.*,
    7, 19. (129)
    [*Trans.*: 'The Sexual Enlightenment of Children', *C.P.*, 2, 36;
    Standard Ed., 9, 131.]
  (1908b) 'Charakter und Analerotik', *G.S.*, 5, 261; *G.W.*, 7, 203.
    (81, 90)
    [*Trans.*: 'Character and Anal Erotism', *C.P.*, 2, 45; *Standard Ed.*,
    9, 169.]
  (1908c) 'Über infantile Sexualtheorien', *G.S.*, 5, 168; *G.W.*, 7,
    171. (89)
    [*Trans.*: 'On the Sexual Theories of Children', *C.P.*, 2, 59;
    Standard Ed., 9, 207.]
  (1909b) 'Analyse der Phobie eines fünfjährigen Knaben', *G.S.*, 8,
    129; *G.W.*, 7, 243. (129)
    [*Trans.*: 'Analysis of a Phobia in a Five-Year-Old Boy', *C.P.*, 3,
    149; *Standard Ed.*, 10, 3.]
  (1911b) 'Formulierungen über die zwei Prinzipien des psychischen
    Geschehens', *G.S.*, 5, 409; *G.W.*, 8, 230. (79)

FREUD, S. (cont.)

[*Trans.:* 'Formulations on the Two Principles of Mental Functioning', *C.P.*, 4, 13; *Standard Ed.*, 12, 215.]

(1911c) 'Psychoanalytische Bemerkungen über einen autobiographisch beschriebenen Fall von Paranoia (Dementia Paranoides)', *G.S.*, 8, 355; *G.W.*, 8, 240. (88)
[*Trans.:* 'Psycho-Analytic Notes on an Autobiographical Account of a Case of Paranoia (Dementia Paranoides)', *C.P.*, 3, 387; *Standard Ed.*, 12, 3.]

(1911e) 'Die Handhabung der Traumdeutung in der Psychoanalyse', *G.S.*, 6, 45; *G.W.*, 8, 350. (13)
[*Trans.:* 'The Handling of Dream-Interpretation in Psycho-Analysis', *C.P.*, 2, 305; *Standard Ed.*, 12, 91.]

(1912f) 'Zur Onanie-Diskussion', *G.S.*, 3, 324; *G.W.*, 8, 332. (112, 137)
[*Trans.:* 'Contributions to a Discussion on Masturbation', *Standard Ed.*, 12, 243.]

(1912–13) *Totem und Tabu*, Vienna, 1913. *G.S.*, 10, 3; *G.W.*, 9. (145, 146, 156)
[*Trans.: Totem and Taboo*, London, 1950; New York, 1932; *Standard Ed.*, 13, 1.]

(1913b) Introduction to Pfister's *Die psychanalytische Methode*, *G.S.*, 11, 224; *G.W.*, 10, 448. (129)
[*Trans.: Standard Ed.*, 12, 329.]

(1913h) 'Erfahrungen und Beispiele aus der analytischen Praxis', *Int. Z. (ärztl.) Psychoanal.*, 1, 377; partly reprinted *G.S.*, 11, 301; *G.W.*, 10, 40. (22)
[*Trans.:* 'Observations and Examples from Analytic Practice', *Standard Ed.*, 13, 193 (in full). Also partly incorporated in *The Interpretation of Dreams, Standard Ed.*, 4, 232, and 5, 409f.]

(1913i) 'Die Disposition zur Zwangsneurose', *G.S.*, 5, 277; *G.W.*, 8, 442. (88)
[*Trans.:* 'The Disposition to Obsessional Neurosis', *C.P.*, 2, 122; *Standard Ed.*, 12, 313.]

(1914c) 'Zur Einführung des Narzissmus', *G.S.*, 6, 155; *G.W.*, 10, 138. (58, 117)
[*Trans.:* 'On Narcissism: an Introduction', *C.P.*, 4, 30; *Standard Ed.*, 14, 69.]

(1914d) 'Zur Geschichte der psychoanalytischen Bewegung', *G.S.*, 4, 411; *G.W.*, 10, 44. (107, 121, 124)
[*Trans.:* 'On the History of the Psycho-Analytic Movement', *C.P.*, 1, 287; *Standard Ed.*, 14, 3.]

(1915c) 'Triebe und Triebschicksale', *G.S.*, 5, 443; *G.W.*, 10, 210. (65, 86)
[*Trans.:* 'Instincts and their Vicissitudes', *C.P.*, 4, 60; *Standard Ed.*, 14, 111.]

(1915d) 'Die Verdrängung', *G.S.*, 5, 466; *G.W.*, 10, 248. (81)

FREUD, S. (cont.)

[Trans.: 'Repression', C.P., 4, 84; Standard Ed., 14, 143.]

(1915e) 'Das Unbewusste', G.S., 5, 480; G.W., 10, 264. (66, 79)

[Trans.: 'The Unconscious', C.P., 4, 98; Standard Ed., 14, 161.]

(1916–17) Vorlesungen zur Einführung in die Psychoanalyse,
Vienna. G.S., 7; G.W., 11. (3–6, 8, 12, 14, 16, 22, 24, 25, 30,
57. 58, 63, 71, 75, 78, 81, 87, 88, 90, 92, 102, 105, 111, 118,
125, 128, 129, 132, 133)

[Trans.: Introductory Lectures on Psycho-Analysis, revised ed.,
London, 1929 (A General Introduction to Psychoanalysis, New
York, 1935); Standard Ed., 15–16.]

(1917c) 'Über Triebumsetzungen insbesondere der Analerotik',
G.S., 5, 268; G.W., 10, 402. (90)

[Trans.: 'On Transformations of Instinct as Exemplified in
Anal Erotism', C.P., 2, 164; Standard Ed., 17, 127.]

(1917d [1915]) 'Metapsychologische Ergänzung zur Traumlehre',
G.S., 5, 520; G.W., 10, 412. (30)

[Trans.: 'A Metapsychological Supplement to the Theory of
Dreams', C.P., 4, 137; Standard Ed., 14, 219.]

(1918a) 'Das Tabu der Virginität', G.S., 5, 212; G.W., 12, 161. (118)

[Trans.: 'The Taboo of Virginity', C.P., 4, 217; Standard Ed.,
11, 193.]

(1920c) 'Dr. Anton von Freund', G.S., 11, 280; G.W., 13, 435. (47)

[Trans.: 'Dr. Anton von Freund', Standard Ed., 18, 267.]

(1920g) Jenseits des Lustprinzips, Vienna. G.S., 6, 191; G.W., 13, 3.
(27, 66, 96)

[Trans.: Beyond the Pleasure Principle, London, 1961; Standard
Ed., 18, 7.]

(1921c) Massenpsychologie und Ich-Analyse, Vienna. G.S., 6, 261;
G.W., 13, 73. (36, 57, 60, 118, 119)

[Trans.: Group Psychology and the Analysis of the Ego, London
and New York, 1959; Standard Ed., 18, 69.]

(1922a) 'Traum und Telepathie', G.S., 3, 278; G.W., 13, 165. (33)

[Trans.: 'Dreams and Telepathy', C.P., 4, 408; Standard Ed., 18,
197.]

(1923b) Das Ich und das Es, Vienna. G.S., 6, 353; G.W., 13, 237.
(51, 57, 58, 64, 70, 71, 75, 79, 81, 91, 93, 97, 98)

[Trans.: The Ego und the Id, London and New York, 1962;
Standard Ed., 19, 3.]

(1923c) 'Bemerkungen zur Theorie und Praxis der Traumdeutung',
G.S., 3, 305, G.W., 13, 301. (11, 13)

[Trans.: 'Remarks on the Theory and Practice of Dream
Interpretation', C.P., 5, 136; Standard Ed., 19, 109]

(1923e) 'Die infantile Genitalorganisation', G.S., 5, 232; G.W., 13,
293. (00)

[Trans.: 'The Infantile Genital Organization', C.P., 2, 244;
Standard Ed., 19, 141.]

FREUD, S. *(cont.)*
　(1924c) 'Das ökonomische Problem des Masochismus', *G.S.*, 5, 374;
　　G.W., 13, 371. (57, 96, 98)
　　[*Trans.*: 'The Economic Problem of Masochism', *C.P.*, 2, 255;
　　Standard Ed., 19, 157.]
　(1924d) 'Der Untergang des Ödipuskomplexes', *G.S.*, 5, 423; *G.W.*,
　　13, 395. (82)
　　[*Trans.*: 'The Dissolution of the Oedipus Complex', *C.P.*, 2, 269;
　　Standard Ed., 19, 173.]
　(1925a) 'Notiz über den "Wunderblock" ', *G.S.*, 6, 415; *G.W.*, 14,
　　3. (67)
　　[*Trans.*: 'A Note upon the "Mystic Writing-Pad" ', *C.P.*, 5, 175;
　　Standard Ed., 19, 227.]
　(1925d [1924]) *Selbstdarstellung*, Vienna, 1934. *G.S.*, 11, 119; *G.W.*,
　　14, 33. (107)
　　[*Trans.*: *An Autobiographical Study*, London, 1935 (*Autobiog-
　　raphy*, New York, 1935); *Standard Ed.*, 20, 3].
　(1925f) Preface to August Aichhorn's *Verwahrloste Jugend*, Vienna.
　　G.S., 11, 267; *G.W.*, 14, 565. (129, 133)
　　[*Trans.*: Preface to Aichhorn's *Wayward Youth*, *C.P.*, 5, 98;
　　Standard Ed., 19, 273.]
　(1925h) 'Die Verneinung', *G.S.*, 11, 3; *G.W.*, 14, 11. (79)
　　[*Trans.*: 'Negation', *C.P.*, 5, 181; *Standard Ed.*, 19, 235.]
　(1925i) 'Einige Nachträge zum Ganzen der Traumdeutung', *G.S.*,
　　3, 172; *G.W.*, 1, 561. (12, 36)
　　[*Trans.*: 'Some Additional Notes on Dream-Interpretation as a
　　Whole', *C.P.*, 5, 150; *Standard Ed.*, 19, 125.]
　(1925j) 'Einige psychische Folgen des anatomischen Geschlechts-
　　unterschieds', *G.S.*, 11, 8; *G.W.*, 14, 19. (58, 99)
　　[*Trans.*: 'Some Psychical Consequences of the Anatomical Dis-
　　tinction between the Sexes', *C.P.*, 5, 186; *Standard Ed.*, 19, 243.]
　(1926d) *Hemmung, Symptom und Angst*, Vienna. *G.S.*, 11, 23;
　　G.W., 14, 113. (55, 68, 75–8, 80–1, 84, 139)
　　[*Trans.*: *Inhibitions, Symptoms and Anxiety*, London, 1960 (*The
　　Problem of Anxiety*, New York, 1936); *Standard Ed.*, 20, 77.]
　(1926e) *Die Frage der Laienanalyse*, Vienna. *G.S.*, 11, 307; *G.W.*,
　　14, 209. (68)
　　[*Trans.*: *The Question of Lay Analysis*, London, 1947; *Standard
　　Ed.*, 20, 179.]
　(1927c) *Die Zukunft einer Illusion*, Vienna. *G.S.*, 11, 411; *G.W.*,
　　14, 325. (32, 129, 148, 151, 158)
　　[*Trans.*: *The Future of an Illusion*, London, 1962; New York,
　　1928; *Standard Ed.*, 21, 3.]
　(1930a) *Das Unbehagen in der Kultur*, Vienna. *G.S.*, 12, 29; *G.W.*,
　　14, 421. (98, 102, 118, 148, 158)
　　[*Trans.*: *Civilization and its Discontents*, London and New York,
　　1930; *Standard Ed.*, 21.]

FREUD, S. (*cont.*)

(1930*b*) Preface to *Zehn Jahre Berliner Psychoanalytisches Institut*, Vienna. *G.S.*, **12**, 388; *G.W.*, **14**, 572. (134)
[*Trans.:* In 'Personal Memories', in *Max Eitingon In Memoriam*, Jerusalem, 1951, 47; *Standard Ed.*, **21**, 257.]

(1931*b*) 'Über die weibliche Sexualität', *G.S.*, **12**, 120; *G.W.*, **14**, 517. (99, 107)
[*Trans.:* 'Female Sexuality', *C.P.*, **5**, 252; *Standard Ed.*, **21**.]

(1931*e*) Letter to the Burgomaster of Příbor, *G.S.*, **12**, 414; *G.W.*, **14**, 561. (124)
[*Trans.: Standard Ed.*, **21**, 259.]

(1932*a*) 'Zur Gewinnung des Feuers', *G.S.*, **12**, 141; *G.W.*, **16**, 3. (91)
[*Trans.:* 'The Acquisition and Control of Fire', *C.P.*, **5**, 288; *Standard Ed.*, **22**, 185.]

(1933*a*) *Neue Folge der Vorlesungen zur Einführung in die Psychoanalyse*, Vienna. *G.S.*, **12**, 151; *G.W.*, **15**, 207.
[*Trans.: New Introductory Lectures on Psycho-Analysis*, London and New York, 1933; *Standard Ed.*, **22**, 3.]

(1933*b* [1932]) *Warum Krieg?*, Paris. *G.S.*, **12**, 349; *G.W.*, **16**, 13. (158)
[*Trans.: Why War?*, Paris, 1933; *C.P.*, **5**, 273; *Standard Ed.*, **22**, 197.]

(1933*c*) 'Sándor Ferenczi', *G.S.*, **12**, 397; *G.W.*, **16**, 267. (135)
[*Trans.:* 'Sándor Ferenczi', *Int. J. Psycho-Anal.*, **14**, 297; *Standard Ed.*, **22**, 227.]

(1937*c*) 'Die endliche und die unendliche Analyse', *G.W.*, **16**, 59. (80, 129, 138)
[*Trans.:* 'Analysis Terminable and Interminable', *C.P.*, **5**, 316; *Standard Ed.*, **23**.]

(1939*a* [1937–39]) *Der Mann Moses und die monotheistische Religion*, *G.W.*, **16**, 103. (143, 148)
[*Trans.: Moses and Monotheism*, London and New York, 1939; *Standard Ed.*, **23**.]

(1940*a* [1938]) *Abriss der Psychoanalyse*, *G. W.*, **17**, 67. (79, 99)
[*Trans.: An Outline of Psycho-Analysis*, London and New York, 1949; *Standard Ed.*, **23**.]

(1940*c* [1922]) 'Das Medusenhaupt', *G.W.*, **17**, 47. (22)
[*Trans.:* 'Medusa's Head', *C.P.*, **5**, 105; *Standard Ed.*, **18**, 273.]

(1941*d* [1921]) 'Psychoanalyse und Telepathie', *G.W.*, **17**, 27. (28, 36–43, 49)
[*Trans.:* 'Psycho-Analysis and Telepathy', *Standard Ed.*, **18**, 177.]

(1950*a* [1887–1902]) *Aus den Anfängen der Psychoanalyse*, London. Includes *Entwurf einer Psychologie* (1895). (79, 107)
[*Trans.: The Origins of Psycho-Analysis*, London and New York, 1954. (Partly, including 'A Project for a Scientific Psychology', in *Standard Ed.*, **1**.)]

FREUD, S. (*cont.*)

(1960*a*) *Briefe 1873–1939* (ed. E. L. Freud), Berlin. (122)
[*Trans.: Letters 1873–1939* (ed. E. L. Freud) (trans. T. and J. Stern), New York, 1960; London, 1961.]

GRODDECK, G. (1923) *Das Buch vom Es*, Vienna. (64)

HARTMANN, H., and BETLHEIM, S. *See* BETLHEIM, S., and HARTMANN, H.

JONES, E. (1912) *Der Alptraum in seiner Beziehung zu gewissen Formen des mittelalterlichen Aberglaubens* (tr. H. Sachs), Leipzig and Vienna. (45–7)
[*English Text: In On the Nightmare*, London and New York, 1931.]

(1953) *Sigmund Freud: Life and Work*, Vol. 1, London and New York. (Page reference is to the English edition.) (141)

(1955) *Sigmund Freud: Life and Work*, Vol. 2, London and New York. (Page reference is to the English edition.) (141)

(1957) *Sigmund Freud: Life and Work*. Vol. 3, London and New York. (Page references are to the English edition.) (3, 28, 122)

LAMPL-DE GROOT, J. (1927) 'Zur Entwicklungsgeschichte des Ödipus-komplexes der Frau', *Int. Z. Psychoan.*, 13, 269. (115)
[*Trans.:* 'The Evolution of the Oedipus Complex in Women', *Int. J. Psycho-Anal.*, 9 (1928), 332.]

PFISTER, O. (1913) *Die psychanalytische Methode*, Leipzig and Berlin. (129)
[*Trans.: The Psychoanalytic Method*, New York and London, 1917.]

RANK, O. (1924) *Das Trauma der Geburt*, Vienna. (78)
[*Trans.: The Trauma of Birth*, London, 1929.]

REIK, T. (1920) 'Völkerpsychologische Parallelen zum Traumsymbol des Mantels', *Int. Z. Psychoan.*, 6, 350.

SCHRÖTTER, K. (1912) 'Experimentelle Träume', *Zbl. Psychoan.*, 2, 638. (21)

SILBERER, H. (1909) 'Bericht über eine Methode, gewisse symbolische Halluzinations-Erscheinungen hervorzurufen und zu beobach-ten', *Jb. psychoan. psychopath. Forsch.*, 1, 513. (21)

(1912) 'Symbolik des Erwachens und Schwellensymbolik über-haupt', *Jb. psychoan. psychopath. Forsch.*, 3, 621. (21)

LIST OF ABBREVIATIONS

G.S. = Freud, *Gesammelte Schriften* (12 vols.), Vienna, 1924–34
G.W. = Freud, *Gesammelte Werke* (18 vols.), London, from 1940
C.P. = Freud, *Collected Papers* (5 vols.) London, 1924–50
Standard Ed. = Freud, *Standard Edition* (24 vols.), London, from 1953
Almanach 1933 = *Almanach der Psychoanalyse 1933*, Vienna, Inter-nationaler Psychoanlytischer Verlag, 1932

GENERAL INDEX

This index includes the names of non-technical authors. It also includes the names of technical authors where no reference is made in the text to specific works. For references to specific technical works, the Bibliography should be consulted.—The compilation of the index was undertaken by Angela Richards.

Abraham, K. (see also Bibliography), 47
Abstract ideas represented in dreams, 19, 21
Active and passive, 85, 100–3, 106, 113, 116
Adler, A., 58 *n.* 2, 124–6
Affect
  anxiety as, 72, 74
  in dreams, 19
  quota of, 19, 74
Aggresive instincts *(see also* Destructive instinct), 92–8
Aggressiveness, 156–7, 159
  in females, 101–6, 109–10
  in males, 101–2, 109–10, 116
Agoraphobia, 74–5
Alexander the Great, 91
Ambition
  and urethral erotism, 90
  in women, 118
Ambivalence, 88, 106, 109–10, 117–18
America, 124, 126, 127
Amnesia, infantile, 26
Anal *(see also* Sadistic-anal)
  birth, 23, 89
  character, 90
  erotism, 89–91, 90 *n.* 4
  impulses, 87–8
Analogies
  alkali in mother-liquor, 11
  'bewitched' as diagnosis, 125
  breaking a crystal, 52
  conjuror and pigeon-breeding, 32
  core of the earth, 29
  draining Zuider Zee, 71
  driver and traffic regulations, 150
  cat or be eaten, 98

elected representatives, 11
general shifting figures on a map, 79
inoculation against diphtheria, 131
mixed population, 64–5
pillory in the Middle Ages, 121
primitive language, 18
rider and horse, 68
sculptor and clay model, 153
witches, detection of, 137
Anarchism, 150, 154–5
Animals
  as gods, 143, 146
  behaviour of, 50, 101
  instinct in, 91–2; 94
Animism, 108, 145–6, 147
Anticathexis, 80 and *n.* 1
Anus and primtive mouth, 90
Anxiety, 'conscience', 55 and *n.* 1
Anxiety, moral, 55, 69–70, 76, 78
Anxiety, neurotic *(see also* Fear; Fright; Phobias), 3, 69–70, 72–6, 78–9, 83–4, 106, 125
  and birth-trauma, 72, 77–8, 83–4, 126
  and expectation, 126
  and repression 78–4, 79–82, 84
  and separation from mother, 77–8
  as affect, 72, 74
  as transformed libido, 73–5, 84 *n.*
  theory of libidinal causation dropped, 81, 84 and *n.*
Anxiety, realistic, 3, 55, 69–70, 72–3, 74–7, 83–4
Anxiety attacks, 74, 80
Anxiety dreams, 8, 16, 25–7
Anxiety hysteria, 76

Anxiety neurosis, 73–4, 83–4 and 84 *n.*
Ariadne's thread, myth of, 23
Archaic
 character of dreams, 18
 communication, telepathy as, 50
Aristarchus of Samos, 153
Aristotle, 15
Art and science, 141
Artemis, Temple of, 91
Association of ideas (*see* Free association)
Astronomy, 6, 21, 153
Attention, distraction of, 36 *n.* 1
Automatic actions, 36 *n.* 1

Babylonians, the, 153
Bedouin bridal ceremonial, 22
Bennett, Arnold, 44
Berlin Psycho-Analytic Institute, 134
Bible, the, 158
Biological factors, 59, 78, 85, 91, 94, 100–01, 116, 136
Birth
 infantile theories of, 89
 trauma of, 72, 77–8, 83–4, 126
 symbols for, 22–3
Bisexuality, 100–03, 116
Blériot, L., 157
Bolshevism (*see also* Communism; Marxism), 158–60
Bowels, symbols for, 23
Boys'
 castration complex, 110–11, 114
 Oedipus complex, 76–7, 104–5, 114–15
 relation to father, 76, 114
 relation to mother, 59, 76, 104–5, 110, 114, 118 and *n.* 2
 sexuality compared with girls', 103–05, 109–11, 112, 114
Brandes, G., 122 and *n.* 1
Breast, child's relation to, 88, 89, 108
Breuer, J. (*see also* Bibliography), 66 *n.* 2, 68 *n.* 1, 128 and *n.*
Bullitt, W. C., 65 *n.* 1

Cases
 of '*Herr P.*' and *Dr. Forsyth*, 43–8
 of '*Katharina*', 106–7 *n.*
 of '*Little Hans*', 129 *n.* 2

 of *Rosalia H.*, 106–7 *n.*
 of *Senatspräsident Schreber*, 88
Cases (unnamed)
 of child and gold coin, 50
 of childless wife and fortune-teller, 36–8
 of physical suffering replacing neurosis, 96–7
 of prophetic graphologist, 40–2
 of student and fortune-teller, 39–40
Castration
 complex, 77, 110–15
 fear of, 76–9, 110, 114
 fright at, 22
Cathexis
 experimental, by ego, 79–80
 instinctual, and the id, 66–7, 68, 80–2, 91 and *n.* 3
 of dream-thoughts, 19
 of objects, 57, 68, 91 and *n.* 3, 104, 109
 of repressed wishes, 66, 111
Censor (*see also* Censorship), 14 and *n.*
Censorship, 14 and *n.*
 of dreams, 14–15, 17–19, 25–6
Character
 'anal', 90
 disorders of, 137, 138
 formation of, 57, 81, 89, 90–91, 110–11, 114–15, 116–17, 118
Charcot, J.-M., 83 *n.*
Charing Cross Hospital, 43 *n.* 2
Childhood impressions
 analysis of, 126, 130
 as source of dreams, 26–7, 94
 pathogenic, 130, 131–2
 repression of, 26, 130
Children (*see also* Boys'; Girls'; Infantile)
 amoral nature of, 54
 and parents, 50, 55–8, 59–60, 97, 129–31, 136, 143–4
 education of, 4, 60, 98, 129–33
 helplessness of, 143–4, 147
 neuroses of, 73–5, 129–31, 148
 play in, 104, 113
 psycho-analysis of, 50, 130–31, 136
Church, the (*see also* Religion), 158
Circumcision and castration, 76–7

Civilization
  history of, 128
  instinctual restrictions and, 98,
    130, 144, 157–8, 159–60
  process of, 158 and n. 2
  use of term, 179 n. 1
  women's contribution to, 117
Clitoris, 58, 87, 104, 112–13
Cloaca theory, 89
Communism (see also Marxism),
  4, 156–60
Complemental series, 111
Compromises
  dreams as, 14, 18
  neuroses as, 14
Condensation
  characteristic of the id, 66–7
  in dreams, 19
Conscience (see also Super-ego),
  53–6, 58, 97, 144
  Conscience anxiety', 55 n. 1
Conscious, the, 14–15
Conscious thinking and uncon-
    scious processes, 16–17, 61–4
Conservative nature of instincts,
  94–6
Constitutional factors, 102, 115,
  116, 182, 136
Contradiction unknown to id, 65
Copernicus, 153
Cortical layer ego, compared to, 67
Cosmogonies, 142–3, 146–7
Crime, 98, 133
Culture (see also Civilization)
  psycho-analytic therapy as, 71
  use of term, 158 n. 1
Curie, P., 153

Danger
  anxiety and, 72–3, 75–9
  internal (instinctual, and exter-
    nal (real), 75, 76–9, 83–4
Day's residues, 10, 18, 19–20
Death
  instinct, 4, 95–6, 96 n.
  neurotic's attitude to, 108
  primitive view of, 108
  symbol for, 22
Deities (see Gods)
Delinquency, 60, 98, 133
Delusions, 14–15, 53
Demons, 145–6
Depression, 54 n.

Destructive
  instinct, 91 n. 3, 92–8, 125
  trends, 88, 92
Dialectical materialism (see Marx-
    ism)
Displacement
  characteristic of the id, 66–7
  in dreams, 19, 23
  in jokes, 19
Disposition to illness, 130
Dispositional points, 88 and n. 2
Distortion
  in dreams, 14, 17, 19, 21, 26–7,
    35
Divination, 140
Dream-content (manifest)
  censorship and, 14–15, 19, 25–6
  effect of distortion upon, 14, 19,
    35
  relation to latent dream-
    thoughts, 8–14, 16, 19, 24–5
Dream-day, 11
Dream-interpretation
  assists occultism, 34–5, 42–3
  elucidates mythology, 23
  importance of, in psycho-analy-
    sis, 7–8
  lay attitude to, 8, 23
  technique of, 8–17, 24
Dreams
  and occultism, 28–50
  as psychopathological structures,
    14–15
  theory of, 4, 7–27, 82, 99, 141
    n.
Dreams, individual
  disobliging secretary, 21–2
  father's repeated appearance,
    23–4
  'Ladies Only' traveling bag, 21
  planing wood, 21
  wife bears twins, 34–5
Dream-thoughts (latent), 8–14, 16–
    20, 24–5
Dream-thoughts, preconscious, 17
Dream-work, 8, 9, 16–27, 35, 65

Economic conditions and human
    behaviour, 60, 156, 157–60
Economy, psychical, 65–6
Education, 4, 60
  Bolshevist, 159–60
  psycho-analysis and, 98, 129–33
  translation of word, 130 n.

Educators
  as models, 57, 60
  psycho-analysis of, 131–2
Ego
  alteration of, 56, 80 and n. 1
  and the external world, 15, 67–
    70, 76, 83, 98
  and the id, 64–5, 67–71, 75–6,
    79–82
  and the instincts, 68–9, 79–82,
    93
  and the super-ego, 53–5, 58–60,
    69–71, 75–6
  as reservoir of libido, 91 and
    n. 3
  as seat of anxiety, 75
  compared to cortical layer, 67
  reaction-formations of, 80–1, 91
  repressive forces of, 51–2, 83, 85
  splitting of, 52
  synthetic tendency of, 68 and n.
    1
  unconscious portions of, 61–3,
    66–7, 69–70
  weakness of immature, 74, 78,
    130
Ego ideal, 57–9
  and enforcing agency, 58 n. 1
Ego-instincts (see also Self-preser-
    vation, instinct of), 51, 84–7,
    91
Ego libido, 91
Ego-syntonic character of dreams,
    18 and n.
Einstein, A., 127
Eitingon, M., 134
Embryology, 94
Energy, instinctual (see also Psy-
    chical energy), 91
  mobility of, 66 and n. 2, 67
  England, 44, 45 n., 47, 156–7
Ephesus, 91
Epimenides, the (paradox), 155
    and n.
Eros (see also Sexual instincts),
    92, 93, 95
Erotogenic zones, 87–90, 104, 105
Ethnology, 128
Evil Spirit, the 146
Excitation, sum of, 83–4
Excretory function, 87, 89–90, 103,
    109
Expectation and anxiety, 73–4

Experimental dreams, 21–2
External world (see Reality)

Faeces, equated with baby and
    penis, 89–90, 103
Fairy tales, 23
Family, the, 118–19, 144, 146
Father
  and God, 143–4
  boy's relation to, 76, 114
  girl's relation to, 23–4, 104–6,
    106 n., 113–15, 117–18
Father-transference to doctor, 43
Faust (Goethe), 30 and n. 3
Fear (see also Anxiety; Phobias)
  of castration (see Castration)
  of demons, 145–6
  of incest, 22
  of loss of love, 55, 77–8
  of the mother, 22, 106, 108
  of the super-ego, 78
Female (see also Girls'; Mascu-
    line and feminine; Mother;
    Women)
  deities, 143
  psychology, 4, 56, 77, 99–120
Ferenczi, S. (see also Bibliography),
    135 and n.
Fire and micturition, 91
Fixation
  of libido, 88–9, 97, 106, 111,
    114–16
  to traumas, 26–7
Fliess, W., 107 n., 122 n. 1
Folklore, 22–3
Fore-pleasure, 87 and n. 2
Forsyte Saga, The (by Galsworthy),
    44, 45–6
Forsyth, D., 43–4, 44 n. 2, 44–8
Fortune-tellers, 36 and n. 1, 37–
    40
Francis Joseph, The Emperor, 152
    and n. 1
Free association, 8, 10–13, 43–8,
    61, 131
Freiberg (Příbor), Moravia, 124
    and n. 2
Frequent occurrence, symbol for,
    23–4
Freud, Anna (see also Bibliogra-
    phy), 129
Freud, Martha, 122 n. 1, 141 n.

Freud, Sigmund
  and *Georg Brandes*, 122 and *n*. 1
  and Vienna University, 5
  in Moravia, 124 and *n*. 2
  phonographic memory, 5
  surgical operation on, 5
Freud-Ottorego, 45, 46
Freund, A. von 44 and *n*., 47 and *n*.
Fright at castration (*see also* Fear), 22
Frigidity, 116
Frustration
  in aetiology of neuroses, 132
  libidinal, in children, 108–10
'Functional phenomenon' (*Silberrer*), 21

Gain from illness, secondary, 125
Galsworthy, J., 44, 45
Genital phase, 88, 90
Genitals, female, 58, 88, 90, 100–101, 104, 111–13
  and castration complex, 77, 110
  symbols for, 22, 23, 90
Genitals, male (*see* Castration; Penis; Phallic symbols)
Girls' (*see also* Women)
  aggressiveness, 103–6, 109–10
  castration complex, 110–15
  intelligence, 104
  masculinity complex, 111, 114–15
  masturbation, 104, 112, 113
  Oedipus complex, 104–6, 113–15
  penis-envy, 90, 110–14
  phantasies, 23, 106
  pre-Oedipus phase, 4, 108–15, 118
  relation to father, 104–6, 106 *n*., 113–15, 117–18
  relation to mother, 105–10, 112–15, 117–18
  wish for a baby, 90, 106, 113–15, 118
God
  and morality, 54–5, 144
  belief in, 143–4
  omniscience of, 50
Gods
  animal, 143, 146
  female, 143
  nature-, 145

Goethe, 30 and *n*. 3
Gold, value set on, 89
Gravitation, theory of, 152
Greece
  myths of Ancient, 91
Groddeck, G. (*see also* Bibliography), 64 and *n*. 1
Group psychology, 49–50, 60, 121–22, 124, 125, 155–60
Guilt, sense of, 54, 58, 69
  unconscious, 96–8

Hallucinations, 53
Hallucinatory character of dreams, 10, 15–16, 18
Hegelian philosophy, 156
'Heimkehr, Die' (by *Heine*), 141 and *n*.
Heine, H., 100 and *n*., 141 and *n*.
Hereditary factors, 72
Heresy, 158
Hermes of Praxiteles, 23
Herostratus, 91
'Herr P.' and *Dr. Forsyth*, case of, 43–8
Homosexuality, 90, 125
  in women, 115
Hordes, human (*see also* Group psychology), 156 and *n*.
Hormones, 136
Hugo, Victor, 137
Hypnosis, 21, 36 *n*. 1
Hysteria
  aetiology of, 106, 125
  anxiety-, 76
  anxiety in, 73–4
  curability of, 137
  traumatic, 26–7
Hysterical attacks, 72

Id, the
  characteristics of, 65–7
  relation to the ego, 64–5, 67–71
  relation to the super-ego, 71
  use of term, 64 and *n*. 2
Ideas and affects separated, 19, 74
  'incompatible', 68 *n*. 3
Identification, 57 and *n*. 2, 60, 81, 113, 115, 118
Illusions, 92, 140–1, 155, 159–60
Imago, 129
Imagos, parentral, 57 and *n*.

174   GENERAL INDEX

Incestuous impulses *(see also* Oedipus complex), 22
'Incompatible' ideas, 68 *n.* 3
'Individual Psychology' *(Adler)*, 58 *n.* 2, 124–6
Infantile *(see also* Childhood; Children)
amnesia, 26
attitude of neurotics, 78–9
features of religion, 143–8
phobias, 73–5
sexual theories, 89, 104–5
sexuality, 26–7, 55, 76–8, 87–91, 103–15, 127, 130
Inferiority
complex, 58
sense of, 58–9, 69, 125
Inhibitions *(see also* Censorship; Repression), 55, 112, 151
Insects, 49, 101
Instincts *(see also* Aggressive instincts; Death instinct; Destructive instinct; Ego-instincts; Self-preservation, instinct of; Sexual instincts)
'active' and 'passive', 85–6
aim inhibited, 86
and civilization, 98, 130, 131, 144, 157–8, 159–60
conservative nature of, 94–6
for recovery, 104
fusions and defusions of, 93
in animals, 92, 94
organic, 94
physical nature of, 65 and *n.* 2, 85–6
popular view of, 84
sublimation of, 86, 87, 111, 119
theory of, 4, 51, 84–98
transformations of, 85–91
use of term, 85 and *n.*, 94 *n.*
Instinctual
forces and dreams, 15–20
needs and the id, 65–9
Intellect *(see also* Reason)
activity of, in dreams, 20
strengthening of, in civilization, 158
Internationale Zeitschrift für (ärztliche) Psychoanalyse, 7–8
Interpretation of dreams *(see* Dream-interpretation)
Interpretation of Dreams, The (by Freud), 4, 122 *n.* 1

Intuition, 140, 141
Inversion, sexual *(see* Homosexuality)
Involution in psychical development, 70–1

Jealousy, 46, 48, 109, 110–12
Jews, 159
Jokes, 10, 19, 30, 36 *n.* 1
Jones, Ernest (see also Bibliography), 45–7
Jung, C. G., 124 *n.* 1, 126 and *n.* 3, 141 *n.*
Justice *(see also* Law; Right), Universal, 147

Kant, I., 55, 66 and *n.* 1, 144
'*Katharina*', case of, 106–7 *n.*
Kepler, 152
Koran, the, 158

Labyrinth, legend of, 23
Latency period, 78, 114
Lavoisier, A.-L., 153
Legends *(see* Mythology; Myths)
Libido *(see also* Sexual instincts)
and masculine and feminine functions, 116
ego as objects of, 68
ego as reservoir, 91
fixation of, 88–9, 97, 105, 111, 114–15
object, 91
phases of organization of, 4, 87–91, 103–16, 118
quota of, unemployable, 74–5
regression of, 57, 82, 88–9, 111, 115
theory, 84–98
transformed into anxiety, 73–4, and *n.* 75, 81, 84
'*Little Hans*', case of, 129 *n.* 2
London, 43 and *n.* 2, 45, 157
Lourdes, 134
Ludwig, E., 59 *n.* 1
Lupus, 138

Magic, 145–6
Man of Property, The (by Galsworthy), 44
Manic states, 55
Marriage, 113, 117–18

Marxism *(see also* Communism), 156–60
Masculine and feminine, 93, 100–103, 106, 113, 116, 125
Masculinity complex, 111, 114–15, 118
Masochism, 92–6, 96 n., 102, 125
Masochistic wishes, 96–7
Masturbation, 77, 112–13
  infantile, 77, 104, 109, 112–13
Mediums, 31–2
Medusa's head, 22
Melancholia, 54, 88
Men *(see also* Masculine and feminine)
  Oedipus complex in, 118
  symbol for, 23
Messiah, 159
Micturition and fire, 91
Middle Ages, the, 121, 159
Mind, structure of, 4, 57–71, 99
Miracles, 31, 134, 146
Miraculous, attraction of, 30, 48
Mnemic
  image, 144
  residues, 67
Mobs *(see also* Group psychology), 50, 121, 125–6
Moral, anxiety, 55, 69, 75–6, 78
Morality
  and religion, 54–5, 142–4, 146–8
  and super-ego, 54–60
  and unconscious sense of guilt, 97–8
  unknown to children, 55
  unknown to id, 66
Moravia, 124
Mother
  boys' relation to, 59, 76, 104–5, 110, 114, 118 and n. 2
  child and, 59, 101, 109–10
  fear of, 22, 106, 108
  girls' relation to, 105–10, 112–15, 117–18
  separation from, 77–8
  symbol for, 22
Mystical practices, 71
Mysticism *(see also* Occultism), 28, 49
Mythology, 22–3, 128
  dream-interpretation and, 23
  theory of instincts, 84

Myths, 90–1

Narcissism, 58n. 1, 91, 177
Narcissistic illness, 137
Narcissus, 91 n. 2
Nature, man's control over, 152–3, 156–7, 160
Nature-gods, 145
Necrophilia, 125
Negative therapeutic reaction, 97–8
Neuroses *(see also* Anxiety neurosis; Children, neuroses of; Hysteria; Obsessional neurosis; Phobias; Transference neuroses; Traumatic neuroses)
  aetiology of, 51, 77, 111, 132
  and ego-psychology, 52
  and tendency to conflict, 51
  compared to dreams, 14–15, 25
  curability of, 135–8
  of society, 148 and n.
  physical treatment, 134–5
  prevention of, 131–3
  religion and, 148 and n.
  theory influences treatment of, 126–7
  unconscious need for punishment in, 96–8
Neurotics
  infantile characteristics of, 78–9, 131
  masturbation in, 112–13
  psycho-analysis of, 51, 96–8, 128, 129–31, 133–8
  psychological treatment of, 134–5
Newton, 152
Nietzsche, F., 64
Nihilism, intellectual, 154–5
Nonsense, pleasure in, 30 and n. 2
Nordsee (by *Heine*), 100 and n.

Object-cathexes, libidinal, 86, 89
  identifications as precipitates of, 57, 68
  infantile, 76, 104, 109
  source of, 68, 91 n. 3
Object-choice
  homosexual, 115
  identification distinguished from, 56–7
  in children, 56, 76, 88, 103–7, 115

in women, 105, 113, 115, 117–18
narcissistic, 91, 116–17
regressive, 56
Object libido, 91
Obsessional neurosis, 74, 82, 88, 125, 137, 145
Obsessions, 14–15, 148 n.
Occultism
  difficulties in studying, 28–32
  dreams and, 28–50, 99
  psycho-analysis assists, 35, 38, 42
  religion and, 31
  science and, 49
Oedipus complex
  dissolution of, 81–2, 114
  in boys, 76–7, 104–5, 114–15
  in girls, 104–6, 113–15
  in women, 106, 117–18
  super-ego as heir to, 57, 59–60, 70, 114
Opposites, representation by (see Reversal)
Oral phase, 87–8, 89, 105–6, 108–9
Oral-sadistic phase, 88
Oral tendencies in identification, 56
Organic instincts, 94
Organic process
  civilization as, 158 and n. 3
  repression as, 158 n. 3
Organ-pleasure, 87 and n. 1
Oxygen, discovery of, 153

Paranoia, 106, 115
Parapraxes, 63
Parental agency and super-ego, 55–60, 81
Parents (see also Father; Mother; Oedipus complex) and children, 50, 55–8, 59–60, 97, 129–31, 136, 143–4
Pathology throws light on normal, 52–3, 54, 107, 128
Penis (see also Castration), 87–90
  clitoris as atrophied, 57
  symbols for (see Phallic symbols)
Penis-envy, 90, 110–14, 117, 118
Perceptual system (system Pcpt.-Cs.) 67–70
Personality
  dissection of psychical, 51–71, 99
Perversions, 92–4, 111

Phallic
  mother, 22, 112, 115
  phase, 77, 78, 87–8, 104–6, 109–14
  symbols, 22
Phantasies, 23, 26, 77, 90, 106 and n.
Philology, 22, 89
Philosophy, 140–2, 146, 154
Phobias, 73–5, 76, 137
Phormio (Terence), 126 and n. 2
Physics, 92
Plaiting, invention of, 117
Plastic art, 23
Play in children, 104, 113
Pleasure principle, 65–6, 67, 82–3, 94–5
Pleasure-unpleasure principle, 80–2
Praxiteles, 23
Prayer, 144
Preconscious, the, 62–4
Preconscious dream-thoughts, 18
Pregenital phases of the libido, 4, 87–91, 104–15, 118
Pressure technique, 36 n. 1
Příbor, Moravia, 124 and n. 2
Primal
  family, 77
Primitive
  mouth, anus corresponds to, 89
  nature of id, 67
  peoples (see also Primal), 77, 108
  quality of dreams, 17–8
  religions, 143, 145–7
Prophecies, 30, 36–42
Prophylaxis, psycho-analysis as, 130–32
Psychiatry and psycho-analysis, 8, 134–5
Psychical
  agencies, two, 14
  and physical, 49, 65 and n. 2, 68, 85
  binding, 75, 80, 146
  economics, 65–6, 83
  energy, 15, 17, 79 and n., 91
  personality, dissection of, 51–71, 99
  plasticity and rigidity, 119, 136
  processes, primary and secondary, 67 and n. 3, 79 n.

Psycho-analysis
  and education, 98, 129–33
  and official science, 8, 121–2, 126
  and psychotherapy, 7, 8, 134–5
  and scientific *Weltanschauung*,
    139–40, 147–8, 154, 160
  assists occultism, 34–5, 38, 42
  criticisms of, 6, 20–1, 23, 29–30,
    51, 120–4, 126, 134, 137
  difficulty of understanding, 62,
    120–1
  dream-theory as basis of, 7, 21,
    25–6
  first work of, on symptoms, 51,
    128, 138
  London Society for, 43 n. 2
  negative reaction to, 97–8
  non-medical applications of,
    98, 128–33
  prophylactic, 130–2
  resistance in, 61, 96–8, 121–2,
    131, 135
  secessions from, 123–4
  uncovers unconscious mental
    processes, 26, 66, 94
Psycho-analysts, women as, 103,
  115, 129, 131
Psycho-Analytic Institute in Berlin, 134
Psycho-Analytic Publishing Company, 3, 47
Psycho-analytic therapy, 66, 71,
  128, 130–31, 133–8
Psycho-analytic treatment, communications in, 8–11, 16
Psychology
  female, 4, 56, 77, 99–119, 151
  group, 50, 60, 121, 124, 125–6,
    156–60
  'Individual', 58, 124–6
  sociology as applied, 158
Psychoses
  compared to dreams, 14–15
  delusions in, 53
  psycho-analysis and, 136–7
  turning away from external re-
    ality in, 15, 52–3, 140
Psychotherapy, 7, 8, 134–5
Puberty, 88
  rites, 77
Pubic hair, 117
Punishment, unconscious need for,
  96–8, 125
Punishment dreams, 25–6

Quality, 66
Quantity, 66, 83, 136–7

Radium, discovery of, 153
Rank, O. (see also Bibliography),
  126 and n. 4
Reaction-formations of the ego,
  80–1, 91
Reality
  and anxiety, 3, 55, 69–70, 72–3,
    74–7, 83–4
  and the ego, 15, 67–70, 76, 83,
    98
  and science, 150–1, 153–5, 160
  turning away from, in psychoses,
    15, 52–3
  turning away from, in sleep, 15,
    17–18
Reality principle, 67
Reality-testing, 30 and n. 1, 67,
  79 n.
Reason *(see also* Intellect)
  advance of, 151
  ego stands for, 68
  man's hostility to, 30–1
Recovery, instinct for, 94
Reflection, analyst curbs powers
  of, 10 and n.
Regression
  in dreams, 17–18
  libidinal, 56, 82, 88–9, 111, 115
Relativity, theory of, 127
Religion, 4
  and Bolshevism, 158
  and occultism, 31
  and scientific *Weltanschauung*,
    31, 141–55
  science of, 128
Religious education, 129 n. 2
Repeat, compulsion to, 95–6, 96 n.,
  118, 126
Repressed, the, 51, 69
  unaltered by time, 66
Repression, 123
  and anxiety, 73–4, 79–82, 84
  and civilization, 98
  and dreams, 14–18, 27
  and self-preservative instinct, 86
  as organic process, 158 n. 2
  as work of ego, 51–2, 82, 85
  as work of super-ego, 61
  in sexual development of girls,
    111, 113
  lifted in psycho-analysis, 66, 94

of childhood experiences, 26, 130
of Oedipus complex, 114
resistance demonstrates, 14–15, 18, 61, 69
Resistance
and dream-interpretation, 12–15
demonstrates repression, 14–15, 18, 61, 69
in psycho-analysis, 61, 96–8, 121–2, 131, 135
to instinctual life, 51
varying pressure of, 12–14
Revelation, divine, 140, 148, 149, 154, 158
Ritual, 22
Rosalia, H., case of, 106–7 *n.*
Russian
Bolshevism (*see also* Communism), 158–60
Tsars, 156

Sadism, 92–4
Sadistic-anal phase, 88, 103–4, 106
Sadistic impulses, infantile, 87
Salzburg, 5
Schiller, 126 and *n.*
Schopenhauer, A., 95
Schreber, Senatspräsident, case of, 88 *n.* 2
Science (*see also Weltanschauung*, scientific)
and occultism, 30–1, 49
and psycho-analysis, 139–40, 147–8, 154, 160
and religion, 31
official, and psycho-analysis, 8, 121–2, 126
Scientific research
aims and methods of, 150, 152–5
man's unfitness for, 6, 30, 125–6
Scientific spirit, strengthening of, in civilization (*see also* Intellect; Reason), 146, 151, 158
Séances, occult, 31–2
Secondary revision of dreams, 19–20, 141 *n.*
Seduction
by adults, 106 and *n.*, 110
phantasy of, 106 and *n.*
Self-detruction, instinct of (*see also* Death instinct), 92–5

Self-injury, neurotic, 125
Self-observation and super-ego, 53, 59
Self-preservation
anxiety serves, 75
instinct of, 83–4, 125, 157
Sensory strength of dreams, 10–11
Sex education, 129 *n.* 2
Sexual intercourse
infantile theories of, 104
symbols for, 21
Sexual
characters, secondary, 100–1
factors in anxiety neurosis, 73–4, 83–4
instincts, 85–96, 98
products, 100–1
relations, dissocial nature of, 119
symbolism, 21–3
theories of children, 89, 104
Sexuality
female, 56, 100–19, 151
infantile, 26–7, 55, 76–8, 87–91, 103–15, 127, 130
theory of, unpopular, 122, 125, 127
Shame, 117
Signal, anxiety as, 16, 73, 75–6, 77 *n.* 1, 80, 82–4
Sleep and dreams, 15–16, 17–18
Social
character of women, 117, 118–19
influences on women, 101–2, 117, 151
structure, 156–60
Society, individuals and, 78, 130
Sociology, 60, 158
Specialization in medicine, 135
Spiritualism, 48–9
Stekel, W., 127 and *n.* 1
Stimuli, sensory, and dreams, 15, 18
Sublimation, 86, 87, 111, 119
Suicidal impulses, 41–2, 133
Super-ego, 5, 25, 97–8, 131
as heir to Oedipus complex, 57, 59–60, 70, 114
as heir to parental authority, 55–60, 81
as vehicle of ego ideal, 57–8, 58 *n.* 1, 59
as vehicle of tradition, 60, 157

distinguished from conscience, 53, 57–8, 59
fear of, 78
in girls and boys compared, 114
partly unconscious, 61–4, 66–7, 69–70
relation to ego, 53–5, 58–60, 69–71, 75–6
relation to id, 71
repression as work of, 61
self-observation as function of, 53, 59
severity of, 54–6, 69, 97
Superstition, 146
Symbolism, 89–90, 113–14, 122, 127
in dreams, 11–12, 18, 20–4, 89–90
Symbols, list of
Ariadne's thread, 23
bridge, 22–3
cloak, 22
Labyrinth, legend of, 23
Medusa's head, 22
multiplicity, 23–4
overcoat, 22
room, 23, 90
spatial relations, 24
spider, 22
staircase, 21
travelling-bag, 21
Symptom-formation
and anxiety, 74–7, 80
and dreams, 14–15
Symptoms, neurotic
and phantasies, 106 and n.
and repression, 51
first work of psycho-analysis on, 51, 128, 138
in hysteria, 125
mechanisms of, compared to dream-work, 17
Syphilidophobia, 78

Taboos, 146
Teachers (see Educators)
Telegraphy and telepathy, 32–3, 49
Telepathy (see also Thought-transference), 4, 32–5, 49
Terence, 126 and n. 2
Thought
as experimental action, 79 and n., 80

postponing activity of, 67, 79
prohibition of by Bolshevism, 159
prohibition of by religion, 149–51
Thoughts, omnipotence of, 145–6
Thought-transference (see also Telepathy), 35–50
Time
idea originates from perceptual system, 67 and n. 2
meaningless to the id, 66 and n. 2
represented by space, 24
Toilet, as source of genital excitement, 106, 109
Totemism, 143, 146
Tradition, super-ego as vehicle of, 60, 157
Transference, 43, 48, 94, 131, 135, 136
neuroses (see also Hysteria; Obsessional neurosis; Phobias), 137
of thought (see Thought-transference)
Traumas
fixation to, 26–7
infantile, 27, 106, 130, 132
Traumatic
moment, 83 and n., 83–4
neuroses, 26–7
Truth, 148, 150, 151, 155, 160
Tuberculosis, 138

U-boats, 157
Ucs., use of abbreviation, 64
Unconscious, the, 30, 111, 122, 125, 139
and dreams, 15–20, 27, 34
and telepathy, 49–50
development of concept, 64
Unconscious
and repressed do not coincide, 62
feelings, 123
in descriptive, dynamic and systematic senses, 62–4
instinctual forces, 15–20, 26
mental processes and attention, 36 n. 1
need for punishment, 96–8, 125
portions of ego and super-ego, 61–3, 66–7, 69–70

resistance, source of, 61, 96
sense of guilt, 97–8
system, 16, 62–4, 69
'Unconscious repressed,' the, 14
Urethral erotism, 90–1

Vagina, 88, 90, 104
Vienna, 122 n. 1
    Psychiatric Clinic, 5
    Univeristy of, 5
    Volksuniversität, 45 and n.
Virgin, The Blessed, 134
Visual imagery in dreams, 18–19

Wallenstein (Schiller), 126
War
    of 1914–18, 43, 156–7
Weaving, invention of, 117
Weltanschauung, use of term, 139
    and n.
Weltanschauung, scientific, 49
    and art, 141
    and intellectual nihilism, 154–5
    and Marxism, 156–60
    and philosophy, 141–2, 145–6,
    154
    and psycho-analysis, 139–40, 147–
    8, 154, 160
    and religion, 141–54
    described, 139–41
Wilhelm II, 59 and n. 1
Wilson, President Woodrow, 65
    and n. 1
Wish-fulfilment
    and sources of knowledge, 140
    and sublimation, 111
    in animism, 145–6
    in dreams, 8, 17–20, 24–7, 34
    in religion, 140, 147–8, 154

Witchcraft, belief in, 125
Womb, symbol for, 23
Women (see also Girls)
    and childbirth, 118
    as analysts, 103, 115, 129–30, 131
    attitude to husband of, 113,
    117–18
    castration complex in, 77, 110
    contribution to civilization of,
    117
    dreams of, 21, 22–3, 22 and n.
    2
    ego influenced by object in, 56–
    7
    envy in mental life of, 110–12,
    119
    frigidity in, 116
    homosexuality in, 115–16
    inhibitions in, 151
    masculinity complex in, 111,
    114–15, 118
    narcissism in,
    Oedipus complex in, 106, 117–
    18
    penis-envy in, 90, 110–14, 117,
    118
    psychical rigidity of, 119
    relation to father of, 105, 117,
    119
    relation to mother of, 107–8,
    118
    social character of, 117, 119
    social influences on, 102, 117,
    151
    sublimation in, 111, 119
    super-ego in, 114
Words, magical power of, 146
Working-over, 80 and n. 2

Zeppelin, 157

Norton Paperbacks
PSYCHIATRY AND PSYCHOLOGY

Adorno, T. W., et al. *The Authoritarian Personality.*

Alexander, Franz. *Fundamentals of Psychoanalysis.*

Alexander, Franz. *Psychosomatic Medicine.*

Bruner, Jerome S. *The Relevance of Education.*

Bruner, Jerome S. *Toward a Theory of Instruction.*

Cannon, Walter B. *The Wisdom of the Body.*

English, O. Spurgeon, and Gerald H. J. Pearson. *Emotional Problems of Living* (3d Ed.).

Erikson, Erik H. *Childhood and Society.*

Erikson, Erik H. *Gandhi's Truth.*

Erikson, Erik H. *Identity: Youth and Crisis.*

Erikson, Erik H. *Insight and Responsibility.*

Erikson, Erik H. *Life History and the Historical Moment.*

Erikson, Erik H. *Young Man Luther.*

Francher, Raymond E. *Psychoanalytic Psychology: The Development of Freud's Thought.*

Ferenczi, Sandor. *Thalassa: A Theory of Genitality.*

Field, M. J. *Search for Security: An Ethno-Psychiatric Study of Rural Ghana.*

Freud, Sigmund. *An Autobiographical Study.*

Freud, Sigmund. *Beyond the Pleasure Principle.*

Freud, Sigmund. *Civilization and its Discontents.*

Freud, Sigmund. *The Ego and the Id.*

Freud, Sigmund. *The Future of an Illusion.*

Freud, Sigmund. *Group Psychology and the Analysis of the Ego.*

Freud, Sigmund. *Inhibitions, Symptoms and Anxiety.*

Freud, Sigmund. *Introductory Lectures on Psychoanalysis*

Freud, Sigmund. *Jokes and Their Relation to the Unconscious.*

Freud, Sigmund. *Leonardo da Vinci and a Memory of His Childhood.*

Freud, Sigmund. *New Introductory Lectures on Psychoanalysis.*

Freud, Sigmund. *On Dreams.*

Freud, Sigmund. *On the History of the Psycho-Analytic Movement.*

Freud, Sigmund. *An Outline of Psycho-Analysis* (Rev. Ed.).

Freud, Sigmund. *The Psychopathology of Everyday Life.*

Freud, Sigmund. *The Question of Lay Analysis.*

Freud, Sigmund. *Totem and Taboo.*

Haley, Jay. *Uncommon Therapy: The Psychiatric Techniques of Milton B. Erikson, M.D.*

Horney, Karen (Ed.). *Are You Considering Psychoanalysis?*

Horney, Karen. *Feminine Psychology.*

Horney, Karen. *Neurosis and Human Growth*

Horney, Karen. *The Neurotic Personality of Our Time.*

Horney, Karen. *New Ways in Psychoanalysis.*

Horney, Karen. *Our Inner Conflicts.*

Horney, Karen. *Self-Analysis*

Inhelder, Bärbel, and Jean Piaget. *The Early Growth of Logic in the Child.*

James, William. *Talks to Teachers.*

Kagan, Jerome, and Robert Coles (Eds.). *Twelve to Sixteen: Early Adolescence.*

Kasanin, J. S. *Language and Thought in Schizophrenia.*

Kelly, George A. *A Theory of Personality.*

Klein, Melanie, and Joan Riviere. *Love, Hate and Reparation.*

Komarovsky, Mirra. *Dilemmas of Masculinity: A Study of College Youth.*

Lasswell, Harold D. *Power and Personality.*

Levy, David M. *Maternal Overprotection.*

Lifton, Robert Jay *Revolutionary Immortality: Mao Tse-tung and the Chinese Cultural Revolution.*

Lifton, Robert Jay *Thought Reform and the Psychology of Totalism.*

Meehl, Paul E. *Psychodiagnosis: Selected Papers.*

Piaget, Jean. *The Child's Conception of Number.*

Piaget, Jean *Genetic Epistemology.*

Piaget, Jean. *Play, Dreams and Imitation in Childhood.*

Piaget, Jean. *Understanding Causality.*

Piaget, Jean, and Bärbel Inhelder. *The Child's Conception of Space.*

Piaget, Jean, and Bärbel Inhelder. *The Origin of the Idea of Chance in Children.*

Piers, Gerhart, and Milton B. Singer. *Shame and Guilt.*

Piers, Maria W. (Ed.). *Play and Development.*

Raymond, Margaret, Andrew Slaby, and Julian Lieb. *The Healing Alliance.*

Ruesch, Jurgen. *Disturbed Communication.*

Ruesch, Jurgen. *Therapeutic Communication.*

Ruesch, Jurgen, and Gregory Bateson. *Communication: The Social Matrix of Psychiatry.*

Sullivan, Harry Stack. *Clinical Studies in Psychiatry.*

Sullivan, Harry Stack. *Conceptions of Modern Psychiatry.*

Sullivan, Harry Stack. *The Fusion of Psychiatry and Social Science.*

Sullivan, Harry Stack. *The Interpersonal Theory of Psychiatry.*

Sullivan, Harry Stack. *The Psychiatric Interview.*

Sullivan, Harry Stack. *Schizophrenia as a Human Process.*

Walter, W. Grey. *The Living Brain.*

Watson, John B. *Behaviorism.*

Wheelis, Allen. *The Quest for Identity.*

Williams, Juanita H. *Psychology of Women: Behavior in a Biosocial Context.*

Zilboorg, Gregory. *A History of Medical Psychology.*